T0140997

Viella Historical Research

6

Tommaso Detti   Giuseppe Lauricella

The Origins of the Internet

viella

Copyright © 2017 - Viella s.r.l.
All rights reserved
First edition: July 2017
ISBN 978-88-6728-870-0

Originally published as:
Tommaso Detti, Giuseppe Lauricella, *Le origini di Internet*, Milano 2013
Copyright © 2013 - Bruno Mondadori
All rights reserved

Translated by Anna Di Biase and Nick Dines

viella
libreria editrice
via delle Alpi, 32
I-00198 ROMA
tel. 06 84 17 758
fax 06 85 35 39 60
www.viella.it

Contents

Introduction

Internet, the Web and Contemporary Globalization

As a phenomenon that occupies growing centrality in today's world, there are obvious reasons for studying the Internet. Its users – who numbered just 16 million in 1995 – surpassed 2.7 billion in March 2013 (almost 40% of the world's population) and continue to rise (Figure 1).

The distribution of "Internauts" is somewhat uneven. As of June 2012, 78.6% of North Americans were users in contrast to just 15.3% of Africans (Figure 2). Nevertheless, although the so-called "digital divide" reflects the imbalances between the Global North and Global South that characterize the contemporary world,[1] it is rapidly diminishing: in fact, the number of users in African countries, who in September 2009 included just 6.8% of the continent's population, increased by 148.4% in less than three years.

As depicted in Figure 3, the growth of "hosts" (computers connected to the network) has been even more pronounced: between 1995 and 2000 this number increased from 6.6 to 93 million, while in July 2012 it reached 908.6 million (+876.4% in twelve years).[2]

In the year 2000 there were approximately 350 to 500 million webpages in existence.[3] By comparison, in 2013 it was estimated that this number could have been as high as 4.7 billion,[4] although one should bear in mind the limits of such data. One should also consider the enormous quantities of documents contained in databases that are not accessible through search engines and are thus much more difficult to count. In 2001 this "deep web" may have hosted something like

---

1. See, for example, Giovanni Gozzini, *Un'idea di giustizia: Globalizzazione e ineguaglianza dalla rivoluzione industriale a oggi*, Torino, Bollati Boringhieri, 2010.

2. Internet Systems Consortium, "Internet Host Count History," http://ftp.isc.Org/www/survey/reports/2012/07/.

3. Rita Tehan, "Internet Statistics: Explanation and Sources," CRS Report for Congress, 6 February, 2002: pp. 8-9, http://digital.library.unt.edu/ark:/67531/metacrs3473/. Peter Lyman and Hal Varian reported 2.1 billion static web pages for a total of circa 21 terabytes and 100% growth per year, Peter Lyman and Hal R. Varian, "Reprint: How Much Information?," *The Journal of Electronic Publishing*, 6, no. 2 (2000), http://dx.doi.org/10.3998/3336451.0006.204,

4. See "The Size of the World Wide Web (The Internet)," 5 June 2013, http://www.worldwidewebsize.com.

Figure 1 – Internet Users, 1995-2013

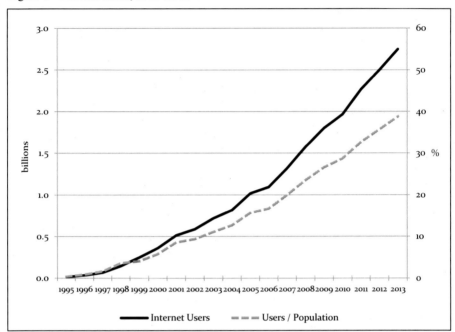

Source: "Internet World Stats. Internet Growth Statistics" (data from March 2013), http://www. internetworldstats.com/emarketing.htm. Other sources present different but not contradictory data. See, for example, data from the International Telecommunication Union at http://www.itu.int/en/ITU-D/ Statistics/Pages/default.aspx and from the World Association of Newspapers and News Publishers at http:// www.wptdatabase.org/summaries/internet-users-0. See also Sara Leckner and Ulrika Facht, "A Sampler of International Media and Communication Statistics, 2010", Göteberg, Nordicom, 2010, http://www. nordicom.gu.se/common/publ_pdf/NMT 12.pdf.

7,500 terabytes of data, compared to the 19 terabytes published on the Internet's "surface"[5] (a single terabyte can contain 300 million pages of text, or alternatively 250 films, or 100,000 medical x-ray images). The fact remains that between 2006 and 2012 the international band's capacity increased from 5 to 77 terabytes per second and in 2012 had registered a 40% growth rate, irrespective of the economic and financial crises of the same period. Since 2007, the costs sustained by providers to connect to the network's backbone in a large city like London

5. Michael K. Bergman, "White Paper: The Deep Web: Surfacing Hidden Value," *The Journal of Electronics Publishing*, 7, no. 1 (2001), http://dx.doi.org/10.3998/3336451.0007.104. Estimates have been reported that suggest more than 1/6 of the web has yet to be indexed and that there are more than 200,000 deep sites, for a total of 550 billion documents, compared to the 1 billion documents that exist on the indexed web, Denis Shestakov, "Search Interfaces on the Web: Querying and Characterizing," University of Turku, Centre for Computer Science, Dissertation n. 104, May 2008: pp. 1, 9, 20, https://www.doria.fi/bitstream/handle/10024/38506/ diss2008shestakov.pdf?Sequence=3.

Figure 2 – Distribution of Internet Users, 2012

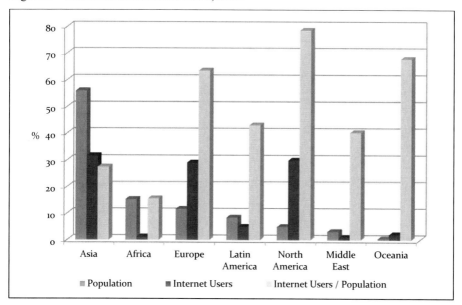

Source: "Internet World Stats. Usage and Population Statistics" (data from June 30, 2012), http://www. internetworldstats.com/stats.htm. The data are shown as percentages in order to be comparable.

have fallen each year by 31%, while they have decreased by 26% in Hong Kong and 22% in New York and São Paulo.[6]

Furthermore, the Internet's role in the contemporary world cannot be measured just in terms of its users, hosts or webpages. Indeed, every day and with increasing frequency the Net is used for commercial and financial transactions, while continuing to absorb all other forms of communication and information management, and above all allowing and favouring the development of new social relations. It is therefore necessary to account for such phenomena, if only very briefly and by way of example.

Like nearly every aspect of Internet, e-commerce cannot be measured easily. Assessments vary to such an extent that absolute figures for both business-to-business (B2B) and business-to-consumer (B2C)[7] transactions are unreliable. However the total number of commercial exchanges is clearly increasing rapidly.[8]

6. Telegeography, "Global Internet Geography Executive Summary," 2012, http://www. telegeography.com/page_attachments/products/website/research-services/global-internet-geography/0003/1871/GIG_Executive_Summary.pdf.

7. Barbara Fraumeni presents, for example, data indicating that estimates for the year 2000 range from 52 to 406 billion dollars for B2B transactions, and between 7 and 200 billion for B2C transactions, Barbara M. Fraumeni, "E-commerce: Measurement and Measurement Issues," *The American Economic Review*, 91, no. 2 (2001): p. 319.

8. See David L. Banks and Yasmin H. Said, "Data Mining in Electronic Commerce," *Statistical Science*, 21, no. 2 (2006): pp. 234-246.

Figure 3 – Internet Hosts, 1995-2012

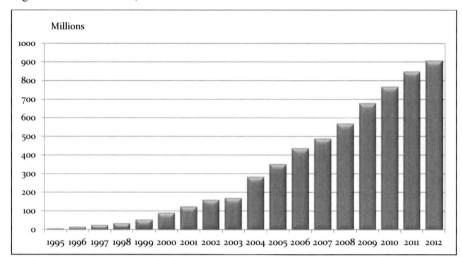

Source: Internet Systems Consortium, "Internet Host Count History," http://ftp.isc.org/www/survey/reports/2012/07/.

In the United States, B2B e-commerce rose from 3,161 to 3,705 billion dollars between 2009 and 2010 (from 33 to 34.7% of the total), and B2C e-commerce increased from 385 to 424 billion dollars (from 42.8 to 46.4%).[9] E-commerce is especially advanced in the US, which is home to a very large number of active online hosts, users and agencies;[10] however the EU also accounted for 13.9% of the total transaction value in 2010,[11] while the number of individuals who made online purchases rose from 20 to 43% between 2004 and 2011.[12] Similar patterns were observed to various degrees in numerous other countries.

Such phenomena are an integral part of the sweeping process of globalization that has unfolded in international economy and finance over the last forty years, and since the 1990s the Internet has precisely been the prime site of this process. Direct foreign investments (net inflows), that rose from 10.4 billion dollars in 1970 to 1.62 trillion in 2000, began rising once again following a recession between 2001 and 2002, and by the year 2007 reached a total of 2.35 trillion. Between 1992 and 2007 the value of stock exchanges rose from 4.78 to 98.82

9. US Census Bureau, "E-Stats," 10 May 2012, http://www.census.gov/econ/estats/2010/2010reportfinal.pdf.

10. According to data from the OECD, "Business-to-Consumer E-commerce Statistics," 2001, http://www.oecd.org/dataoecd/34/36/1864439.pdf), in the year 2000 the US was responsible for 65.4% (39.5 billion dollars) of the total transaction value among 19 participating countries, as well as 68.8% (28.5 million dollars) among online buyers.

11. OECD, "E-commerce Uptake," in "OECD Science, Technology and Industry Scoreboard 2011," http://dx.doi.org/10.1787/888932488027.

12. European Commission, Eurostat, "Information Society," updated 25 June 2012, http://epp.eurostat.ec.europa.eu/portal/page/portal/information_society/data/database.

trillion dollars, from 21% to 182% of the gross world product.[13] Global financial flows are also difficult to quantify; some have hypothesized in very general terms that at the end of the 20th century the global value of so-called "cyber-economics" amounted to a figure 50-100 times greater than that the actual economy. It has also been estimated that in this same period the daily volume on currency exchange markets was 60 times greater than the exportation of commercial goods.[14]

In the United States, where in 1999 financial activity was equivalent to 951% of GDP,[15] in 2007 gross inflows of 2.13 trillion dollars and outflows of 1.47 trillion dollars were recorded (without taking derivatives into account), against a current account deficit of 730 billion. The United Kingdom in the same year had an 80 billion dollar current account deficit and at least two trillion in gross financial outflows; Switzerland, with a 43 billion dollar surplus saw 325 billion dollars in gross financial inflows.[16]

The list of more or less partial data could be much longer, but the Internet's fundamental role in the growth of the flows that rendered the world economy increasingly transnational is completely clear. This is enough to affirm that the Internet and the Web are of the utmost importance in the modern world and in the globalization processes that are central to the current era. "The ubiquity," wrote Christopher T. Marsden, "rapid penetration and commonplace necessity of international data flows over digital communications networks (consider Internet email), combined with the economic and social effects of such flows, makes the Internet the paradigm of globalization."[17] In other words, the Internet is the reason for the most distinctive features that since the 1990s have differentiated modern-day globalization from what was previously observed during the 19th and 20th centuries, as well as during a new phase of the process that began in 1945, following the period of crisis and de-globalization that occurred between the two world wars.[18] These features have been aptly illustrated by Moisés Naím, who,

13. World Bank, "World Development Indicators & Global Development Finance," http://databank.worldbank.org/data/views/variableselection/selectvariables.aspx?Source=world-development-indicators#. Furthermore, the economic-financial crisis that broke out in 2007 caused investments to drop to 1.4 trillion dollars in 2011 and stock market exchanges to fall to 66.4 trillion dollars (98% of the global GDP).

14. See Luciano Gallino, "Su alcune trasformazioni del lavoro," in *Alla ricerca del lavoro. Tra storia e sociologia: bilancio storiografico e prospettive di studio*, ed. by Angelo Varni, Turin, Rosenberg & Sellier, 1998, p. 45; Robert Gilpin, *The Challenge of Global Capitalism: The World Economy in the 21st Century*, Princeton, NJ, Princeton University Press, 2000, p. 18.

15. Elvio Dal Bosco, *La leggenda della globalizzazione*, Turin, Bollati Boringhieri, 2004, p. 77, table 2.5.

16. Karen H. Johnson, "Gross or Net International Financial Flows: Understanding the Financial Crisis," Working Paper, July 2009, Council on Foreign Relations, Center for Geo-economic Studies, http://www.cfr.org/international-finance/gross-net-international-financial-flows-understanding-financial-crisis/p19726.

17. Christopher T. Marsden, "Hyperglobalized Individuals: the Internet, Globalization, Freedom and Terrorism," *Foresight*, 6, no. 3 (2004): p. 130.

18. See Kevin H. O'Rourke and Jeffrey G. Williamson, *Globalization and History: The Evolution of a Nineteenth-Century Atlantic Economy*, Cambridge, MA, MIT Press, 1999. For the various forms of globalization observed throughout history, see Anthony G. Hopkins, ed.,

disputing the idea that "the printing press, the telegraph, and the telephone were technologies as disruptive in their day as the Internet," has written:

> As Internet access penetrates the most remote corners of the globe, it is transforming the lives of more people, in more places, more cheaply than ever before – and the pace of change is accelerating faster than we can hope to chronicle it.
> Today's globalization is also more individualized than ever. The telegraph was most intensively used by institutions, but the Internet is a truly personal tool that allows Spanish women to find marriage prospects in Argentina, and South African teenagers to share music files with peers in Scotland. Contemporary globalization is also different in that the speed at which it is integrating human activities is often instantaneous and almost costless. Moreover, the quantitative change in each of globalization's components – economic, cultural, military, etc. – is so enormous that it creates a qualitative change.[19]

Of the three aspects highlighted by the author – individualistic qualities, speed and low costs – we believe that the first one is the discriminating factor. The online transmission of documents is indeed so rapid as to be considered real time, and the resulting acceleration undoubtedly produced a fundamental qualitative change. However, speed is not an attribute that only the Internet possesses (certain analogous media are even faster), and changes of a similar importance, relatively speaking, have also occurred in the past. In fact, increasing speeds have characterized the history of communication for centuries and were a crucial factor in earlier forms of globalization, defined by Christopher A. Bayly as "a progressive increase of the scale of social processes from a local or regional to a world level."[20]

In 1949, Fernand Braudel wrote that in the age of Philip II the Mediterranean was 60 days long,[21] thus measuring a physical space in terms of time. In the 18th century, progress made in sailing capabilities "shrunk" the Atlantic Ocean to the size of the Mediterranean of two centuries prior, and by the mid-nineteenth century steam ships had further reduced journey times to just two weeks.[22] At the same time, the electric telegraph made it possible for information to travel independently from its messengers,[23] and after 1865 – when an underwater cable connected the old and new worlds – it "miniaturized" the Atlantic Ocean, slashing communication times from weeks to minutes. It is no coincidence that Reinhart Koselleck established that modernity (*Neuzeit*) took root between the sixteenth and eighteenth centuries and identified acceleration as the general and "infallible" criterion that defined it.[24]

Globalization in World History, New York, Norton, 2002; Christopher A. Bayly, *The Birth of Modern World, 1780-1914: Global Connections and Comparisons*, Malden, MA, Blackwell, 2004; Peter N. Stearns, *Globalization in World History*, London – New York, Routledge, 2010.

19. Moisés Naím, "Think Again: Globalization," *Foreign Policy*, 171 (16 February 2009), http://www.foreignpolicy.com/articles/2009/02/16/think_again_globalization.

20. Christopher A. Bayly, "'Archaic' and 'Modern' Globalization in the Eurasian and African Arena, ca. 1750-1850," in Hopkins, ed., *Globalization in World History*, p. 47.

21. Fernand Braudel, *The Mediterranean and the Mediterranean World in the Age of Philip II*, vol. 1, Berkeley, University of California Press, 1995 [1949], pp. 360-371.

22. Asa Briggs and Peter Burke, *A Social History of the Media: From Gutenberg to the Internet*, Cambridge, Polity Press, 2009, pp. 23, 126-127.

23. Terhi Rantanen, *The Media and Globalization*, London, Sage, 2005, p. 49.

24. Reinhart Koselleck, "The Eighteenth Century as the Beginning of Modernity," [1987] in R. Koselleck, *The Practice of Conceptual History: Timing History, Spacing Concepts*, preface

Of course, Internet's speed – along with its low access costs for private citizens – has made it a means of communication that is more personal than institutional, and this sets it apart from past forms of communication. Yet neither low costs nor speed alone can account for its distinctiveness: to explain this, we must also consider that the Internet has created new forms of social communication, in as much as it is a distributed network.[25] Television is hierarchical and unidirectional, since information is transmitted from the center to the periphery and not vice versa, while the telephone establishes an equal connection but is limited to just two people. The Internet interconnects a large number of individuals and at the same time is also interactive, as each of these connections transmits and receives; each apparatus and everyone using them have equal possibilities. As such, the web lends individualistic traits to contemporary globalization, and this, more than any other element, is what distinguishes it from past forms.

These traits have come into sharp focus since the web has entered a period defined as 2.0.[26] Generally speaking, this term refers to certain changes that have taken place in the ways in which web programmers and end users make use of the Internet. These new uses include the possibility of adding comments to pages published online. In this way an enormous quantity of information that was once reserved to two-person exchanges, or at most to closed groups such as mailing lists (offhand comments, outbursts or knee-jerk reactions), is now accessible through search engines and visible to everybody. Websites such as eBay, Wikipedia, YouTube, Facebook and blogs are also expressions of this shift, allowing every user to share and exchange goods, knowledge, video clips, images, personal data, opinions and thoughts. As such, the information regarding these sites is extremely significant.

Since its founding in 1995, eBay's users have grown from 340,000 in 1997 to more than 100 million in 2011, and the value of their tradings has increased from 100 million to 92 billion dollars. In addition, the online communication programme Skype was a part of eBay Inc. between 2005 and 2009, and in this four-year period the number of users grew from 171 to more than 400 million.[27] However, these absolute figures are meaningful only in part. The Skype blog reported peak moments in 2012 when 45 million users were connected simultaneously, for on average over 200 million connections per month. A quarter of all international telephone calls are now made using Skype.[28] Similarly, articles published on the English language

by Hayden White, Stanford, Stanford University Press, 2002, p. 165; Reinhart Koselleck, "'Neuzeit:' Remarks on the Semantics of the Modern Concepts of Movement," in R. Koselleck, *Futures Past: On the Semantics of Historical Time*, introduction by Keith Tribe, New York, Columbia University Press, 2004, pp. 222-254.

25. On this see below, pp. 32-33.

26. Tim O'Reilly, "What Is Web 2.0: Design Patterns and Business Models for the Next Generation of Software," in "O'Reilly," 30 September 2005, http://oreilly.com/web2/archive/what-is-web-20.html.

27. ebay Inc.'s annual reports from 1998 to 2011, http://investor.ebayinc.com/annuals.cfm. Data on ebay from 1996 to 2006, and on others later in the text, are contained in Johnny Ryan, *A History of the Internet and the Digital Future*, London, Reaktion Books, 2010, pp. 125, 138, 150-154.

28. http://skypenumerology.blogspot.it.

version of Wikipedia increased from 19,700 in January 2002 to 4.3 million in June 2013.[29] The number of hours of video uploaded every minute on YouTube stood at 48 in 2011 (already eight times greater than in June 2007),[30] and in 2013 it rose to 72, for a total of more than 4 billion hours of video per day.[31]

Among the most widely used social networks, between September 2012 and May 2013 Facebook and Twitter had 927.4 and 554.8 million members, respectively,[32] but by 2009 Facebook had recorded nearly 1.2 billion visits a months, with an additional 810,000 visits to Myspace and 425,000 to the other most widely used social networks.[33] As for blogs, which are increasingly relevant in social network activity, from 2003 to 2006 the total number rose from less than two million to 34.5 million, and by 2011 the number was hovering around 160 million. In 2008 there were 900,000 messages posted every 24 hours on the so-called "blogosphere" and 77% of active Internet users read blogs.[34]

The impact of these phenomena – as well as others that are too numerous to count – on social relations between individuals and more or less large groups has been enormous and has also had highly relevant repercussions in the so-called public sphere. The literature on this subject is too extensive to summarize even just its central themes,[35] but according to many scholars the web – in addition to infringing upon the pre-existing separation between the private and public spheres – has revitalized the latter, following a period in which, according to Jürgen Habermas, it had been colonized and deprived by mass media such as the radio and television.[36] Different opinions are held in this respect as well. In 2006, Jürgen Habermas, referring to the theme of the network "that counterbalances the seeming deficits that stem from the impersonal and asymmetrical character of broadcasting by reintroducing deliberative elements in electronic communication," wrote that Internet "has

29. "Size of Wikipedia," http://en.wikipedia.org/wiki/Wikipedia:Size_of_Wikipedia.

30. "You Tube Gets 48 Hours of Video Every Minute!," 25 May 2011, http://www. Youtube.com/watch?V=vqibgvxdg90.

31. http://www.youtube.com/t/press_statistics/.

32. Internet World Stats, "Facebook Growth Stats for 2011-2012," http://www. internetworldstats.com/facebook.htm; Statistic Brain, "Twitter Statistics," 9 May 2012, http://www.statisticbrain.com/twitter-statistics/.

33. http://blog.compete.com/2009/02/09/facebook-myspace-twitter-social-network/ (data from January 2009).

34. Technorati, "State of the Blogosphere," 2004-2011, http://technorati.com/state-of-the-blogosphere/; Rightmix Marketing, "2011 Blogging Statistics [Infographic]," http://www. rightmixmarketing.com/right-mix-blog/blogging-statistics/.

35. On the subject, see among others "Digitising the Public Sphere," *Javnost – The Public*, 16, no. 1 (2009); Paolo Jedlowski and Olimpia Affuso, eds., *Sfera pubblica. Il concetto e i suoi luoghi*, Cosenza, Luigi Pellegrini, 2010; João C. Correira and Rousiley C. Maia, eds., *Public Sphere Reconsidered: Theories and Practices*, Covilhã, labcom Books, 2011, http://www.livroslabcom.ubi.pt/pdfs/20120305-public_sphere_reconsidered_ebook.pdf.

36. See, in particular, Jürgen Habermas, *The Structural Transformation of the Public Sphere: An Inquiry Into a Category of Bourgeois Society*, Cambridge, MA, MIT Press, 1989 [1962]); *The Theory of Communicative Action*, Boston, Beacon Press, 1984-1987 [1981]; *Between Facts and Norms: Contributions to a Discourse Theory of Law and Democracy*, Cambridge, MA, MIT Press, 1996 [1992].

certainly reactivated the grassroots of an egalitarian public of writers and readers." It was his belief however that the web could boast of "unequivocal democratic merits" only within the context of authoritarian regimes that attempt to control and repress public opinion because it undermines censorship. In liberal regimes:

> the rise of millions of fragmented chat rooms across the world tend instead to lead to the fragmentation of large but politically focused mass audiences into a huge number of isolated issue publics. Within established national public spheres, the online debates of web users only promote political communication, when news groups crystallize around the focal points of the quality press, for example, national newspapers and political magazines.[37]

As Terje Rasmussen has observed, Habermas is interested primarily in political aspects of the public sphere, but also favours the national dimension "that *directly* influences legitimate, political decision-making" with respect to local, regional and global public spaces.[38] If the fragmentation of the public sphere on the Net is a given fact (which also coexists with a trend toward globalization), in reality at a political level the Internet's role is anything but marginal. This is apparent not just in authoritarian regimes such as those that were challenged by the so-called Arab Spring, but also in democratic contexts, as seen in the Pirate Parties of Sweden, Germany and other countries, Occupy Wall Street, Spain's "Indignados" or the Italian "Five Star Movement."

The fact is that ever since news and opinions have become freely accessible online, the circulation of newspapers and magazines – which had been steadily increasing since the 1940s – has entered a period of decline. This drop has been particularly pronounced in the United States, where the number of newspaper copies in circulation had reached a high of 63 million in 1988 but subsequently fell to 48.5 million in 2011, reaching levels that were lower than those seen in the 1950s.[39] A similar – if much less marked – trend has also characterized the markets of other OECD countries: from 2007 to 2009 Great Britain registered a 21% drop, followed by Greece, Italy, Canada, Spain, Turkey and Japan, in that order, which saw decreases of between 20-15%.[40]

According to some estimates, it is true that newspaper circulation rose from 425.8 to 463.3 million copies between 2000 and 2004 in 65 countries on various continents, but this growth was the total sum of a 12.9 million copy decrease in 23 countries and a 51.2 million copy increase in 40 other countries. In addition, if China and India are eliminated from this calculation the final balance would

37. Jürgen Habermas, "Political Communication in Media Society: Does Democracy Still Enjoy an Epistemic Dimension? The Impact of Normative Theory on Empirical Research," *Communication Theory*, 16, no. 4 (2006): p. 423 note 3.

38. Terje Rasmussen, "The Significance of Internet Communication in Public Deliberation," *Javnost – The Public*, 16, no. 1 (2009): p. 19.

39. Newspaper Association of America, "Newspaper Circulation Volume," http://www.naa.org/Trends-and-Numbers/Circulation-Volume/Newspaper-Circulation-Volume.aspx; Ryan, *A History of the Internet and the Digital Future*, p. 162.

40. OECD, Directorate for Science, Technology and Industry, "The Evolutions of News and the Internet," 2010, http://www.oecd.org/dataoecd/30/24/45559596.Pdf.

be negative, since these two countries account for an increase of 40.4 million copies.[41] From 2006 to 2010 newspaper circulation increased by 15% in Asia and 5% in Latin America, however these rates of growth could not compensate for the decline experienced in North America and Europe (by 20 and 10 per cent respectively). As a result, the total of copies sold in the world decreased from 540 million in 2008 to 519 million in 2010.[42]

Internet's influence even on the more established institutional forms of politics has been notable. As Johnny Ryan has written, the Net has become increasingly the "nervous system" of American presidential campaigns, and indeed played an important role in the nomination of Barack Obama and his 2008 victory. In addition to facilitating the inflow of a considerable number of small donations from the public in the place of fewer large contributions, the use of Internet and the web by some candidates has substituted the traditional "one to many" unidirectional communication with a conversational, interactive and decentralized logic that has favoured active mass participation and the development of "two-way politics."[43]

Moreover, it was the Internet that allowed for the formation and development of transnational movements such as the so-called "no global" or "new global" movements, which were founded on "organizational and membership structures, each one constituting an assemblage of various networks and coalitions, with an absence of a centralized body or hierarchy."[44] Active primarily in the fields of human and civil rights, the environment, peace, justice and global inequality, these "movements of movements" – for which the botanical metaphor of the rhizome has been attributed[45] – reflect the structure of the "network of networks" that made them possible.[46]

41. UNESCO Institute for Statistics, "Public Reports, Newspapers," http://stats.uis. unesco.org/unesco/tableviewer/tableview.aspx?Reportid=398.

42. World Association of Newspapers and News Publishers, "World Press Trends 2011," http://www.wan-ifra.org/articles/2012/04/17/world-press-trends-2011.

43. Ryan, *A History of the Internet and the Digital Future*, pp. 164-177. See also Aaron Smith, "The Internet's Role in Campaign 2008," April 2009, http://web.pewinternet.org/~/media/Files/Reports/2009/The_Internets_Role_in_Campaign_2008.pdf. Certain limits to the political use of the Internet in the US have been underlined in Stephen Zavestoski, Stuart Shulman and David Schlosberg, "Democracy and the Environment on the Internet: Electronic Citizen Participation in Regulatory Rulemaking," *Science, Technology, & Human Values*, 31, no. 4 (2006): pp. 383-408.

44. Kléber G. Ghimire, "The Contemporary Global Social Movements: Emergent Proposals, Connectivity and Development Implications," UN Research Institute for Social Development, Programme on Civil Society and Social Movements, Paper n. 19, 2005: p. 9, http://www.unrisd.org/80256B3C005BCCF9/%28httpauxpages%29/F0F8C2DF84C2FB2DC 1257088002BFBD9/$file/ghimire.pdf.

45. See Oliver Froehling, "The Cyberspace 'War of Ink and Internet' in Chiapas, Mexico," *Geographical Review*, 87, no. 2 (1997): pp. 291-307. Rhizome is an extension of the roots of certain herbaceous plants; it generally grows horizontally and underground.

46. See, among others, Jennifer Earl and Alan Schussman, "The New Site of Activism: On-line Organizations, Movement Entrepreneurs, and the Changing Location of Social Movement Decision Making," in "Consensus Decision Making, Northern Ireland and Indigenous Movements," ed. by Patrick G. Coy, *Research in Social Movements, Conflicts and Change*, 24 (2002): pp. 155-187; John Clark and Nuno Themundo, "The Age of Protest:

It is in the relations between individuals and groups, however, that this enormous change has had the most substantial effect. The web has given a voice to subjects who in the past could only be heard in exceptional circumstances and/ or in geographically or socially limited circles. It has connected a multitude of persons in an open global space, breaking down the distances that separate them in the physical world. Taken together, the various kinds of social relations that have arisen from the web amount to a significant and undeniably novel phenomenon.

The extent of this change can be understood thoroughly by using the historiographical category of "sociability," which was accredited to Maurice Agulhon in his studies of eighteenth and nineteenth century France.[47] This concept, which recalls the microsociology of groups that was developed by Georges Gurvitch in the 1930s, describes the intensity of life through inter-individual relations and the ways in which these relations are manifested. It is a particularly useful tool for analyzing the networks of relations that have developed online, as it refers to the forms and organization of these relations rather than to social structures (such as class and profession), underlines the permeability of social fields and establishes the need to define various groups on the basis of their function and the spaces that they occupy.[48]

Every kind of activity and sociability that we have summarized here arose from a "hyperglobalization of the individual,"[49] which has been further reinforced by the strong growth in the number of cellular phones that are able to connect to the Internet: in 2011 5.8 billion cell phones were estimated to exist, of which 940 million could access 3G services.[50] This has given rise to a "hyperglobalized interdependent Internet planet,"[51] and has launched a new phase of contemporary globalization. Many potentially harmful pursuits, including terrorist activities, have also found a home within this "Internet-connected planet," and as such the question of a different and more rigorous regulation of the network has been repeatedly discussed.[52]

Internet-Based 'Dot Causes' and the 'Anti-Globalization' Movement," in *Globalizing Civic Engagement: Global Society and Transnational Action*, ed. by John Clark, London, Earthscan, 2003, pp. 109-126; Sidney Tarrow, *The New Transnational Activism*, Cambridge, Cambridge University Press, 2005; Sidney Tarrow and Donatella Della Porta, eds., *Transnational Protest and Global Activism: People, Passions, and Power*, Lanham, MD, Rowman & Littlefield, 2005. See also *Rassegna italiana di sociologia*, 46, no. 2 (2005) with essays by Tarrow, Della Porta, Massimiliano Andretta and Dieter Rucht.

47. Maurice Agulhon, *Pénitents et Francs-Maçons de l'ancienne Provence: Essai sur la sociabilité méridionale*, Paris, Fayard, 1968; Maurice Agulhon, *Le Cercle dans la France bourgeoise: 1810-1848. Étude d'una mutation de sociabilité*, Paris, A. Colin, 1977.

48. See Giuliana Gemelli and Maria Malatesta, "Le avventure della sociabilità," in *Forme di sociabilità nella storiografia francese contemporanea*, ed. by Giuliana Gemelli and Maria Malatesta, Milano, Feltrinelli, 1982 and the bibliographical references cited within.

49. Marsden, "Hyperglobalized Individuals," p. 130.

50. International Telecommunications Union, "The World in 2011: ICT Facts and Figures," http://www.itu.int/ITU-D/ict/material/factsfigures2011.pdf.

51. Marsden, "Hyperglobalized Individuals," p. 138.

52. Marsden himself has raised the issue. For some positions on this matter, see for example Saskia Sassen, *Territory, Authority, Rights: From Medieval to Global Assemblages*, Princeton, NJ, Princeton University Press, 2006.

Without delving too extensively into the debate, we believe that the governance of Internet has, thus far, been generally consistent with its characteristics, because it is based on a flexible decision-making model that equally engages all public and private stakeholders, assigns a central role to those who develop the network and is essentially user-oriented.[53] As it is largely self-regulated and can be viewed as "an orderly anarchy,"[54] Internet possesses a non-hierarchical, acephalous, open and individualistic nature. These qualities are a mirror of its users and, above all, are the basis for the peculiarities of contemporary globalization that we have already indicated.

It is thus even more essential that we understand Internet's characteristics and workings. However, a synchronic analysis of Internet in its current state is inadequate. Internet is the final product of a process that has been anything but linear and has developed over the course of many decades, over the course of which certain alternatives have been adopted and others have been discarded. Therefore, we must ask ourselves when, how and why the Internet's current characteristics were established. In order to respond to these questions we need to reconstruct the network's history.

Toward a History of the Net

In truth, since the 1990s a number of histories of the Internet have been written. However these histories have tended to focused on and emphasize single aspects of the process. In a perceptive review in 1998, Roy Rosenzweig identified four different approaches to capturing the history of the Internet, all of which he held to be partial and inadequate. He defined these approaches, respectively, as biographic, bureaucratic, ideological and social.[55]

In the first approach, the history of the Internet's origins ultimately boils down to a parade of inspired geniuses, with each one laying a brick for a building still under construction. The brilliant book by Katie Hafner and Matthew Lyon joins this "great man approach" with an emphasis on the civil goals of the Net since its origins, which in truth are mostly military.[56] Arthur L. Norberg and Judy

53. On the governance of the Internet see below, pp. 155-159.
54. A. Michael Froomkin, "Habermas@Discourse.Net: Toward a Critical Theory of Cyberspace," *Harvard Law Review*, 116, no. 3 (2003): p. 756.
55. Roy Rosenzweig, "How Will the Net's History Be Written? Historians and the Internet," in *Academy & the Internet*, ed. by Helen F. Nissenbaum and Monroe E. Price, New York, Peter Lang, 2004, pp. 1-34. The first version of this essay, ("Bureaucrats, Warriors, and Hackers: Writing the History of the Internet," *The American Historical Review*, 103, no. 5 (1998): pp. 1530-1552) is published in Roy Rosenzweig, *Clio Wired: The Future of the Past in the Digital Age*, introduction by Anthony Grafton, New York, Columbia University Press, 2011, pp. 179-202. See also the critical analysis by Jon Guice, "Looking Backward and Forward at the Internet," *The Information Society*, 14, no. 3 (1998): pp. 201-211.
56. Katie Hafner and Matthew Lyon, *Where Wizards Stay Up Late: The Origins of the Internet*, 2nd ed., New York: Simon & Schuster, 1998 [1996]. On the same topic, see John Naughton, *A Brief History of the Future: The Origins of Internet*, London, Weindefeld & Nicholson, 1999.

E. O'Neill's perspective is in turn bureaucratic-institutional,[57] which conversely highlights the positive role of the military institution and endorses what Rosenzweig defined as a "marriage of computer and defence." Hafner and Lyon deemphasize the military, technical and intellectual aspects of the Internet's history, while Norberg and O'Neill focus less on its political and economic context. Although his approach does not greatly differ from the latter authors, Thomas P. Hughes does dedicate ample space to context in a comparative study of the first network – Arpanet – and three other complex systems, adopting a system approach that is more focused "upon management rather than upon engineering and science."[58]

The Closed World by Paul N. Edwards is focused to an even greater extent on context. This original cultural study well exemplifies the ideological approach, although it addresses the network only marginally. Edwards considers the computer to be both the cause and the effect of the "closed world" of the Cold War, and he argues that the transition from analogical to digital occurred not because of the technological superiority of the latter, but because it catered to the need for centralized command and control that existed in the United States at that time.[59]

Finally, Michael and Ronda Hauben took a social approach that insists on "the bottom-up" origins of the Net, its connections to the "counterculture" of the 1960s and 1970s, and its ability to produce a new type of "online citizen," the "netizen."[60] Rosenzweig considered such a perspective to be incomplete as well: "some of them may have had beards, but most were also willing to take defense department funding," he wrote of the young people who took part in the creation of the first network: "maybe the closed world of the military and the open world of the hippies were not as separate as we sometimes think." Despite this, it was his view that "it offers an interpretive perspective that should be central to any future Net history."[61] These are his conclusions:

> Any history of the Internet will have to locate this story within its multiple social, political, and cultural contexts. This is particularly true since the Internet [...] seems to be emerging as a "meta-medium" that combines aspects of the telephone, post office, movie theater, television set, newspaper, shopping mall, street corner, and a great deal more. Such a profound and complex development cannot be divorced from the idiosyncratic and personal

57. Arthur L. Norberg and Judy E. O'Neill, with contributions by Kerry J. Freedman, *Transforming Computer Technology: Information Processing for the Pentagon, 1962-1986*, Baltimore – London, Johns Hopkins University Press, 1996.

58. Thomas P. Hughes, *Rescuing Prometheus*, New York, Vintage Books, 2000 [1998], p. 5. See also Thomas P. Hughes, "The Evolution of Large Technological Systems," in *The Social Construction of Technological Systems*, ed. by Wiebe E. Bijker, Thomas P. Hughes and Trevor Pinch, Cambridge, MA, MIT Press, 1987, pp. 51-82; Agatha C. Hughes and Thomas C. Hughes, eds., *Systems, Experts, and Computers: The System Approach in Management and Engineering, World War II and After*, Cambridge, MA – London, MIT Press, 2000.

59. Paul N. Edwards, *The Closed World: Computers and the Politics of Discourse in Cold War America*, Cambridge, MA – London, MIT Press, 1996.

60. Michael and Ronda Hauben, *Netizens: On the History and Impact of Usenet and the Internet*, Los Alamitos, CA, IEEE Computer Society Press, 1997, available for consultation at http://www.columbia.edu/~hauben/book-pdf/.

61. Roy Rosenzweig, "How Will the Net's History Be Written?," pp. 21, 24, 16.

visions of some scientists and bureaucrats whose sweat and dedication got the project up and running, from the social history of the field of computer science, from the Cold Warriors who provided massive government funding of computers and networking as tools for fighting nuclear and conventional war, and from the countercultural radicalism that sought to redirect technology toward a more decentralized and nonhierarchical vision of society.[62]

Among the publications that appeared after 1998, *Inventing the Internet* by Janet Abbate is particularly noteworthy. It presents a history of technology that resists the progressive determinism that is often seen in this field, and emphasizes rather the "protean" nature of the Net, which allowed it to develop in directions that were neither predictable nor predetermined. Abbate addresses the political and economic contexts of the period from the 1960s to the 1980s and successfully resolves the apparent paradox of a network that is both civil and essentially private, the first embryo of which was created with public funds and by a military institution no less. However, her work does not shed light on the complex cultural background of the origins of the Internet: intellectuals such as Vannevar Bush, Norbert Wiener and others who influenced the progression of events are not cited here. At the same time the role of a key figure such as Joseph C.R. Licklider is decidedly undervalued.[63]

Among recent studies, a comprehensive essay by Hans Dieter Hellige published in 2008 deserves mention. Based on a meticulous critical analysis of existing literature, the author interprets the history of Internet from its origins as a *Lernprozess*, or learning process. More specifically, he believes that Internet's development was complex and not preordained, and was made possible by the flexibility of the system that was adopted. Multiple elements contributed to the system, including military and university research, the user community and the coexistence of varying models during the course of a process that presented many choices and conflicts.[64] We were particularly persuaded by this interpretation to the extent that in a later section of our study we have adopted the metaphor coined by Hellige – a strange alliance between "uniforms and sneakers" – to illustrate the primary reason for the success and historical significance of the network.[65] "The Internet," Hellige wrote, "is not a garage or lab invention; rather, it is a complex system development that emerged in multiple stages at the conjunctions between large scale academic and military research and the information technology cultures of users."[66]

Finally, Martin Campbell-Kelly and Daniel D. Garcia-Swarz have offered a stringent critique of studies on the Internet's history, many of which they believe

---

62. *Ibid.*, pp. 26-27.

63. Janet Abbate, *Inventing the Internet*, Cambridge, MA – London, MIT Press, 1999. M. Mitchell Waldrop dedicated an exhaustive and well-documented biography to Licklider in *The Dream Machine: J.C.R. Licklider and the Revolution That Made Computing Personal*, New York, Viking, 2001. On the original period, a brief but well-balanced summary containing numerous references is provided by Ryan, *A History of the Internet and the Digital Future*.

64. Hans Dieter Hellige, "Die Geschichte des Internet als Lernprozess," in *Informatik und Gesellschaft: Verflechtungen un Perspektiven*, ed. by Hans-Jörg Kreowski, Münster – Hamburg – Berlin, LIT Verlag, 2008, pp. 121-170.

65. *Ibid.* See also below, p. 147.

66. *Ibid.*, p. 123.

amount to teleologies or "Whig histories," as they retrace Internet to a single origin – Arpanet, the first packet switching network that began operating in 1969 – while overlooking other existing technologies. Indeed, many studies (including ours) devote little attention to the alternatives that for one reason or another failed to take off. However, Campbell-Kelly and Garcia-Swarz also clearly explain the reasons why Arpanet prevailed.[67]

The additional problems that arise when approaching some of these texts and the events depicted reflect familiar issues to scholars of contemporary history; nonetheless, two caveats in particular need to be highlighted. The first regards the need to avoid an excessive dependency on the way in which the protagonists of Internet's history have represented themselves. Most of these individuals were active in the field for a long time or are still working in it, and they have written memoirs, animated meetings, given interviews and responded to emails. These constitute important and extremely interesting material, but they need to be thoroughly and critically verified against contemporary sources, in the absence of which memory tends to overlap with and condition history. The overestimation of these documents is favoured by the fact that they have been frequently consulted online, which is further confirmation of the need for attentive verification.[68]

The second caveat concerns archival sources. In addition to the fact that the breadth of this topic makes the systematic consultation of these sources an arduous task – particularly for someone who does not live in the United States – a portion of them remain inaccessible. The archives of the US Defence Department's Advanced Research Project Agency (ARPA) in particular are only partially accessible, because some of the sources dealing with the Internet's origins remain classified or have not been deposited in the public section of the National Archives and Records Administration (NARA).[69] Therefore, we were only able to work with documents that were available at NARA, along with Licklider's papers, which are kept at the Massachusetts Institute of Technology (MIT).[70] In addition to these sources, there are

---

67. Martin Campbell-Kelly and Daniel D. Garcia-Swartz, "The History of the Internet: The Missing Narratives," *Journal of Information Technology*, 28, no. 1 (2013): pp. 18-33. We were less convinced by arguments in Paul N. Edwards, "Some Say the Internet Should Never Have Happened," in *Media, Technology, and Society: Theories of Media Evolution*, ed. by W. Russell Neuman, Ann Arbor, University of Michigan Press, 2010, pp. 141-160, and not just because Edwards believed that Internet was "utterly inevitable" (p. 157). He writes that "the Internet's history lies shrouded in myth" and that by filling in the various pieces of the puzzle a surprisingly different image emerges. Ultimately, however, he does not add much to this image and he concludes that the myth largely corresponds to reality (pp. 141, 143-144, 146).

68. For example, the interviews used by Arthur Norberg and Judy O'Neill are available on the website of the Charles Babbage Institute, University of Minnesota, http://www.cbi.umn.edu/oh/index.phtml, while the materials gathered by Katie Hafner and Matthew Lyon can be consulted at http://www.archive.org/details/arpanet.

69. In 2007 and 2009, at the National Archives in College Park, MD, only some of the resources used by Norberg and O'Neill were available. It is likely that the scholars had access to these sources because they had done research in contract with the Defence Department.

70. MIT Libraries, Institute Archives and Special Collections, J.C.R. Licklider Papers 1938-1995, Manuscript Collection MC 499 (from here on: Licklider Papers).

many others that are readable online, including documents on the Internet Archive and those published by a number of universities, the Defence Technical Information Centre (DTIC) and by many other official and unofficial sites.[71]

The origins of the Internet can be traced to the 1960s; although it goes without saying that it did not come out of nowhere and was, in fact, preceded by a number of developments. In the early 1960s the structure of a distributed digital network was defined, and in 1966 the project to produce the first network, Arpanet, was launched, which became operational three years later. In keeping with other scholars, we attribute a decisive importance to this period, because we believe that the nature and functioning of Internet largely derive from a series of choices that were made during these and subsequent years. Without entering too deeply into topics that will be addressed later on in this study, suffice it to say that in addition to the configuration of the network, the 1960s saw the development of the mechanism for the transmission of documents within the network (the so-called "packet-switching" method), while the protocols that oversaw its operation were developed in the following decade.

However, in order to justify an emphasis on the importance of the period of Internet's origins, it is imperative that we first address a fundamental question of method and formulate a clear interpretative hypothesis. "The explanation of the very recent in terms of the remotest past, naturally attractive to men who have made of this past their chief subject of research," wrote Marc Bloch, "has sometimes dominated our studies to the point of a hypnosis. In its most characteristic aspect, this idol of the historian tribe may be called the obsession with origins." Because the term is contaminated by two different meanings (beginnings and causes), Bloch believes that the notion of origins is commonly and mistakenly considered to be "a beginning which explains. Worse still, a beginning which is a complete explanation. There is the ambiguity, and there the danger! [...] In any study, seeking the origins of a human activity, there lurks the same danger of confusing ancestry with explanation."[72]

As Charles S. Maier has noted, the usual method for explaining the past consists in essentially connecting "short term events with long term developments." The historian makes an event "accountable" by establishing that it follows a series of preceding events; in other words, that it is part of a sequence, or part of an interlinking set of relations usually defined as a "structure."[73] The fact that every phenomenon is in some way shaped by those that preceded it and by the networks of relations to which it belongs is obvious. However, it is also clear that no phenomenon can be considered predetermined. Before it occurs, any event may be more or less probable, but it is nonetheless possible. As for unforeseen occurrences that lead to breaks and discontinuities in the course of events, these are perceived as interruptions only

71. We have indicated the documents that were procured online in the respective footnotes. Unless otherwise specified, all of the URLs cited were verified on 4 June 2013.

72. Marc Bloch, *The Historian's Craft*, preface by Peter Burke, Manchester, Manchester University Press, 1992 [1949], pp. 24-25, 27.

73. Charles S. Maier, "I paradossi del 'prima' e del 'poi.' Periodizzazioni e rotture nella storia," *Contemporanea*, 2, no. 4 (1999): p. 717.

because the sequence of events considered significant is the product of ex-post selections made by historians. However, in such cases, it is not the past that surprises historians; rather, to draw again on Maier's words, it is their oversights.[74]

In reference to the "embryogenic obsession" that was common in an old tradition of research on Christianity, Bloch wrote: "Great oaks from little acorns grow. But only if they meet favourable conditions of soil and climate, conditions which are entirely beyond the scope of embryology."[75] His metaphor is useful as we introduce the interpretive hypothesis that is the foundation of our study. Arpanet already possessed the "original characteristics" of the current "network of networks," of which it was the first embryo, and these characteristics were preserved and developed through to the present thanks to a series of favourable political, institutional, economic, cultural and social conditions. It is because these conditions were present that since its origins the Net and the network's uses have been shaped – to use economic terminology – by demand rather than supply, and that this user-centric approach has always prevailed.

Despite being promoted and financed by a military institution, Arpanet was actually constructed by its users – who were a community of university researchers, in other words a scientific network – and its configuration was the product of autonomous decisions made by these user-designers. There were many possible options as Arpanet took shape, but the ones that were chosen were those that best responded to the needs and expectations of the users, or appeared the most likely to guarantee the network's development within a specific context or environment that was shaped by those needs. Thus, we believe that in order to fully comprehend the history of the Internet, this must be read as a sort of evolutionary process, which includes the idea of natural selection.[76]

While it is certainly reasonable to consider the effects of the advent and growth of the Net to be a revolution, applying such a label to the innovations that shaped the network's history would unduly re-establish a "heroic" vision of technology, according to which "inventions emerge in a fully developed state from the minds of gifted inventors […], small improvements in technology are ignored or discounted and all emphasis is placed upon the identification of major breakthroughs by specific individuals."[77] Furthermore, it almost goes without

74. *Ibid.*, p. 719.

75. Bloch, *The Historian's Craft*, p. 27.

76. Tao Gong, Lei Qi and Long Li also insist on the crucial role played by the users of two more networks that took shape in the 1980's and take on an "evolutionary" approach, Tao Gong, Lei Qi and Long Li "Lifelike Evolution of csnet and Bitnet: Birth to Death," in *Seventh International Conference on Natural Computation (ICNC 2011) Volume 3*, ed. by Yongsheng Ding, Haiying Wang, Ning Xiong, Kuangrong Hao and Lipo Wang, IEEE, 2011, pp. 1532-1536, http://ieeexplore.ieee.org/stamp/stamp.jsp?Tp= &arnumber=6022261&isnumber=60222 59. Similar observations are made but are neither discussed nor developed in Hafner and Lyon, *Where Wizards Stay Up Late*, pp. 52-53 and in James Gillies and Roger Cailliau, *How the Web Was Born*, Oxford – New York, Oxford University Press, 2000, p. 64.

77. This statement was made by George Basalla, who appropriately enough adopts an evolutionary perspective, George Basalla, *The Evolution of Technology*, Cambridge, Cambridge University Press, 1988, p. 21.

saying that to avoid this tendency does not mean that individual actors in Internet's history go unrecognized; on the contrary, in this way the many lesser known or unknown protagonists are taken into consideration in addition to the recognized protagonists of twentieth-century culture. Historical knowledge is intrinsically individualizing[78] and the network of social relations from which this knowledge is weaved is made up of single individuals.

It has long been a common practice to resort to evolutionary theories in studies on the development of culture, knowledge and technology. This is particularly true of the analogical or metaphorical forms that are imposed by the fundamental difference between biological and cultural evolution (the former occurs by chance, while the latter is conscious and intentional). The literature on these themes is vast and incorporates disciplines from biology to genetics to psychology that lie beyond the realm of our competence. We therefore make only limited references to the ongoing debate within these fields, which primarily serve to point out how the range of theories on this topic presents significant problems for historians. Indeed, often the conversation shifts, without mediation, from the cultural analogues of genes of single individuals – "memes," ideas or otherwise[79] – to the entire cultural evolution (or biological-cultural co-evolution) of the human species. Between these two extremes, historically determined phenomena are utilized merely as examples and are lined up one after the other, even when they belong to completely different contexts that differ enormously in space and time.

It is therefore unsurprising that these theories were authoritatively criticized for having caused a "disappearance of the social," and more generally for their "transhistorical and therefore ahistorical" character, which prevents them from responding to "many crucial questions pertaining to the particularity, the uniqueness, of all historical phenomena."[80] For historians these caveats are obvious, however we don't believe that they invalidate the adoption of an "evolutionary"

---

78. See Carlo Ginzburg, *Clues, Myths, and the Historical Method*, Baltimore, MD, Johns Hopkins University Press, 2013.

79. The idea of a "meme" as a cultural "replicator" was proposed by Richard Dawkins, *The Selfish Gene*, 2nd ed., Oxford – New York, Oxford University Press, 2006 [1989], pp. 191-192: "Examples of memes are tunes, ideas, catch-phrases, clothes fashions, ways of making pots or of building arches. Just as genes propagate themselves in the gene pool by leaping from body to body via sperms or eggs, so memes propagate themselves in the meme pool by leaping from brain to brain via a process which, in the broad sense, can be called imitation". More simply according to Luigi L. Cavalli Sforza, ideas are "objects that evolve" in culture, like DNA in biology: they are "a cultural DNA," L.L. Cavalli Sforza, *L'evoluzione della cultura*, 2nd ed., Turin, Codice, 2010 [2004], pp. 10, 128. Elsewhere, Cavalli Sforza, together with Marcus Feldman, has spoken of "cultural entities," with reference to ideas, languages, values, behaviors, skills, rules, tools and technologies that can be learned and transmitted, L.L Cavalli Sforza and M.W. Feldman, *Cultural Transmission and Evolution: A Quantitative Approach*, Princeton, NJ, Princeton University Press, 1981, pp. 10, 70.

80. These points were made by Joseph Fracchia and Richard C. Lewontin, "Does Culture Evolve?," in "The Return of Science: Evolutionary Ideas and History," *History and Theory*, 38, no. 4 (1999): pp. 69, 71, 77. The essays in this special issue were republished with other articles in Philip Pomper and David G. Shaw, eds., *The Return of Science: Evolution, History, and Theory*, Lanham, MD, Rowman & Littlefield, 2002.

interpretive hypothesis, as long as this hypothesis is not used as a pre-formed prescriptive interpretation, and it stands up to problematic contexts and specific spatio-temporal frameworks.

This is what, for example, Joel Mokyr has done with regard to the role of scientific and technological knowledge in economic development. In his model, the analytical unit is not physical, but epistemological (the technique as a set of instructions), and the genotype analogue is the whole of existing "useful knowledge," from which a set of possible techniques, or phenotypic manifest entities, is mapped. As the result of a kind of Malthusian "superfecundity," the selection includes chance and contingency, which both play an important role. It is Lamarckian rather than Darwinian, both because it is the work of conscious agents and because the acquired "traits" are transmittable. Cultural evolution occurs by way of "mutations" that create entirely new knowledge, "recombinations" that apply this knowledge to different fields and "hybridizations" that connect varying inventions in new ways. It also includes forms of exaptation (when the object that is selected as a characteristic takes on different roles.) Certain evolutionary systems change rapidly whereas others remain stagnant for a long time, and the evolutionary trajectories begin with "macro-inventions" that are in some ways similar to speciation. These are discoveries that indicate decisive interruptions, giving way to new technological "species," and are subsequently refined by a series of "micro-inventions."[81] This metaphor is highly useful, as Mokyr highlights its limitations almost obsessively, and we have sought to adhere to it during the course of our study.

81. Joel Mokyr, *The Lever of Riches: Technological Creativity and Economic Progress*, New York, Oxford University Press, 1990. Additional essays by the same author are consultable at http://sites.northwestern.edu/jmokyr/research/.

1. Baran and Davies: Spanning the Atlantic

The Sputnik Challenge

"SOVIET FIRES EARTH SATELLITE INTO SPACE; IT IS CIRCLING THE GLOBE AT 18,000 M.P.H.; SPHERE TRACKED IN 4 CROSSINGS OVER U.S.". It was with this front-page headline on 5 October 1957 that *The New York Times* announced the Soviet Union's previous day's launch of the world's first orbital satellite, Sputnik 1. The event, which was accompanied by the Soviet leader Nikita Khrushchev's bombastic, if unfounded, declarations about the technological and scientific superiority of his country, had enormous psychological and political fallout across the globe. Occurring as it did at the peak of the Cold War, the event's impact on American public opinion was particularly pronounced. Although president Dwight D. Eisenhower asserted that the achievement did not increase his concerns about national security "by one iota,"[1] the notion – confirmed one month later with the launch of a second Sputnik – that the USSR was capable of striking American territory with intercontinental ballistic missiles equipped with nuclear warheads, conjured memories of Pearl Harbour and triggered a wave of fear across the country.[2]

The event reinforced the positions within the administration, armed forces and democratic opposition that were critical of the president's cautious stance, and pressure mounted to continue nuclear testing and close the so-called "missile gap." In reality, American dominance in the field was undisputed, and shortly after these events this was fully confirmed when the United States succeeded in producing its own intercontinental missiles. Nonetheless, what came to be known as the "Sputnik Challenge"[3] led to a sudden intensification of the USA's commitment to scientific and military innovation. The end of the 1950s saw a major expansion of the university system, including an increase in federal funds

---

1. William H. Lawrence, "President Voices Concern on U.S. Missiles Program, But Not on the Satellite," *The New York Times*, 10 October 1957.

2. For a press review see Marta Wheeler George, "The Impact of Sputnik 1: Case-Study of American Public Opinion at the Break of the Space Age," NASA Historical Staff, Washington, DC, 15 July 1963, http://ntrs.nasa.gov/archive/nasa/casi.ntrs.nasa.gov/19650069476_1965069476.pdf (accessed 30 November 2012).

3. Robert A. Divine, *The Sputnik Challenge*, New York, Oxford University Press, 1993.

directed at the "research and development" of national defence, which more than doubled from 14.7 billion dollars in 1958 to 31.5 billion dollars in 1959.[4]

Meanwhile, in late 1957, the president of MIT, James R. Killian Jr. was nominated Eisenhower's special assistant for science and technology.[5] On 7 February 1958 an agency within the Department of Defence (DoD) was created with the goal of advancing the United States' space and missile programmes: the Advanced Research Projects Agency (ARPA). Finally, on 29 July the National Aeronautics and Space Administration (NASA) was founded, and became operational on 1 October of the same year.[6] ARPA was created to manage defence, and it aimed to synchronize the various initiatives of the Army, Navy and Air Force so as to reduce rivalry between them. NASA, in turn, was intended to be responsible for civil issues but in fact came to occupy a "dominating position,"[7] and ultimately assumed control of projects that had initially been entrusted to ARPA; in other words projects related not just to space technology and solid fuel chemistry, but also to antiballistic defence.[8]

Without entering into the long-running debate on Eisenhower's national security politics,[9] it is significant that the US president considered deterrence to be

4. Federico Romero, *Storia della guerra fredda: L'ultimo conflitto per l'Europa*, Turin, Einaudi, 2009, p. 145; American Association for the Advancement of Science, "R&D Budget and Policy Program, Guide to R&D Funding Data – Historical Data, Trends in Federal R&D Function, FY 1949-2009 Outlays for the Conduct of R&D," http://www.aaas.org/spp/rd/histda09tb.pdf (data in 2008 U.S.D.).

5. See James R. Killian, *Sputnik, Scientists, and Eisenhower: A Memoir of the First Special Assistant to the President for Science and Technology*, Cambridge, MA, MIT Press, 1977.

6. The NASA Act of 29 July 1958 can be consulted at http://www.nasa.gov/offices/ogc/about/space_act1.html.

7. *Memorandum of Conference with the President*, Dr. Killian et al., 5 March 1958, *Dwight D. Eisenhower's Papers as President*, DDE Diary Series, Box 31, "Staff Notes March 1958 (2)," http://www.eisenhower.archives.gov/research/online_documents/nasa/Binder12.pdf.

8. See ARPA, "Statement of R.W. Johnson, Director, 15 June 1959," in DoD Appropriations for 1960, *Hearings Before the Subcommittee of the Committee on Appropriations, United States Senate, Eighty-Six Congress, First Session on H.R. 7454*, Washington, DC: US Government Printing Office, 1959, pp. 1393-1399.

9. See John L. Gaddis, *Strategies of Containment: A Critical Appraisal of American National Security Policy During the Cold War*, Oxford – New York, Oxford University Press, 1982; Peter J. Roman, *Eisenhower and the Missile Gap*, Ithaca, Cornell University Press, 1995; Saki Dockrill, *Eisenhower's New-Look National Security Policy, 1953-61*, New York, St. Martin's Press, 1996; David Callahan and Fred I. Greenstein, "The Reluctant Racer: Eisenhower and U.S. Space Policy," in *Spaceflight and the Myth of Presidential Leadership*, ed. by Roger D. Launius and Howard E. McCurdy, Urbana: University of Illinois Press, 1997; Andreas Wenger, *Living with Peril: Eisenhower, Kennedy, and Nuclear Weapons*, Boston – Oxford, Rowman & Littlefield, 1997; Campbell Craig, *Destroying the Village: Eisenhower and the Thermonuclear War*, New York: Columbia University Press, 1998; Robert R. Bowie and Richard H. Immermann, *Waging Peace: How Eisenhower Shaped an Enduring Cold War Strategy*, Oxford: Oxford University Press, 1998; Benjamin P. Greene, *Eisenhower, Science Advice, and the Nuclear Test-Ban Debate, 1945-1963*, Stanford, Stanford University Press, 2007; Nina Tannenwald, *The Nuclear Taboo: The United States and the Non-Use of Nuclear Weapons Since 1945*, Cambridge, Cambridge University Press, 2007; Ira Chernus, *Apocalypse*

the somehow automatic result of the nuclear capabilities of the two rival powers. He also knew that the idea of Soviet superiority was a myth, even if he could not publicly declare as much since he was receiving his information from the secret flights of U-2 spy planes. Indeed, Eisenhower did not embrace the Gaither Report – presented in November 1957 at the National Security Council – which placed heavy emphasis on the US's vulnerability.[10] Nonetheless, the "Sputnik Shock" provided ammunition to those who disagreed with his vision of deterrence, and for such individuals the RAND Corporation became an important point of reference.

RAND stands for Research and Development. "Project RAND" was the name of a contract stipulated in 1946 between the United States Air Force (USAF) and the Douglas Aircraft Company, which had been turned into a private, independent non-profit organization in 1948. Thanks in part to its privileged relationship with the US Air Force, the RAND Corporation became the primary think tank of Cold War America,[11] and in the 1950s it focused considerable attention on the problem of the country's vulnerability to a Soviet missile attack. This gave rise to a perspective that clashed sharply with that of the president; a perspective exemplified in the words of one of the corporation's leaders, Albert Wohlstetter in 1959: "To deter an attack means being able to strike back in spite of it. It means, in other words, a capability to strike second." But in order to do this, he added, there was need for stable deterrent systems that were able "to survive enemy attacks" and "to make and communicate the decision to retaliate".[12]

Regardless of whether or not a Soviet attack was likely to occur, the US nuclear forces' complex system of command and control did not come close to meeting the requirements identified by Wohlstetter. According to Paul Bracken, a "small, inaccurate Soviet nuclear weapon" would have been sufficient to destroy the Strategic Air Command, while the Ballistic Missile Early Warning System was vulnerable even to a conventional attack.[13] These represented two of the USAF's six "Big L" (Logistic) Systems, but similar considerations also held true for other command centres and for the system as a whole. From this perspective

Management: Eisenhower and the Discourse of National Insecurity, Stanford, Stanford University Press, 2008.

10. See Lawrence Freedman, *The Evolution of Nuclear Strategy*, London – Basingstoke, Macmillan, 1981, pp. 160-163; David L. Snead, *The Gaither Committee, Eisenhower, and the Cold War*, Columbus, Ohio State University Press, 1999; Valerie L. Adams, *Eisenhower's Fine Group of Fellows: Crafting a National Security Policy to Uphold the Great Equation*, Lanham, MD, Lexington Books, 2006, ch. VI; Zuoyue Wang, *In Sputnik's Shadow: The President's Science Advisory Committee and Cold War America*, New Brunswick, NJ, Rutgers University Press, 2009, pp. 80-82.

11. See David Hounshell, "The Cold War, RAND, and the Generation of Knowledge, 1946-1962," *Historical Studies in the Physical and Biological Sciences*, 27, no. 2 (1997): pp. 237-267; Martin J. Collins, *Cold War Laboratory: Rand, the Air Force, and the American State, 1945-1950*, Washington, DC – London, Smithsonian Institution Press, 2002.

12. Albert Wohlstetter, "The Delicate Balance of Terror," *Foreign Affairs*, 37, no. 2 (January 1959): pp. 213, 216.

13. Paul Bracken, *The Command and Control of Nuclear Forces*, New York – London, Yale University Press, 1983, p. 186.

Figure 4 – A centralized command system

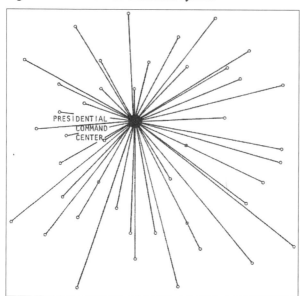

Source: Bracken, *The Command and Control of Nuclear Forces*, p. 191.

the National Security Reorganization Act, which restructured the system in 1958, entrusting the power to give the order "to go or not to go" directly to the president through the Secretary of Defence, simply exacerbated the situation. Indeed, it only would have taken one hit to paralyze a centralized command system such as the one represented in Figure 4.

The United States responded to the need for a survivable communications system "by deciding to exploit the most redundant, geographically dispersed communications system ever built: the American common carrier network, and especially the Bell Telephone system."[14] However, not even the National Communications System, established on this basis in 1963, was able to provide a fully satisfying solution to the problem. Indeed, the telephone network was decentralized and differed from the US nuclear command and control system of the 1950s (outlined in Figure 5) primarily in its dimension and the number of nodes. It remained however hierarchically organized on multiple levels with only a few "primary command posts," and as such it maintained a high degree of vulnerability. The same can be said of the Autovon network created by the American Telephone and Telegraph Company (AT&T), for the Defence Department. This network was more solid, but still "not completely invulnerable to a massive attack."[15] Basically, the function of the presidential centre's command procedures "was not to act as *a*

14. *Ibid.*, pp. 206-207.
15. Frederick T. Andrews, "The Telephone Network of the 1960s," *IEEE Communications Magazine*, 40, no. 7 (2002): p. 51.

Figure 5 – A decentralized command system

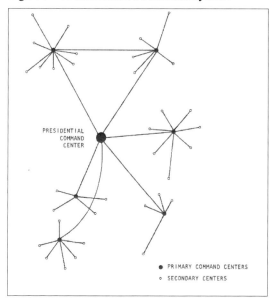

Source: Bracken, *The Command and Control of Nuclear Forces,* p. 193. The image reproduces a diagram developed by the National Military Command System.

trigger to launch nuclear weapons, but as *a safety catch preventing other triggers from firing.*"[16] The problem thus remained unresolved.

Baran

However, during this period an alternative solution already existed: this had been discovered by Paul Baran, an engineer born in Poland in 1926, who at the age of two emigrated with his family to the United States. He had joined the RAND Corporation in late 1959, and his first contributions on the topic appeared shortly afterwards in the organization's publications.

Baran claimed himself on numerous occasions that his starting premise had been to devise a communication system that could survive a nuclear attack. Notably, in the first of his contributions – produced on his own personal initiative – Baran emphasized the need to "minimize potential destruction and to do all those things necessary to permit the survivors of the holocaust to shuck the ashes and reconstruct the economy swiftly,"[17] and in doing so contribute to the

16. Bracken, *The Command and Control of Nuclear Forces*, p. 196.
17. Paul Baran, "Reliable Digital Communications Systems Using Unreliable Network Repeater Nodes," The RAND Corporation, Paper P-1995, 27 May 1960, http://www.rand.org/pubs/papers/P1995.html.

Figure 6 – Centralized, decentralized and distributed networks

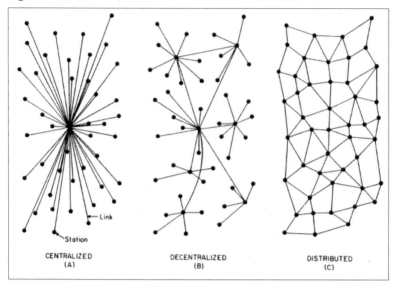

Source: Baran, "On Distributed Communications: I. Introduction to Distributed Communication Networks," p. 2.

protection of the country's democratic institutions following a nuclear attack.
In his second paper, written under the auspices of the USAF, he insisted above
all on the assumption of invulnerability as a "necessary requirement for certain
command and control systems," drawing inspiration from – among others –
Herman Kahn, the expert on thermonuclear military strategy who was the object
of Stanley Kubrick's satirical film *Dr. Strangelove*.[18]

In order to achieve invulnerability, between 1960 and 1962 Baran laid the
theoretical foundations for a new communication system, which was presented
in its entirety in eleven detailed memoranda in 1964.[19] The system was based on

18. Baran, "On a Distributed Command and Control System Configuration," USAF,
Project RAND, Research Memorandum RM-2632, 31 December 1960, http://www.rand.org/
pubs/research_memoranda/RM2632.html. The work cited by Baran (Herman Kahn, "The
Nature and Feasibility of War and Deterrence," The RAND Corporation, Paper P-1888-RC,
20 January 1960, http://www.rand.org/pubs/papers/P18 88.html) was publihed prior to Herman
Kahn, *On Thermonuclear War*, Princeton, NJ, Princeton University Press, 1960. On Kahn, see
Sharon Ghamari-Tabrizi, *The World of Herman Kahn: The Intuitive Science of Thermonuclear
War*, Cambridge, MA, Harvard University Press, 2005.

19. Nine of these memoranda were signed by Baran, one was written in collaboration
with Sharla P. Bohem and one was authored by Joseph W. Smith. See "On Distributed
Communications," The RAND Corporation, 1964, http://www.rand.org/about/history/baran-
list.html. A synthesis was also published: Baran, "On Distributed Communications Networks,"
IEEE Transactions on Communications Systems, 12, no. 1 (1964): pp. 1-9. Two other memoranda
on the system's weaknesses and message decryption remained classified.

three basic options regarding its form, its essential characteristics and the means of message transmission. The first option favoured a distributed network that was much less vulnerable than the other options for two reasons: first, and as a celebrated image from his work shows (Figure 6), it was a non-hierarchical network in which the status and functioning of all its nodes were equal ("each station is fully equivalent to all others"); second, its greater security was due to its redundancy, which Baran defined as the measure of the network's connectivity that was provided by the relation between the number of links and stations.[20]

In other words, since every station in a distributed network is directly connected to many others, a message can reach its destination by taking any number of paths, bypassing stations that have been destroyed. The author firmly insisted on the redundancy of the command structures, the "computational apparatus" and the communication system, and believed this notion to be "fundamental to continued system performance."[21] According to Baran, a criterion for survivability was "the percentage of stations both surviving the physical attack and remaining in electrical connection with the largest single group of surviving stations."[22] However, it is significant that Baran's first paper evoked an image that was undoubtedly effective, and seemed to assert a strong connection between military research and the defence of American democracy during the Cold War, as was common during the era:

> To better visualize the operation of the network, a hypothetical application is postulated: a congressional communications system where each congressman may vote from his home office. The success of such a network may be evaluated by examining the number of congressmen surviving an attack and comparing such number to the number of congressmen able to communicate with one another and vote via the communications network. Such an example is, of course, farfetched but not completely without utility. Such a system would do much to help preserve our democratic institutions after a possible nuclear attack.[23]

Baran's second option was for a digital rather than analogue network, which would have made the system safer, more reliable and fast enough to guarantee greater connectivity, in addition to making it less expensive. It represented a much more innovative conceptual breakthrough, since at the time communications and computers were usually treated as two almost entirely separate fields, and moreover computers were then viewed as little more than simple calculating machines. In fact, Baran emphasized that one of the disadvantages was precisely that this was an "all-digital system".[24] At the same time, he warned that by using existing methods of analogue-digital-analogue modulation it would have been possible to transmit one's voice,[25] and, as such, avoid signal deterioration, which in analogue systems occurred with each link between network nodes.

20. Baran, "Reliable Digital Communications," p. 9.
21. Baran, "On a Distributed Command and Control," pp. 1, 17.
22. *Ibid.*, p. 1.
23. Baran, "Reliable Digital Communications," p. 7.
24. Baran, "On Distributed Communications: V. History, Alternative Approaches, and Comparisons," p. 38.
25. Baran, "On Distributed Communications: IV. Priority, Precedence, and Overload," Appendix D.

The choice of an all-digital network was also functional to the third option, which consisted in a method devised by Baran for data transmission. This proposed that data transmission would be safer and faster if messages were sent in separate reduced standard dimension blocks (1,024 bits) and then reassembled upon arrival at their destination. Every message block therefore had to contain, in addition to the text, pieces of information that could be processed by the switching of nodes (departure and arrival addresses, etc.), but the advantages were truly noteworthy. With other systems such as telephones, when the line was engaged or overloaded, one would have to wait and call back. Instead, dividing messages up into small parts allowed multiple users to share the same line: "standardized data blocks permit many simultaneous users, each with widely different bandwidth requirements, to economically share a broadband network made up of varied data rate links."

In contrast to traditional store-and-forward communication networks such as postal and telegraphic systems, waiting times were drastically reduced in the transit between stations. Messages were able to traverse the US in a fraction of a second, practically in real time. As Baran wrote, "each node tries to get rid of its messages as if they were 'hot potatoes' and the node is not wearing gloves." Moreover, in a distributed network "if this preferred link is busy, to not wait, [the message can] choose the next best link that is free."[26]

Although Baran arranged his work around the perspective of military communications and the need for a system capable of surviving a nuclear attack, he tended nonetheless to emphasize that it could be applied across a variety of fields. Indeed, many different subjects could be interested in distributed networks: artificial intelligence scholars; "mathematicians working with optimization of flow in networks" and "using dynamic programming to optimize incompletely understood and changing systems;" "those concerned with communications within organisms and organizations" and "those connected with civilian common carrier telephone plant switching."[27] Based on the hypothesis of a large geographical network of 400 switching nodes capable of supporting 100,000 simultaneous users,[28] Baran imagined a "new common-user system" that went beyond the military sphere. He envisaged "an *ideal* electrical communications system [...] defined as one that permits any person or machine to reliably and instantaneously communicate with any combination of other people or machines, anywhere, anytime, and at zero cost."[29]

Having finished most of his work in 1962, Baran unsuccessfully proposed it to the heads of AT&T, who held a monopoly on telecommunications. One of the key reasons for the company's opposition was the fact that they managed an analogue network, whereas the network proposed by Baran was digital. Furthermore,

---

26. The quotes in this text are taken from Baran, "On Distributed Communications: I," pp. 23, 25; "On Distributed Communications: IV," p. 9; "On Distributed Communications Networks," pp. 27-28, 33.
27. Baran, "On Distributed Communications: V," p. 2.
28. Baran, "On Distributed Communications: X. Cost Estimate," p. III.
29. Baran, "On Distributed Communications: XI. Summary Overview," p. 1.

the project was met at least initially with little enthusiasm within the RAND Corporation, which only formally recommended it to the USAF in 1965, following the publication of Baran's memoranda "On Distributed Communications." The Air Force then submitted it for evaluation to the MITRE Corporation, a spin-off of MIT that worked for the government, which gave it a positive assessment. Due to the different areas of competence, the project's realization was then entrusted to the Defence Communications Agency (DCA), founded in 1960. However, this agency did not possess the know-how necessary to develop the venture, and so in 1966 Baran decided himself to withdraw his proposal. "I recommended that this program not be founded at this time and the program be quietly shelved, waiting for a more auspicious opportunity to resurrect it" he recalled in 1999, observing that "the Cold War at this time had cooled from loud threats of thermonuclear warheads to the lower level of surrogate small wars. And, we were bogged down in Viet Nam."[30]

Indeed, Baran had carried out his research during the years of the two international crises in Berlin and Cuba, both of which ended between 1961 and 1962 with Soviet failure that was attributed to the determination of the new democratic president John F. Kennedy. Never before had the world seemed to be on the cusp of catastrophe as it had been in Cuba, and the highly acute tensions accompanying the crisis had increased awareness that the two superpowers' nuclear escalation would have transformed a potential conflict into mutual destruction. This had created the conditions for a change in direction, which radically modified the bipolar system established following the Second World War. The 1963 treaty that saw the USA, USSR and Great Britain ban nuclear testing in the atmosphere marked the shift from the Cold War in the proper sense of the term to a new period characterized by a regulated and less tense rivalry.[31] Within this context the problem of nuclear vulnerability lost the strategic relevance that American defence theorists had attributed to it in the 1950s.

The system devised by Baran can thus be a considered a sort of false start provoked by a doubly unfavourable context: first, the gap that existed between analogue and digital in the field of communications; and, second, the arrival of what would later be interpreted as the end of the Cold War. Despite this temporary setback, Baran's work would soon be put back on track elsewhere - following a route that was anything but linear – that would see him go on to make a fundamental contribution to the birth of the first network.

Before proceeding however, it is essential that we attempt to answer a question raised by this story: how was this young engineer able to make such a significant improvement to this matter? How did he come to conceive of a distributed digital network that contained a new means of internally transmitting messages? These points require some explanation in order to avoid any suggestion that Baran and his ideas about the network appeared out of nowhere (as the "heroic" histories of technology would have it), but also to understand how, independently from Baran

30. David Hochfelder, "Oral History: Paul Baran," interview conducted on 24 October 1999, IEEE History Center, http://www.ieeeghn.org/wiki/index.php/Oral-History:Paul_Baran (accessed 30 November 2012).

31. Romero, *Storia della guerra fredda*, pp. 164-173.

Figure 7 – An image of the IBM 7090

Source: http://www.computer-history.info/Page4.dir/pages/IBM.7090.dir/images/Picture.9.jpg.

and in a different context, during the same period a project was beginning to take shape that would lead to the creation of Arpanet in 1969.

Moreover, to fully understand the significance of Baran's research it is worth briefly explaining what a mainframe computer was in the early 1960s and how it functioned. This can be done by summarizing a few pages written by Paul E. Ceruzzi[32] about a model launched in 1959, the IBM 7090, and an updated version (7094) that came out in 1962. In place of the thousands of vacuum tubes present in earlier machines, the 7094's processor used a transistor (which had become increasingly reliable and less expensive) and its memory had a capacity of about 150 KB. It was one of the fastest computers of its time, capable of carrying out 150,000 operations a second. To put this into context, consider that its memory was similar to what was available on the first IBM personal computer that came out in 1981, while it was not until the late 1980s that PCs were able to match its speed. The 7094 cost 1.6 million dollars and it could be rented for 30,000 dollars a month.

A mainframe was made up of various metal cabinets connected by cords that were isolated in a climate-controlled room to which only the operators had access. Programmers wrote on perforated cards that were passed onto operators, and then had to wait to see the result to be sure that they had not made any errors. When mistakes were made, the programmers had to restart the entire process. A similar

32. Paul E. Ceruzzi, *A History of Modern Computing*, 2nd ed., Cambridge, MA, MIT Press, 2003, ch. 2.

Figure 8 – Operators at SAGE Consoles

Source: http://webmuseum.mit.edu/grabimg.php?wm=1&kv=131704.

situation occurred in university settings: "a typical transaction began by submitting a deck of cards to an operator through a window (to preserve the climate control of the computer room). Later the user went to the location where printed output was delivered to retrieve the block of fanfold paper that contained the results of his or her work."[33] In many cases this processing of data was performed once a week.

From Radars to the Net via the Brain

As he himself stated in 1960, Baran had already taken an interest in the issue of a reliable communications system prior to arriving at the RAND Corporation, when he worked for a large aerospace agency, the Hughes Aircraft Company, and was taking night classes at the University of California, Los Angeles (UCLA) for a Master's degree in Electronics. Moreover, before this time he had already been dealing with communications at Raymond Rosen Engineering Products as an employee during the Korean War, where he had addressed the problem of noise caused by frequency oscillations on radio tape recordings of instruments on board airplanes and missiles. Following his transfer to the Hughes Aircraft Company, he began to work on processing radar data and participated in what the company called the "vest pocket

33. *Ibid.*, p. 77. See also below, pp. 89-90, for the description that Joseph C.R. Licklider gave for these procedures in 1963.

SAGE" project. This consisted in a defence system that was miniaturized thanks to the use of a transistor and could therefore be "packed inside an Army trailer,"[34] and which was modelled on the Semi-Automatic Ground Environment (hence, SAGE) that had been developed for the USAF by MIT's Lincoln Laboratory.

SAGE was another of the "Big L" military aviation systems: it had a centralized defensive system for intercepting bomber squadrons, which calculated their speed and position on the basis of signals transmitted by radar lines installed in Canada and the North-eastern United States. These signals were processed by a long distance network of computers connected by telephone, using a modem that SAGE had contributed significantly to perfecting. Other pre-existing MIT initiatives came together in the project to develop SAGE, such as Jay W. Forrester's plan to build the Whirlwind digital computer – which became the "brain" of the project – and the so-called Project Charles, a series of courses of study that saw the participation of many eminent scientists of the time. In turn, the MITRE Corporation (which would later be in favour of Baran's distributed network) was created in 1958 with the task of developing SAGE.[35]

The system only became fully operative in the early 1960s, and was considered by many to be failure, since it was made obsolete by the advent of intercontinental ballistic missiles and by the development of nuclear armaments. Despite this, as Paul N. Edwards wrote, "SAGE *did* 'work.' It worked for the research community, which used it to pursue major intellectual and technical goals. It worked as industrial policy, providing government funding for a major new industry."[36] And here again: "what makes SAGE such an interesting case is its origins within the academic science and engineering community – *not* with military imperatives, though its military funding sources and key geopolitical events spurred it on."[37]

The work of Norbert Wiener, in particular, had decisive influence on the SAGE programme, as well the other previous programmes that merged into it.

34. See "An Interview with Paul Baran," conducted by Judy O'Neill, 5 March 1990, University of Minnesota, CBI, Charles Babbage Institute Collections, Oral History 182, http://conservancy.umn.edu/bitstream/107101/1/oh182pb.pdf; Hochfelder, "Oral-History: Paul Baran."

35. See Kent C. Redmond and Thomas M. Smith, *Project Whirlwind: The History of a Pioneer Computer*, Bedford, MA, Digital Press, 1980; Kent C. Redmond and Thomas M. Smith, *From Whirlwind to MITRE: The R&D Story of the SAGE Air Defense Computer*, Cambridge, MA, MIT Press, 2000.

36. Paul N. Edwards, *The Closed World*, p. 110. Edwards further notes: "Perhaps most important, SAGE worked as ideology, creating an impression of active defense that assuaged some of the helplessness of nuclear fear. SAGE represented both a contribution and a visionary response to the emergence of a closed world."

37. *Ibid.* See also Stuart W. Leslie, *The Cold War and American Science: The Military-Industrial-Academic Complex at MIT and Stanford*, New York, Columbia University Press, 1993, pp. 32-43; Hans Dieter Hellige, "From SAGE via Arpanet to Ethernet: Stages in Computer Communications Concepts Between 1950 and 1980," *History and Technology*, 11, no. 1 (1994): pp. 49-75; Thomas P. Hughes, *Rescuing Prometheus: Four Monumental Projects that Changed the World*, New York, Vintage Books, 1998; Stephen B. Johnson, *The United States Air Force and the Culture of Innovation, 1945-1965*, Washington, DC, Air Force History and Museums Program, 2002.

Formerly a scholar of probability calculus, during the Second World War he had worked to improve US antiaircraft defence and went on to found cybernetics (his book, published in 1948, bears the same title).[38] In short, Wiener envisioned a cybernetic system or "servo-mechanism" – mechanical, but also animal or human – as functioning by absorbing input from the exterior, processing the data received and providing instructions to interact with the environment through an output apparatus. In other words, it was based on an information feedback cycle and was conceived as a system of both control and information exchange. As Antoine Bousquet wrote, citing Wiener himself, "in cybernetics, control and communication are inextricably linked since control 'is nothing but the sending of messages which effectively change the behaviour of the recipient.'"[39]

It was therefore not a surprise when, a couple of decades later, Baran claimed to have developed an interest in the issues of vulnerability and of command and control during his work on radars. The working group, which until 1959 included Baran, that handled command and control within the Ground Systems Division of the Hughes Aircraft Company, studied human and mechanical risk factors connected to the control of Minuteman intercontinental ballistic missiles, which was especially delicate because of the speed with which the missiles' solid propellants were refuelled. The study in which Baran reformulated the problem of a survivable network originated from this period. In 1999 he recalled that

> Prof. Warren McCollough [*sic*] of MIT, a brain-researcher who was a combination of electrical engineer and psychiatrist was a consultant on this project. He brought a range of insights into the risk factors on the extreme fallibility of human beings. My interest further increased in the issues of command and control and techniques to ameliorate these risk factors.[40]

Indeed, in 1960 Baran cited three "foundation papers."[41] The first paper was by the neurophysiologist Warren McCulloch, who would later become in 1964 the first president of the American Society for Cybernetics. The second one was by John von Neumann, the Hungarian scientist who had conducted important studies in mathematics and quantum mechanics before seeking refuge in the United States to escape Nazi anti-Semitic persecution. Later in 1944 he developed game theory with the economist Oskar Morgenstern, which during the Cold War would have innumerable applications for the management of crisis situations on the basis of calculated risk strategies.[42] Among his many activities, von Neumann had served as a consultant for Project Charles.

38. Norbert Wiener, *Cybernetics: Or Control and Communication in the Animal and the Machine*, New York, MIT Press, 1961 [1948].

39. Antoine Bousquet, "Cyberneticizing the American War Machine: Science and Computers in the Cold War," *Cold War History*, 8, no. 1 (2008): p. 79. See also Antoine Bousquet, *The Scientific Way of Warfare: Order and Chaos on the Battlefields of Modernity*, New York, Columbia University Press, 2009, ch. 5.

40. Hochfelder, "Oral History: Paul Baran."

41. Baran, "Reliable Digital Communications," p. 6.

42. John von Neumann and Oskar Morgenstern, *Theory of Games and Economic Behavior*, Princeton, NJ, Princeton University Press, 1944.

The third essay mentioned by Baran was by Edward F. Moore and Claude E. Shannon, who both worked in the field of the mathematical aspects of machine automation. Shannon in particular had contributed to the construction of Vannevar Bush's analogical calculator (Bush was a scientist who had been the principal figure in organizing research in the US research during the years of the Roosevelt administration and the Second World War)[43] and in 1949 he published a basic mathematical theory of information.[44] It is also significant that Baran, retracing the steps of those who came before him, began from Theseus, the electro-mechanic mouse invented in 1950 by Shannon that "learned" to move around a maze in search of the perfect piece of cheese.[45] All three of the papers cited by Baran dealt with "infallible" or "reliable" networks based on "fallible" or "unreliable" units, and all three of them lead us into the field of neurophysiology.[46]

The image of the brain as a network of neurons took on board the method invented by Camillo Golgi in 1873 for selectively colouring areas of the nervous fabric, and which had made it possible to analyze its structure. Through the application of this method another great histologist, Santiago Ramón y Cajal, had discovered the existence of connections between nervous cells, which in 1891 were first referred to as "neurons" by Wilhelm Waldeyer. Once the concept of a neural network had been established in the scientific community, it was subsequently discovered that neurons responded to chemical stimuli (synapses), which modifies their condition and put them in communication with other neurons.

What the synapses were transmitting from one neuron to another remained to be understood. In 1943 Warren McCulloch, along with the mathematician Walter H. Pitts, made an important contribution to the topic by suggesting that neurons did not emit energy but rather information of a logical nature ("and-or-not").[47]

43. See G. Pascal Zachary, *Endless Frontier: Vannevar Bush Engineer of the American Century*, Cambridge, MA, MIT Press, 1999.

44. Claude E. Shannon, *The Mathematical Theory of Communication*, Urbana, University of Illinois Press, 1949. The first version of this book is available for consultation at http://cm.bell-labs.com/cm/ms/what/shannonday/shannon1948.pdf.

45. Baran, "On Distributed Communications: V," p. 16; Claude E. Shannon, "Presentation of a Maze Solving Machine," in *Cybernetics: Circular, Causal and Feedback Mechanisms in Biological and Social Systems*, ed. by Heinz von Foerster, Margaret Mead and Hans Lukas Teuber, New York, Josiah Macy Jr. Foundation, 1952, pp. 169–181.

46. These papers were, in order, as follows: John von Neumann, "Probabilistic Logics and the Synthesis of Reliable Organisms from Unreliable Components," in *Automata Studies* ed. by Claude E. Shannon and John McCarthy, Princeton, NJ, Princeton University Press, 1956, pp. 43-98 (the paper is the revision of a series of conferences from 1952); Edward F. Moore and Claude E. Shannon, "Reliable Circuits Using Less Reliable Relays," *Journal of the Franklin Institute*, 261, no. 3 (1956): pp. 191-208 and n. 4 (1956): pp. 281-297; Warren S. McCulloch, "Infallible Nets of Fallible Formal Neurons," MIT Research Laboratory of Electronics, Quarterly Progress Report, n. 53, 15 April 1959. An online version of report n. 54 of 15 July, in Warren S. McCulloch, Humberto R. Maturana, Jerome Y. Lettvin and Walter H. Pitts, "Neurophysiology," MIT Research Laboratory of Electronics can be consulted at http://dspace.mit.edu/bitstream/handle/1721.1/52294/RLE_QPR_054_XVI.pdf?sequence=1.

47. Warren S. McCulloch and Walter H. Pitts, "A Logical Calculus of the Ideas Immanent in Nervous Activity," *Bulletin of Mathematical Biophysics*, 5 (1943): pp. 115-133, re-printed in *Bulletin of Mathematical Biology*, 52, no. 1-2 (1990): pp. 99-115.

Although it would subsequently be proven that neurons were not actually logical switches, McCulloch and Pitts' essay paved the way for a thriving branch of studies that explored the similarities between the brain and the computer, as well as opening up research on artificial intelligence.[48]

In the text cited by Baran, von Neumann (who was in turn cited by Moore and Shannon) drew on McCulloch and Pitts to establish an analogy between "relays in electrical circuits and neurons in the nervous system." His other primary reference was the key 1936 essay in which Alan M. Turing had devised a "universal machine" capable of performing every kind of calculation and dividing them into operations "so elementary that it is not easy to imagine them further divided."[49] This essay, which is the foundation of every computer in existence, had also influenced McCulloch and Pitts.[50] The analogy between machine parts and nervous cells can also be found in another essay by Turing in 1950, which opened with the following words: "I propose to consider the question, 'Can machines think?'"[51] An analysis of this network of cross-references clearly illustrate the close-knit nature of the interdependencies between neurophysiology, information technology, information theories and, as we will see later on, even psychology.

For our present purposes, it is sufficient to add that, starting from the analogies and the differences between the brain and machines, von Neumann made a considerable contribution to the design of the first American digital computers.[52] First of all, he had provided a consultation for the Electronic Numerical Integrator and Calculator (ENIAC) project, launched in 1943 at the University of Pennsylvania Moore School under the management of J. Presper Eckert and John W. Mauchly (incidentally, Baran's first job was with the agency that these two men founded in 1946).[53] From the ENIAC experience the idea of a new machine

48. See Manfred Spitzer, *The Mind Within the Net: Models of Learning, Thinking, and Acting*, Cambridge, MA, MIT Press, 1999, pp. 5-6.

49. Alan M. Turing, "On Computable Numbers, with an Application to the Entscheidungsproblem," *Proceedings of the London Mathematical Society*, s2-42, no. 1 (1937): p. 250.

50. McCulloch himself affirmed as much in a debate with von Neumann in 1948: "It was not until I saw Turing's paper that I began to get going the right way around, and with Pitts' help formulated the required logical calculus. What we thought we were doing (and I think we succeeded fairly well) was treating the brain as a Turing machine:" quoted in B. Jack Copeland, ed., *The Essential Turing: Seminal Writings in Computing, Logic, Philosophy, Artificial Intelligence, and Artificial Life: Plus the Secrets of Enigma*, Oxford – New York, Oxford University Press, 2004, p. 408.

51. Alan M. Turing, "Computing Machinery and Intelligence," *Mind*, 59, no. 236 (1950): p. 433.

52. See William Aspray, *John von Neumann and the Origins of Modern Computing*, Cambridge, MA, MIT Press, 1990.

53. On the Eckert-Mauchly Computer Corporation see Arthur L. Norberg, *Computers and Commerce: A Study of Technology and Management at Eckert-Mauchly Computer Company, Engineering Research Associates, and Remington Rand, 1946-1957*, Cambridge, MA, MIT Press, 2005. This agency produced the first American commercial computer (UNIVAC, Universal Automatic Computer), which Baran worked on between 1949 and 1950.

was born: the Electronic Discrete Variable Calculator (EDVAC). In 1945 von Neumann composed the first "Draft Report on the EDVAC" and anticipated a "neuron analogy," in reference to the work of McCulloch and Pitts.[54]

Finally, in 1946 von Neumann began work on another computer for the Princeton University Institute for Advanced Study (IAS), directed by J. Robert Oppenheimer, with whom he had previously participated in the Manhattan project. Out of the development of the "IAS Machine" (which involved the collaboration of two of Baran's professors at UCLA, Willis H. Ware and his advisor Gerald Estrin) derived von Neumann's so-called architecture, which is still in use to this day in the majority of computers. Its primary components included a central processing unit (the CPU) and a structure for storage that contained instructions and data (the memory), in addition to input and output devices and a connecting channel between the various parts (BUS).

On this basis, speed, reliability and architecture became the primary elements of evaluation for analyzing analogies and differences between the brain and the computer.[55] Unsurprisingly, studies of the differences between the brain and computers did not generate results that were inferior to those produced by studies of analogies. For example, although neurons are about a million times slower than a 200 Mhz CPU, the human brain is able to carry out certain operations much more quickly than a computer, such as reading words or recognizing a face. However the differences that help us better understand Baran's reasons for choosing to favour a distributed network have to do with reliability and architecture. In his lectures at Yale on *The Computer and the Brain*, published posthumously in 1958, von Neumann estimated that the brain, in addition to being much slower than a computer,[56] was also much less accurate. Despite this, he wrote, the nervous system leads "to a rather high level of reliability." If in the case of a digital system "a single pulse is missing, absolute perversion of meaning, i.e. nonsense, may result." In the nervous system, on the other hand, if "a single pulse is lost, or even several pulses are lost – or unnecessarily, mistakenly, inserted," the meaning of the message "is only inessentially distorted."[57]

Indeed, mistakes do not prevent the brain from continuing to work at perfectly acceptable levels. This depends on its architecture: in a computer an error in one of the main components causes an immediate crash. In neural networks this is not the case because their nodes operate simultaneously as processing and storage units; in other words, they perform all the functions that are assigned to different components in the case of machines. In addition, as previously noted, neural networks possess a high level of redundancy. Finally, the human brain has the

---

54. John von Neumann, "First Draft of a Report on the EDVAC," reproduced in *IEEE Annals of the History of Computing*, 15, no. 4 (1993): pp. 27-75.

55. See Spitzer, *The Mind within the Net*, pp. 12-14.

56. John von Neumann, *The Computer and the Brain*, preface by Ray Kurzweil, 3rd ed., New Haven – London, Yale University Press, 2012 [1958], p. 47. Von Neumann wrote that a neuron's reaction time is "somewhere between 10^{-4} and 10^{-2} seconds, but the more significant definition is the latter one. Compared to this, modern vacuum tubes and transistors can be used in large logical machines at reaction times between 10^{-6} and 10^{-7} seconds."

57. *Ibid.*, pp. 78-79.

property of neuroplasticity, which allows it activate alternative routes when for some reason – the natural mortality of neurons included – one of its circuits ceases to operate.

Baran introduced a new element – the importance of which can hardly be understated – by relocating the terms of the problem from the "less centralized internal organization" of the new generation computers[58] to a long distance communication network that connected many machines to each other. However, without taking the reference points that we cited into consideration, it is impossible to understand how he was able to devise a much more reliable network, that was able to mimic the fault tolerant architecture of neural networks. As Baran himself mentioned in an interview in 2002,

> No single person ever does anything. It's always groups of people. We wanted to know how to go about building such a system. So I got interested in the subject of neural nets. Warren McCulloch in particular inspired me. He described how he could excise a part of the brain, and the function in that part would move over to another part. As we get older – at least this was thought in those days – the number of brain cells decreases but we're able to use the surviving functionality effectively. As you and I are getting older, we know it takes a little time to remember a word – so we find a synonym. We have more trouble with proper nouns because there's lower redundancy. McCulloch's version of the brain had the characteristics I felt would be important in designing a really reliable communication system.[59]

Davies

Meanwhile, between the autumn of 1965 and the spring of 1966, precisely when Baran's project was running aground, on the opposite side of the Atlantic another young scholar, the Englishman Donald W. Davies, had reached conclusions that were very similar to those of Baran. In the history of science and technology, as well as culture more generally, it is not uncommon for scholars to make the same discoveries or to work on analogous concepts more or less simultaneously and yet independently from one another. The most common explanation for this (which is not completely unfounded) is the notion that "the time is ripe;" since innovation often originates from necessity, and if this necessity is felt at the same time in various environments more than one response may occur. As Carlo Ginzburg wrote after reconstructing a genealogy of microhistory, "the fact that certain ideas are floating around means, after all, that when starting from the same premises it is possible to reach similar conclusions." However, he added, "demonstrating the existence of intellectual convergences and, simultaneously, the absence of direct contacts is often a process that is anything but simple."[60] This

---

58. Baran, "On a Distributed Command and Control," p. 16.

59. Stewart Brand, "Founding Father," interview with P. Baran, *Wired*, March 2001, http://www.wired.com/wired/archive/9.03/baran.html.

60. Carlo Ginzburg, "Microhistory: Two or Three Things That I Know about It," in C. Ginzburg, *Threads and Traces: True, False, Fictive*, Berkeley, University of California Press, 2012, p. 208.

is exactly what needs to be done with the case in hand, although not before having verified that we are indeed referring to similar premises.

We must initially consider the fact that both the political and institutional context within which Davies was developing his work, as well as the objectives that he set for himself, were very different from those of Baran. The priorities of Harold Wilson's Labour Party government (which took office in 1964) did not include antiballistic defence; rather it sought to re-launch the British economy and reduce the technology gap between Great Britain and the United States. As has been noted: "Labour aimed to harness the 'white heat of the technological revolution' especially by the creation of Mintech which eventually took on responsibility for almost all of Labour's industrial policy."[61] In addition, the National Physical Laboratory (NPL) – which was founded at the start of the twentieth century and where Davies began working in 1947, after receiving a degree in Physics and a Master's in Mathematics at London Imperial College – had a civil as opposed to a military mission.

Davies' project for a computer network was first outlined in a seminar that he organized at the NPL in November 1965, which was developed in a paper published a month later. A more complete version of the project was presented in a public lecture in March 1966, and this became a formal proposal in June of the same year.[62] Davies was particularly concerned about the speed needed for a long distance network to allow "a conversation between a computing (or information) system and a human user which can save the human effort." This network, which one day might be able to absorb telegraph and telephone communications, was primarily intended to serve business and commercial systems: "The emphasis on real-time business systems in this report" he wrote, "is due to the belief that they will generate more real-time digital communications traffic than, say, scientific calculations or computer-aided design."[63] To reach an increased speed the information needed to be "carried in relatively small units" of 1,024 bits: the

61. Jim Tomlinson, "The Labour Party and the Capitalist Firm, c. 1950-1970," *The Historical Journal*, 47, no. 3 (2004): p. 699, which refers to Richard Coopey, "Industrial Policy in the White Heat of the Scientific Revolution," in *The Wilson Governments, 1964-1970* ed. by Jim Tomlinson, Steven Fielding and Nick Tiratsoo, London – New York, Pinter, 1993. The Ministry of Technology (Mintech) was created by the Wilson Government. See also Abbate, *Inventing the Internet*, pp. 21-23 and, on British ballistic missile strategy, Kristan Stoddart, "The Wilson Government and British Responses to Anti-Ballistic Missiles, 1964–1970," *Contemporary British History*, 23, no. 1 (2009): pp. 1-33.

62. See M. Campbell-Kelly, "Oral history interview with Donald W. Davies," 17 March 1986, University of Minnesota, CBI Collections, Oral History 189, http://conservancy.umn.edu/bitstream/107241/1/oh189dwd.pdf. These documents are held in the U.K. National Archive for the History of Computing (University of Manchester), and in contrast to Baran's documents, these remained unpublished. Transcriptions of the first two documents can be found in Donald W. Davies, "An Historical Study of the Beginnings of Packet-Switching," *The Computer Journal*, 44, no. 3 (2001): pp. 158-161.

63. Donald W. Davies, "Proposal for a Digital Communication Network," NPL, June 1966: p. 2, http://www.archive.org/details/NationalPhysicalLaboratoryProposalForADigital-CommunicationNetwork.

same dimensions proposed by Baran. Davies called them packets, and it was this term that would come to be used for what, still today, is referred to as "packet switching."

In addition to its civil purposes, Davies' project differed from the work of Baran in terms of its starting points and priorities. Davies' goal, in fact, was to enable a conversation between the user and the computer and thus to tackle the so-called "time-sharing" problem. Machines at the time were enormous and incredibly expensive, and were only able to carry out one operation at a time. Thus, waiting times were very lengthy, and the list of instructions to follow was similarly long. The term "time-sharing" referred to a series of operations intended to give multiple users simultaneous access to one of the machines through interactive terminals, in order to share its calculating power. In this way every user had the impression of having the computer entirely at their disposal, within the limits of its abilities. It was with this prospect in mind that Davies first concentrated on packet switching, in which he identified the definitive requisite for multi-access, real time computer use.

In contrast to Baran, Davies did not elaborate on the question of network redundancy, which he did not define (at least not explicitly) as a distributed network. Consequently, Davies did not establish a strong link between this characteristic and packet switching. From what he wrote at the time and later, one could deduce that he did not attribute prior importance to the network's structure; it was as if a high level of connectivity was not essential to him in a non-military system, and he thought that the problems stemming from malfunctions in one or more of the nodes could be resolved simply by repairing them.

This hypothesis would appear to be supported by the fact that from 1955 one of the focal points of his work was concerned with the planning of cryotrons: elements of commutation within systems designed to make computers much faster by lowering the electric conductors to temperatures as close to absolute zero (-273°C) as possible, thus achieving "superconductivity."[64] In short, it seems that for Davies the speed of communications in the network depended more on packet switching and on the machine's structure rather than on the structure of the network.

As such, a significant aspect of his proposal regarded interface computers provided "between the high level network and the users." Given that very slow terminals would also have to be connected to the network, in order to guarantee their speed Davies distinguished between a fast central system articulated in nodes (N) from interface units for users (I) connected to each node (see Figure 9).[65]

The premises from which Baran and Davies arrived at similar conclusions and the solutions they found to obtain a communication network "in real time"

64. See Roger M. Needham, "Donald Watt Davies, C.B.E. 7 June 1924 – 28 May 2000," *Biographical Memoirs of Fellows of The Royal Society*, 48, no. 1 (2002): p. 91. One of the first cryotrons was developed at MIT's Lincoln Laboratory, see Dudley A. Buck, "The Cryotron: A Superconductive Computer Component," Memorandum 6M-3843, 22 August 1955, http://dome.mit.edu/bitstream/handle/1721.3/40618 /MC665_r15_M-3843.pdf.

65. Donald W. Davies, "Proposal for a Digital Communication Network," pp. 7, 9.

Figure 9 – "A hypothetical communication network"

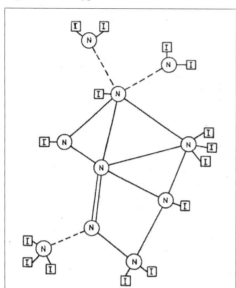

Source: Donald W. Davies, "Proposal for a Digital Communication Network," p. 8.

were therefore in both cases different. In truth, in June 1966 the English physicist did not fail to point out that "a network with many similarities to the present one was described by Paul Baran." Baran's first memorandum and a book by Leonard Kleinrock on *Communication Nets* were the only studies that were cited in his proposal.[66] However, Davies was only informed of Baran's work by a member of the British Ministry of Defence during the March 1966 seminar; in other words, when the bulk of his project had already been developed.[67]

Meanwhile, the other cited text by Kleinrock – who at the time of its publication in 1964 was Assistant Professor of Engineering at UCLA and who would later become one of the authors of Arpanet – was developed from his PhD dissertation, which he had finished at MIT in late 1962 under the supervision of

66. *Ibid.*, p. 13 (which contains a reference to Leonard Kleinrock, *Communication Nets: Stochastic Message Flow and Delay*, New York: McGraw-Hill, 1964) and p. 21. It through referencing Baran, that Davies touched on the problem of redundancy and network connectivity, asserting: "It must be admitted that the redundancy features needed to ensure a service in the presence of faults have not been carefully thought out […]. A large part of that report was concerned with the behaviour of the network when many nodes and links were out of action (in a military context, this is important). The highly-connected networks there considered are not needed in a civil environment, but nevertheless the value of overconnection as a fail-soft feature was well demonstrated."

67. Martin Campbell-Kelly, "Data Communications at the National Physical Laboratory (1965-1975)," *Annals of the History of Computing*, 9, no. 3-4 (1988): p. 226.

Shannon,[68] among others. Kleinrock referred to Baran in an interview in 1990: "I was well aware of his results. In fact I quoted his results in my own dissertation. He had some of the important ideas of packet switching as a system. The thing that really drove my own research was the idea of a message switching network, which was a precursor to the packet switching networks."[69] Yet Kleinrock did not make explicit reference to packet switching or to Baran in either the dissertation or the book.[70]

It can thus be concluded that the American engineer and the English physician indeed made two separate "inventions." The fact that the authors of these inventions had worked independently and without direct contact does not however allow us to exclude the possibility of "intellectual convergences," and therefore it remains to be determined if and to what extent the contexts within which they were working were actually distinct.

Time-Sharing

According to his recollections, Davies had been cultivating an interest in computer communications for some time, but it was a trip to the US in May 1965 to take part in the International Federation of Information Processing (IFIP) conference that made him "sufficiently enthused that I was willing to put a lot of the NPL's effort into it" (he was able to do this only after August 1966, when he became supervisor of the laboratory's Computer Science Division). During the trip Davies had visited some of the places where research programmes on super conductors as well as on time-sharing were in place.[71] Regarding time-sharing, his objectives had been the Johnniac Open Shop System (JOSS) project developed by the RAND Corporation with the sponsorship of the USAF, MIT's Project MAC and another programme managed by Dartmouth College in Hanover, New Hampshire. Each of these projects, which were centred on human-machine interaction, aimed to create time-shared systems made up of interactive consoles connected to a central computer by way of telephone lines.

The JOSS project consisted of a machine based on von Neumann's architecture; and because he had also contributed to its creation, the machine was

68. Leonard Kleinrock, "Message Delay in Communication Nets with Storage," MIT, December 1962, http://dspace.mit.edu/bitstream/handle/1721.1/11562/33840535.pdf.

69. "An Interview with Leonard Kleinrock" conducted by Judy O'Neill, 3 April 1990, University of Minnesota, CBI Collections, Oral History 190, http://conservancy.umn.edu/bitstream/107411/1/oh190lk.pdf.

70. Baran is not mentioned in the bibliography of Kleinrock, *Communication Nets*, pp. 201-204, which makes the following point: "in transmission between two nodes, a message is considered to be received at the second node only after it is fully received." (*ibid.*, p. 15)

71. On the history of time-sharing see Hans Dieter Hellige, "Leitbilder in der Genese von Time-Sharing Systemen: Erklärungswert und Grenzen des Leitbildansatzes in der Computerkommunikation," in *Technikleitbilder auf dem Prüfstand: Das Leitbild-Assessment aus Sicht der Informatik- und Computergeschichte*, ed. by Hans Dieter Hellige, Berlin, Edition Sigma, 1996, pp. 205-234.

called Johnniac in his honor.[72] Project MAC (Multiple Access Computer or also Machine-Aided Cognition) was the name of a laboratory created in the early 1960s and financed by ARPA. The project was directed by Robert M. Fano and included a research sector on artificial intelligence managed by Marvin Minsky, who – before receiving his second PhD on "Neural Nets and the Brain Model Problem" in 1954 from Princeton – had in fact created the first neural network simulator in 1951.[73] The programme developed by Project MAC in the field of time-sharing was called Compatible Time Sharing System (CTSS). Alongside this, in 1965 a more powerful system called Multics was under development.[74]

Dartmouth College's project, which was directed by the mathematicians John G. Kemeny and Thomas E. Kurtz, was "designed for the novice,"[75] and created terminals both for the students on campus and surrounding secondary schools.[76] Here, too, a research project on artificial intelligence was underway, directed by the philosopher James Moor, which, in fact, is often considered the genesis of the discipline. John McCarthy (who before transferring from MIT to Princeton helped to set up Project MAC) organized the first round of the project in 1956, and the proposal to activate it was signed by him, Nathaniel Rochester of IBM, Minsky and Shannon.[77]

Davies was impressed by his experiences especially with Dartmouth College and RAND, for their practical attempts at providing engineers with an instrument for solving numerical problems. Project MAC, on the other hand, made less of an impression for two reasons. As he later noted when discussing the project, at MIT, "all the people worked only on operating systems, and nobody actually used the machine. There were these marvellous operating systems, but nobody was rushing around to actually use them." In other words, there was a greater focus here on the theoretical aspects of interaction with computers than on their applications.

72. See E.P. Gimble, "JOSS: Problem Solving for Engineers," The RAND Corporation, Memorandum RM-5322-PR, May 1967, http://www.rand.org/pubs/research_memoranda/ RM5322.html; Fred J. Gruenberger, "The History of the Johnniac," The RAND Corporation, Memorandum RM-5654-PR, October 1968, http://www.rand.org/pubs/research_memoranda/ RM5654.html.

73. "Marvin Minsky," http://web.media.mit.edu/~minsky/.

74. See Robert M. Fano, "The MAC System: A Progress Report," MIT Project MAC, MAC-TR-12, 9 October 1964, http://publications.csail.mit.edu/lcs/pubs/pdf/MIT-LCS-TR-012.pdf; Jerome H. Saltzer, "CTSS Technical Notes," MIT Project MAC, MAC-TR-16, 1965, http://publications.csail.mit.edu/lcs/pubs/pdf/MIT-LCS-TR-016.pdf.

75. John G. Kemeny and Thomas E. Kurtz, "Dartmouth Time-Sharing," Science, 162, no. 3850 (1968): p. 227.

76. "The Dartmouth Time Sharing System: A Brief Description," 26 March 1965, http:// dtss.dartmouth.edu/ge_dtss.php; Kenneth M. Lochner, "The Evolving Time-Sharing System at Dartmouth College," Computers and Automation, 14, no. 9 (1965), reproduced at http://dtss. dartmouth.edu/evolving/. The project's results also included the BASIC programming language.

77. "July Conference at Dartmouth Commemorates Golden Anniversary of 'Artificial Intelligence,'" March 2006, http://www.dartmouth.edu/~news/releases/ 2006/03/13a.html; John McCarthy, Marvin L. Minsky, Nathaniel Rochester and Claude E. Shannon, "A Proposal for the Dartmouth Summer Research Project on Artificial Intelligence," 31 August 1955, http:// www-formal.stanford.edu/jmc/history/dartmouth.pdf.

From our perspective, however, the second motive is perhaps the more interesting of the two. If at RAND (where he did not meet Baran) Davies came into contact with an environment that was new to him, Project MAC was not as attractive to him because "it also went back to something that I experienced earlier when I had a Commonwealth Fund Fellowship to study at MIT for a year in 1954."[78] Although he subsequently considered his choice to study there a mistake, since most of the work he carried out was of military interest, and thus classified, this precedent is further confirmation of the existing operative connections between the British and American scientific cultures.

Furthermore, the war had just ended, and as a student Davies had already had the opportunity to hear a lecture at Imperial College by Norbert Wiener (who he would later meet at MIT), noting that he was "very inspired by it." In addition, one of his professors was John R. Womersley, who shortly thereafter, as supervisor of the NPL's Mathematics Division, brought in Alan M. Turing to work on the project for a new machine: the Automatic Computing Engine (ACE). It is well known that Turing approached this venture as if he were "building a brain."[79] This is confirmed in a letter in 1946 from Turing to W. Ross Ashby, who would shortly afterwards become the director of the Burden Neurological Institute in Bristol and who is considered another "father" of cybernetics:

The ACE is in fact, analogous to the "universal machine" described in my paper on computable numbers. This theoretical possibility is attainable in practice, in all reasonable cases, at worst at the expense of operating slightly slower than a machine specially designed for the purpose in question. Thus, although the brain may in fact operate by changing its neuron circuits by the growth of axons and dendrites, we could nevertheless make a model, within the ACE, in which this possibility was allowed for, but in which the actual construction of the ACE did not alter, but only the remembered data, describing the mode of behaviour applicable at any time.[80]

Described by James H. Wilkinson – who worked with him at NPL – as "obsessed with the idea of speed on the machine,"[81] Turing had cited the EDVAC

78. Campbell-Kelly, "Oral history interview with Donald W. Davies."

79. See, among others, Andrew Hodges, *Alan Turing: The Enigma*, Princeton, NJ, Princeton University Press, 2012 [1983], kindle loc. 7460-7521; Andrew Hodges, *Alan Turing: A Short Biography*, http://www.turing.org.uk/bio/part6.html. "Building a Brain: Intelligent Machines, Practice and Theory" is also the title of part 2 of S. Barry Cooper and Jan van Leeuwen, eds, *Alan Turing: His Work and Impact*, Waltham, MA, Elsevier, 2012.

80. Correspondence between Turing and W. Ross Ashby, no date (but "about 19 November 1946"), http://www.rossashby.info/letters/turing.html. For publications by Ashby see *Design for a Brain: The Origin of Adaptive Behavior*, 2nd ed., New York – London, John Wiley & Sons – Chapman & Hall, 1960 [1952], http://www.archive.org/details/designfor brainor00ashb and *An Introduction to Cybernetics*, London, Chapman & Hall, 1956, http://pespmc1.vub.ac.be/books/IntroCyb.pdf.

81. Christopher R. Evans, interviewed by James H. Wilkinson, quoted by Copeland, "A Brief History of Computing," 2000, http://www.alanturing.net/turing_archive/pages/Reference%20Articles/BriefHistofComp.html. The interview is part of Christopher R. Evans, *Pioneers of Computing*, a series of cassettes published in 1977 by the London Science Museum. See also C. R. Evans, "Turing's Work at the National Physical Laboratory and the Construction

project in his first report for ACE. In January 1947, just a few months before Davies joined the staff, he went to Harvard and Princeton, where he met with Shannon and various scientists who were working toward the construction of the first American computers.[82] In a lecture after his return at the London Mathematical Society, Turing asserted that ACE could perform the calculating work of 10,000 human beings. But, he added, it would not be necessary for all interested parties to have a computer: "It would be quite possible to arrange to control a distant computer by means of a telephone line."[83] Though his relationship with Davies was not particularly relaxed,[84] this was the atmosphere that the young physician found when he joined the NPL. Even after Turing abandoned the ACE project, when Davies was working on a quicker version called Pilot ACE and on other projects, he was not lacking in contacts with scientists studying the analogies between the computer and human brain; indeed, these were the "main interests" of Albert M. Uttley, his predecessor at the NPL, whose publications included two essays that had appeared in the previously mentioned *Automata Studies,* edited by Shannon and McCarthy.[85]

When Davies returned to the United States in 1965, his travel companion was a psychologist and ergonomist from EMI Electronics, Brian Shackel, who dealt with human-machine interaction in radar control displays and other infrared ray devices.[86] The psychologist Joseph C.R. Licklider was also present at the IFIP conference. As we will see, Licklider had been deeply involved in time-sharing, and in 1962 he had formed ARPA's Information Processing Techniques Office (IPTO), which in 1969 would create the first network. Following a conference given by Davies at MIT, the two would discuss the matter at length with Lawrence G. Roberts, who at the time was working at the Lincoln Laboratory.[87]

of Pilot ACE, DEUCE and ACE," in Nicholas Metropolis, Jack Howlett and Giancarlo Rota, eds, *A History of Computing in the Twentieth Century*, New York, Academic Press, 1980.

82. See Hodges, *Alan Turing*, kindle loc. 8331-8352; Simon Lavington, ed., *Alan Turing and His Contemporaries: Building the World's First Computers*, Swindon, British Informatics Society, 2012.

83. Quoted in Hodges, *Alan Turing*, p. 331. The text of the conference, which was held on 20 February 1947 is reproduced in Brian E. Carpenter and Robert W. Doran, eds., *A.M. Turing's ACE Report of 1946 and Other Papers*, Cambridge, MA, MIT Press, 1986.

84. Davies in fact found some errors in "On Computable Numbers." The paper "On Computable Numbers: Corrections and Critiques" by Turing, Emil Post and Donald W. Davies is included in Copeland, *The Essential Turing*, pp. 91-124.

85. Albert M. Uttley, "Conditional Probability Machines and Conditioned Reflexes" and "Temporal and Spatial Patterns in a Conditional Probability Machine," in Shannon and McCarthy, *Automata Studies*, pp. 253-275 and pp. 277-285. See also A. M. Uttley, "Information, Machines, and Brains," *Transactions of the IRE Professional Group on Information Theory*, 1, no. 1 (1953): pp. 143-149 and A. M. Uttley, "The Transmission of Information and the Effect of Local Feedback in Theoretical and Neural Networks," *Brain Research*, 2, no. 1 (1966): pp. 21-50. As Davies noted, it was thanks to him that the physiology of the brain had become a central concern in this area at the NPL.

86. Donald Day, Gitte Lindgaard and Jan Noves, eds., "In Memoriam: Professor Brian Shackel (1927-2007)," *Interacting with Computers*, 21, no. 5-6 (2009): pp. 323-402.

87. See Lawrence G. Roberts, "The ARPANET and Computer Networks," in *A History of Personal Workstations*, ed. by Adele Goldberg, New York – Reading, MA: ACM Press –

Davies and Shackel subsequently invited some researchers to hold lectures in England.[88] The participants of the seminar organized by Davies at the NPL in November 1965 included various MIT scholars such as Jack B. Dennis, Fernando J. Corbató and Roberts. Dennis and Corbató were part of Project MAC and in early 1967 Roberts transferred to ARPA, where he coordinated the planning of Arpanet. But there were also other scholars in attendance who were active in time-sharing projects sustained by ARPA (which paid for their trips), as well as Ivan Sutherland, who at the time was the director of the IPTO.[89]

In 1986 Davies asserted that Roberts had definitely been sent a copy of his June 1966 "Proposal for a Digital Communication Network."[90] However, their meeting does not appear to have had any significant consequences, although Roberts was already working on a "cooperative network of time-shared computers."[91] A turning point would only take place at the Association for Computer Machinery (ACM) symposium held in 1967 in Gatlinburg, Tennessee, where Roberts outlined the project for Arpanet. An English researcher, Roger A. Scantlebury, presented a report on the work of Davies' group at the NPL,[92] and it was then that he, Roberts and others "spent all night [...] arguing about the thing back and forth."[93] In addition, it was on this same occasion that Roberts learned from Scantlebury of the existence of Baran's work, and so the circle was complete.

From early on Davies had involved certain ministries, the General Post Office (GPO) and the British telecommunications industry in his project. However, to bring the idea of a national network to fruition he resolved first and foremost to create an internal network at the NPL, just as the Americans working on time-sharing had done. This network, referred to as Mark I, became operative in 1971, and two years later it was replaced by a faster and more efficient version, Mark II.

Meanwhile, Davies had accompanied a group of engineers from the GPO to study American data communications, and in 1969 he had made a proposal to Mintech to initiate a public network. As Martin Campell-Kelly has noted, it

---

Addison-Wesley Pub., 1988, p. 144. The volume republishes the acts of a conference that took place in January 1986 which had already appeared in John R. White and Kathi Anderson, eds., *Proceedings of the ACM Conference on The History of Personal Workstations*, New York, ACM, 1986.

88. Needham, "Donald Watt Davies," p. 91.

89. Norberg and O'Neill, *Transforming Computer Technology*, p. 47.

90. Campbell-Kelly, "Oral history interview with Donald W. Davies."

91. Davies was not cited, for example, by Thomas Marill and Lawrence G. Roberts, "Toward a Cooperative Network of Time-Shared Computers," in AFIPS, *Proceedings of the November 7-10, 1966 Fall Joint Computer Conference*, New York, ACM, 1966, pp. 425-443.

92. See Lawrence G. Roberts, "Multiple Computer Networks and Intercomputer Communication," in *Proceedings of First ACM Symposium on Operating System Principles*, ed. by John Gosden and Brian Randell, New York, ACM, 1967, pp. 3.1-3.6; Donald W. Davies, Keith A. Bartlett, Roger A. Scantlebury and Peter T. Wilkinson, "A Digital Communication Network for Computers Giving Rapid Response at Remote Terminals," in *ibid.*, pp. 2.1-2.17.

93. Arthur L. Norberg, "An Interview with Lawrence G. Roberts" conducted 4 April 1989, University of Minnesota, CBI Collections, Oral History 159, http://conservancy.umn.edu/bitstream/107608/1/oh159lgr.pdf.

was a "Trojan horse strategy:" "I am not at all sure" Davies wrote in a letter "that it is the right way to carry out a pilot experiment in store-and-forward type networks. Much better, I think for the Post Office to set up a pilot network to provide a commercial service to all users." The fact remains that the proposal to Mintech "was overtaken by events and did not materialize; if it had done so it would have created a research network contemporary with ARPANET, though on a smaller scale."[94] Rather, it was the GPO that developed a national network – the Experimental Packed Switched Service (EPSS) – but it only became operational (with American technology) in 1977, when various other networks already existed not only in the US, but also in Europe. Meanwhile, as of 1973, NPL's small network had become a node of ARPANET.

Thus it can be said that Davies was faced with a missed opportunity, as opposed to a false start. However, here as well his fate was determined by unfortunate circumstances. The sluggish response to his ideas and the inadequate funds allocated to bring them to reality led to a "national failure to transfer technology successfully."[95] A number of factors led to this outcome. While Davies did not endure the same hostile reception as Baran at AT&T, from early on the GPO did not show much interest in his proposals. The Labour Party's coordination of the English computer industry and focus on a limited number of standard models to be rapidly distributed on the market also proved to be counterproductive. Moreover, because of this approach the Plessey Company did not begin producing the computer chosen by Davies' team for the NPL network. The computer was substituted with a machine from the American company Honeywell – the same machine that was used for Arpanet.[96] To conclude more generally, the funding of base research was much lower in Great Britain than in the United States, and universities were not involved in the net project, whereas on other side of the Atlantic, ARPA made sure they played a decisive role.

The fact remains that regardless of their outcomes, Baran and Davies' projects were born out of such tightly interwoven scientific contexts that they could almost be considered a single cultural environment. Their ideas drew their originality and productiveness from the deeply multidisciplinary nature of this environment, which is characterized by the convergence of various sciences, from physics to mathematics, from computer science to neurophysiology, and from cybernetics to artificial intelligence. As John Ziman wrote, in contrast to what happens in biological evolution, in this technology "'memes' from distant lineages often recombine, and 'multiple parentage' is the norm. No biological organism is like, say, a computer chip, which combines basic ideas, techniques and material from a variety of distinct fields of chemistry, physics, mathematics

94. Campbell-Kelly, "Data Communications at the National Physical Laboratory," pp. 242-243, which also contains the excerpt of Davies' letter cited in the text, addressed on 16 June 1969 to Stanley Gill, leader of the Real Time Club. This club was formed in 1967 as a sort of academic-professional lobby that aimed to support the opportunities to create a British national network.

95. *Ibid.*, p. 245.

96. For further details see below, p. 110.

and engineering."[97] If Baran and Davies' projects were not "selected" and developed as they were, this was attributable to the wide ranging institutional, political and economic contexts within which they were operating, which in both cases were unfavourable. If the projects were not lost it was because, as we will see, within the same cultural milieu they were ultimately recovered in a more auspicious setting.

To conclude with a geographical metaphor, the context in which Baran and Davies' ideas took shape might be said to evoke two connecting lakes (for example Lake Michigan and Lake Huron, joined as they are by the Straits of Mackinac), even if, in reality, we are speaking of a scientific setting with connections that spanned the Atlantic. In turn, the work conducted by the American engineer and the English physicist could be represented as two outflows of this lake basin: each followed different paths, taking on different characteristics along the way, but at a certain point they both converged into a single river. The two had now become tributaries of the third river, and were discharging their water into its course. The moment has thus come to retrace the history of this third outflow: ARPA's Information Processing Techniques Office, which in 1969 created the first embryo of Internet. In a similar way to what we have done with Baran and Davies, it is first necessary to verify whether and to what extent the figure and the work of the founder of this office, Joseph C.R. Licklider, can be situated in the same cultural milieu.

97. John Ziman, "Evolutionary Models for Technical Change," in *Technological Innovation as an Evolutionary Process*, ed. by J. Ziman, Cambridge, Cambridge University Press, 2000, p. 6.

2. Joseph C.R. Licklider

The Birth of the Information Processing Techniques Office

The "Sputnik-generated" Advanced Research Projects Agency had just been set up at the US Department of Defence when President Eisenhower, who like other members of his administration was of the mind "that space should not be dominated by the military,"[1] established NASA. As a result most of the space projects that had been entrusted to ARPA were transferred to NASA. ARPA's budget subsequently dropped from 486 million dollars in 1959 to 260 million in 1961,[2] and it was forced to change its appearance and objectives. In the first half of the 1960s more than two-thirds of the budget was therefore set aside for research and development projects in the fields of antiballistic defence and nuclear test detection. In addition, with the US's growing involvement in the Vietnam War, another 10% of the budget was used for developing anti-guerrilla techniques.

The agency's reorganization continued through early 1961, after which a scientist was made director for the first time: Jack P. Ruina, who had previously worked as a professor of Electronic Engineering at Brown University and the University of Illinois, as well as Assistant Director of the Secretary of Defence. Situated in a wing of the Pentagon and equipped with a relatively small staff comprised primarily of scientists and technicians, under Ruina's guidance ARPA took on a flexible and nonbureaucratic approach to work that prioritized basic research and engaged the most important university and agency research centers in existence.

Command and control was one of the few new sectors of activity during this period, assigned to the agency in 1961 by Harold Brown, a physicist from Berkeley who had, himself, just been nominated director of the Department of Defence's Research and Engineering Office by the new Secretary of Defence, Robert S.

1. Richard H. Van Atta, Seymour J. Deitchman and Sidney G. Reed, "DARPA Technical Accomplishments," vol. 3, "An Overall Perspective and Assessment of the Technical Accomplishments of the Defense Advanced Research Projects Agency: 1958-1990," IDA Paper P-2538, Alexandria, VA, Institute for Defense Analyses, 1991, p. III-3, www.darpa. mil/WorkArea/DownloadAsset.aspx?id=2680. The "D" at the beginning of "ARPA" in the publication's title stands for "Defence" after the agency was renamed in 1972.
2. Richard J. Barber Associates, *The Advanced Research Project Agency, 1958-1974*, Washington, DC, Barber Associates, 1975, App. A-1. Other spatial projects also returned to the various armed forces.

McNamara. Brown and his colleague Eugene G. Fubini (an Italian physicist who emigrated to the US in 1939) were interested "in computer applications to war gaming, command systems studies and information processing related to command and control," and were also saddled with the task of reallocating a very expensive computer built for SAGE that the US Air Force no longer believed was necessary to the programme.[3]

It was primarily with this task in mind that the agency gave 5.8 million dollars to the Santa Monica Systems Development Corporation (SDC), which until 1957 had been a division of RAND involved with SAGE, for an information processing project in command and control systems. Moreover, a study commissioned by ARPA at the Institute for Defence Analyses (IDA) in 1960 was moving in the same direction.[4] As Ruina said during a hearing at the House of Representatives, "ARPA's programme in command and control deals primarily with fundamental questions related to the use of computers and automatic devices and displays for command and control application. It is a programme in the very fundamentals of the use of computers in such problems."[5]

Created along these lines in 1962, the following year the office designated with ARPA's command and control research was renamed the Information Processing Techniques Office (IPTO), thus reflecting the programme's objectives in its name. Although its budget rose from 9 million dollars in 1963 to 44 million dollars in 1974, as indicated in Figure 10, it nonetheless remained a secondary sector in the agency for a long time; indeed, it did not surpass 10% of the total budget until 1969, and exceeded 20% of the budget only in 1974. Despite this, its resources were undoubtedly considerable.

The man selected by Fubini and Ruina to set up this office was a psychologist, Joseph Carl Robnett Licklider. At first glance this choice may have seemed peculiar. In truth, however, this was not the case, and it was justified only in part by the fact that his tasks included initiating new research in the field of behavioural sciences for ARPA. Certainly, once in the job in October 1962, "Lick" – as all his close associates called him – immediately brought what he termed "interactive computing" to the forefront of his office's projects. He stayed with ARPA only until 1964, but during his twenty-two months of employment, the IPTO became so innovative that all of his colleagues and successors acknowledged their indebtedness to him.

The fact that this could happen means that Licklider must have already possessed a fully developed vision. Since there is no doubt that his role in the

3. *Ibid.*, p. V-49. The expression "war gaming" refers to the simulation of war scenarios that are developed in order to refine strategies that would be applicable in a real conflict.

4. See Norberg and O'Neill, *Transforming Computer Technology*, pp. 9-10; Chigusa I. Kita, "J.C.R. Licklider's Vision for the IPTO," *IEEE Annals of the History of Computing*, 25, no. 3 (2003): pp. 62-63. For a more extensive version of this essay, which appeared in a volume in Japanese, see Chigusa I. Kita, *J.C.R. Licklider and His Age*, Tokyo, Seido-sha, 2003.

5. DoD Appropriations for 1963, *Hearings Before the Subcommittee of the Committee on Appropriations, House of Representatives, Eighty-Seventh Congress, Second Session*, Part 5. *Research, Development, Test, and Evaluation*, Washington, DC, US Government Printing Office, 1962, p. 114.

Figure 10 – ARPA and IPTO's budgets, 1958-1975

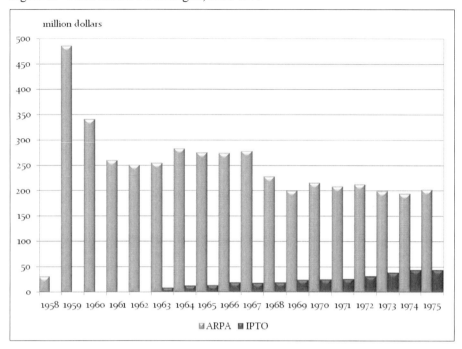

Source: Barber Associates, *The Advanced Research Projects Agency*, App. A-1 (for funds granted by Congress, taking into account the variations occuring throughout each year) and Tab. V-1, VI-1, VII-1, VIII-1, IX-1 (for IPTO's budgets).

origins of the network was fundamental, we must once again look to the past to help us understand what made this possible.

Psychoacoustics and Networks

Licklider was born in 1915 in St. Louis, Missouri, and received his PhD in Psychology from the University of Rochester in 1942.[6] His thesis, "An Electrical Study of Frequency Localization in the Auditory Cortex of the Cat" was an experimental study of "the 'place' and 'frequency' of neural impulse theories about the perception of pitch and loudness. Specifically, he measured the magnitude, frequency, and loci of cortical electro-neural activity in the brain of animals in response to tones presented to the ear."[7] Licklider ultimately never went back

6. This and other information is based on Licklider Papers, Box 1, Folder "Curricula vitae, JCRL." See also Waldrop, *The Dream Machine*.

7. Robert M. Fano, "Joseph Carl Robnett Licklider," in National Research Council, *Biographical Memoirs V.75* (Washington, DC: The National Academies Press, 1998), pp. 191-192, http://www.nap.edu/openbook.php?record_id=9649&page=191.

to this kind of research, but the issue of sound perception long remained at the centre of his interests. In 1942 he became a research associate at Swarthmore College in Pennsylvania, where he studied Gestalt psychology with one of its most authoritative exponents, Wolfgang Köhler.

Shortly after, Licklider transferred from Swarthmore to Harvard University's Psycho-Acoustic Laboratory (PAL), where he worked as a research associate and research fellow until 1946. During the Second World War, with the laboratory primarily focused on military research, Licklider studied the effects of airplane altitudes and related noise distortions on the intelligibility of radio communication.[8] These studies – along with others commissioned by the US Navy such as "Auditory Research and Undersea Warfare" – continued until 1950, when he was made lecturer in Harvard's Department of Psychology.[9]

In a 1948 article, to cite just one work, Licklider adopted the perspective of a communication engineer in order to study the auditory system's performance through headsets when vocal intelligibility is disturbed by noise.[10] At the same time, however, his interests extended from the external communication networks between human beings that are established through the emission and reception of auditory signals, to the internal network that connects the ears to the central nervous system. Indeed, in other studies from this period he addressed "the characteristics of speech as a stimulus" in the study of "brain functions" particularly in neural networks.[11] Licklider's work earned him the Acoustical Society of America's Biennial Award in 1950 and is still today considered a fundamental reference point in the field. One research paper in particular should be mentioned: "The Intelligibility of Interrupted Speech,"[12] which was produced in collaboration with George A. Miller, one of the founders of psycholinguistics and who in the same year published the book *Language and Communication*.[13]

It is significant that the article by Miller and Licklider, alongside another by Shannon, were among only four contributions cited in 1953 by another "classic"

---

8. In Licklider Papers, Box 5, Folders "1943," "1944" and "1946" there are documents on Licklider's studies from these years, including one on speech and sound transmission through gas masks. A list of his publications is in Licklider Papers, Box 1, Folder "List of Papers and Publications, JCRL." See also Mark R. Rosenzweig and Geraldine Stone, "Wartime Research in Psycho-Acoustics," *Review of Educational Research*, 18, no. 6 (1948): pp. 648, 650-651.

9. Licklider Papers, Box 5, Folder "1947". His other studies for the USAF were concluded in 1954.

10. Joseph C.R. Licklider, "The Influence of Interaural Phase Relations Upon the Masking of Speech by White Noise," *The Journal of the Acoustical Society of America*, 20, no. 2 (1948): pp. 150-159.

11. Joseph C.R. Licklider, Dalbir Bindra and Irwin Pollack, "The Intelligibility of Rectangular Speech Waves," *The American Journal of Psychology*, 61, no. 1 (1948): pp. 1-20.

12. George A. Miller and John C.R. Licklider, "The Intelligibility of Interrupted Speech," *The Journal of the Acoustical Society of America*, 22, no. 2 (1950): pp. 167-173. See also George A. Miller and Joseph C.R. Licklider, "The Perception of Speech," in *Handbook of Experimental Psychology*, ed. by Stanley S. Stevens, New York, Wiley, 1951, pp. 1040-1074.

13. George A. Miller, *Language and Communication*, New York, McGraw-Hill, 1951. On Miller's role see Edwards, *The Closed World*, p. 222.

of the period. The author in question was E. Colin Cherry, a scholar of Electronic and Telecommunications Engineering at the Imperial College of London, who in the same year was a visiting professor at MIT. In addition, although not cited, another important study by Licklider from 1951 is today considered a source of its premises.[14]

Cherry's essay inaugurated the study of what is referred to as "selective attention," articulating for the first time a problem that still to this day has not been entirely solved. "How do we recognize" Cherry asked, "what one person is saying when others are speaking at the same time (the 'cocktail party problem')? On what logistical basis could one design a machine ('filter') for carrying out such operation?"[15] In other words, what is the mechanism that allows us to tune into just one of the many conversations that intermingle during a cocktail party, singling it out and treating all the others as interference or background noise? This confirms what was suggested above: that Licklider's psychoacoustic studies involved two communication networks connected with ears; the first formed by multiple human beings linked together through voice and hearing, with the second formed by the nervous system.

One could object that to insist on the concept of network in these studies is in some way finalistic, as it is predetermined by the knowledge of Licklider's role in the process that ultimately led to the realization of Arpanet. This said, it was precisely in such terms that in 1950 Licklider himself summarized the significance of the work conducted by the MIT's Acoustic Laboratory and Research Laboratory of Electronics (where he had just transferred from Harvard and where he would remain until 1957 as an associate professor, first in the Department of Electrical Engineering and then in Economics and Social Science):

> The general problem on which this group is working is somewhat as follows. You have a number of humans beings connected together by communication links to form a network. They have access to certain information and a task to perform that requires action based on the information. The question is: How does their performance of the task depend upon the configuration of the network?[16]

Six years later, an essay by Licklider, "Auditory Frequency Analysis," appeared in a volume edited by Cherry and entitled *Information Theory*.[17] The roles were reversed in this meeting between a scholar of psychoacoustics who

---

14. The study in question is Joseph C.R. Licklider, "A Duplex Theory of Pitch Perception," *Experientia*, 7, no. 4 (1951): pp. 128-134.

15. E. Colin Cherry, "Some Experiments on the Recognition of Speech, with One and with Two Ears," *The Journal of the Acoustical Society of America*, 25, no. 5 (1953): pp. 975-976. On this issue, see, for example, Adelbert W. Bronkhorst, "The Cocktail Party Phenomenon: A Review of Research on Speech Intelligibility in Multiple-Talker Conditions," *Acustica – Acta Acustica*, 86 (2000): pp. 117-128.

16. Abstract of a presentation by Licklider at the Conference on Hearing and Voice Communication of the National Academy of Sciences, Washington, 28 October 1950, in Licklider Papers, Box 5, Folder "1950."

17. Joseph C.R. Licklider, "Auditory Frequency Analysis," in *Information Theory*, ed. by E. Colin Cherry, New York, Academic Press, 1956, pp. 253-268.

reasoned in terms of networks and an engineer specialized in telecommunications who studied the physiology of the auditory system. To understand how this meeting came about, we must first analyze the context in which Licklider was working from 1942 onwards and the circumstances in which Cherry spent his sabbatical year in 1953.

Of course, the most obvious *trait d'union* between the experts of these different disciplines were the electronic devices which they both used to measure the size and frequency of their respective flows, to build models and so on. However, as Edwards has observed in his far-reaching, rigorous reconstruction of the scientific milieu during the Second World War and postwar period, this was not merely an instrumental link. It was primarily the subject of this period's psychology – comprised of the human factor of sophisticated man-machine systems such as airplanes, submarines and tanks, and the servomechanisms that had to control or neutralize them – that placed "the machine in the middle" and contributed to the growth of "cybernetic psychology."[18]

Although communications have always played an essential part in war, their speed and efficiency were especially crucial to the functioning of chains of command and control in a conflict that was more mechanized than ever, as was the case when the United States joined the Second World War at the end of 1941. Yet the noise created by motors and explosions rendered existing communication tools useless. At Harvard, both the Electro-Acoustic Laboratory, directed by Leo L. Beranek, and the PAL, overseen by Stanley S. Stevens, were dedicated to finding a solution to this problem. Licklider worked in the latter laboratory, which was an important testing ground for cognitive psychology. During the final years of the war, the PAL also entered into operative relations with MIT's Radiation Laboratory.

However, there were also other links connecting Cambridge, Massachusetts' two academic communities to each other and to other research centres. Ten conferences were held between 1946 and 1953 that were of fundamental importance to the development of cybernetics and cognitive sciences. They were financed by the Josiah Macy Jr. Foundation and were prepared during the war from the elaborations of a group that included MacCulloch, Wiener, von Neumann, Shannon, Pitts, the neurobiologist Arturo Rosenblueth, the engineer Julian Bigelow as well as various anthropologists, psychologists and psychoanalysts.[19] The main topics discussed included, on the one hand, the similarities and differences between the computer and the human brain, and, on the other, information and communication theories. Psychology played a significant part thanks to contributions by Köhler, John Stroud and others, including Licklider.

In 1950 Licklider gave a keynote guest lecture at the seventh Macy Conference on "The Manner in Which and Extent to Which Speech Can be Distorted and

---

18. See Edwards, *The Closed World*, p. 210, where the author discusses one of the first examples "of what would eventually be labeled 'cyborgs': biomechanical organisms made up of humans and machinery." "The Machine in the Middle" is the title of chapter 6 in this book.

19. See Steve J. Heims, *Constructing a Social Science for Postwar America: The Cybernetics Group, 1946-1953*, Cambridge, MA, MIT Press, 1993; Jean-Pierre Dupuy, *Aux origines des sciences cognitives*, 2nd ed., Paris, La Découverte, 1999.

Remain Intelligible."[20] Licklider's presentation was immediately followed by a report on "The Redundancy of English" given by Shannon, who in the Bell Laboratories had contributed to Project X, the first digital speech transmission system. Shannon considered the written language "as a discrete (discontinuous, or digital) information source" and the 26 letters of the English alphabet to be elements of a "stochastic coding process" (a transmission and reception mechanism based on the frequencies of single characters understood as coders and decoders.)[21] It is also significant that later Licklider contributed alongside Shannon to develop this particular research.[22] Although it is unlikely that Baran and Davies had a particularly close relationship with experimental psychology, this discipline was also at the basis of the issues they would address in the 1960s.

After transferring to MIT – where thanks in part to his interest he was followed by Miller in 1951 – Licklider continued his research on psychoacoustics primarily at a theoretical level,[23] acquiring increasing authority in the field before finally becoming president of the Acoustical Society of America in 1958. However, in this period his interests began to change. In 1950 he participated in Project Hartwell, an undersea war programme, in 1952 he was involved with Project Charles, which instead regarded antiaircraft defence, while between 1953 and 1954 he took part in a summer studies programme at the Hughes Aircraft Company. Both SAGE and MIT's Lincoln Laboratory were born out of Project Charles, and it was in the Lincoln Laboratory that Licklider and Miller created a psychology section, recruiting a group of young researchers from various American universities, half of whom were psychologists and the other half were engineers. These military project collaborations were not in and of themselves new either to Licklider or the universities where he worked. Nonetheless, the projects gave him the chance to broaden his interests from psychoacoustics (although he continued to cultivate this area) to issues that more directly regarded information and communication.

The final Macy Conference was held in 1953. The following year, Licklider, Miller and others organized a similar initiative on "Problems in Human Communication and Control" with the sponsorship of the National Science Foundation (NSF), which included Wiener among its participants. Licklider had become a much more regular member of Wiener's "circle" since he starting to work at MIT, and the many topics discussed therein all rotated around the "active interaction between psychology and cybernetics." The report on the conference was

20. Joseph C.R. Licklider, "The Manner in Which and Extent to Which Speech Can be Distorted and Remain Intelligible," in *Cybernetics: Circular Causal and Feedback Mechanisms in Biological and Social Systems, Transactions of the Seventh Conference, March 23-24, 1950, New York, N.Y.* ed. by Heinz von Foerster, Mead and Teuber, New York, J. Macy Jr. Foundation, 1951, pp. 58-122.

21. See Claude E. Shannon, "The Redundancy of English," in *ibid.*, pp. 123-158; Edwards, *The Closed World*, pp. 200-201, 205; Dupuy, *Aux origines des sciences cognitives*, pp. 125, 128. In probability calculus, "stochastic" is a synonym for "casual" or "random."

22. Nancy G. Burton and Joseph C.R. Licklider, "Long-Range Constraints in the Statistical Structure of Printed English," *The American Journal of Psychology*, 68, no. 4 (1955): pp. 650-653.

23. See for example Joseph C.R. Licklider, "Three Auditory Theories," in *Psychology, A Study of a Science Volume 1*, ed. by Sigmund Koch, New York, McGraw-Hill, 1959, pp. 41-144.

prepared by Licklider – who acted as its chairman and oversaw the transcription and publication of its acts – and insisted that the event "had turned out not to be about information theory as narrowly conceived, but about a broader range of quantitative problems." He further added: "The thing that is basically important in engineering and in psychology is much broader than bits and $p \log p$ [*sic*]. It is a whole complex of quantitative techniques and relations."[24]

The same elements were highlighted in the NSF's official report, which also noted the need to intensify interdisciplinary exchanges both among psychologists, physicists, engineers and mathematicians and between the work being conducted in the US and Great Britain.[25] Wiener and Licklider in effect discussed how to create a geographically dispersed scientific community, and it is also for this reason that Ronda Hauben (who asserted that "Licklider's vision [was] a logical outcome of the cybernetic movement and its concerns") saw the conference as a connection with the project that would ultimately lead to the creation of the first network.[26]

From 1954, Licklider, Miller and Walter A. Rosenblith (who had also come from the PAL) worked on man-machine interfaces and specifically on their audiovisual systems as part of the SAGE project. It was during this period that Licklider's focus of interest shifted increasingly from psychology to communications. At the same time, the need for quantification and data processing that he had already experienced (and that was emphasized by the conference) led him to have direct contact with digital computers, and to follow a path that ran parallel to that of Miller.

> Licklider – wrote John A. Swets – pursued mainly neurophysiological theories of hearing and the role of humans and machines in complex systems. Miller developed his interests in language, memory, and perception and popularized in psychology Shannon's information theory and the linguistic theory of Noam Chomsky. Both Licklider and Miller began thinking about computer models for human cognitive processes and human-computer interaction.[27]

But we should let Licklider speak for himself, who in 1988 recalled:

> About that point I came to realize that my interests just couldn't be furthered. I had a big analogue computer lab, because I was modelling brain stuff, and I realized that I could not do what I was trying to do by analogue computing. I did not know digital computing, but I could see in all this Lincoln context that there were digital computers everywhere. I started

24. Joseph C.R. Licklider, "Report on a Conference Sponsored by the National Science Foundation, 15-17 June 1954, on Problems in Human Communication and Control," in Licklider Papers, Box 5, Folder "Conference on Human Communication and Control." (This folder also contains a copy of the transcription of the acts that he edited.)

25. National Science Foundation, *Fourth Annual Report for the Fiscal Year Ending June 20, 1954*, Washington, DC, US Government Printing Office, 1954, p. 38.

26. Ronda Hauben, "Creating the Vision for the Internet: From the Wiener Circles to Licklider and ARPA's Information Processing Techniques Office (IPTO)" (2004), pp. 267, 271, http://www.columbia.edu/~rh120/other/misc/Beitrag_RHauben_korrigiert.pdf.

27. John A. Swets, "The ABC's of BBN: From Acoustics to Behavioral Sciences to Computers," *IEEE Annals of the History of Computing*, 27, no. 2 (2005): p. 16.

to go tinker and learn how they work. Wes Clark got a hold of me one day and gave me a lecture about it. He said, "Why don't you take a couple of hours everyday and go work at this TX2 computer that we put together?" So I saw that I had really got to do that, and I also saw that I was not going to do that trying to build a psychology department at MIT. Just about that same time, George Miller got an offer from Harvard to go be a professor.[28]

Miller left MIT in 1956 and Licklider also departed a short while later to accept Leo L. Beranek's proposal to join the acoustic consulting company he had founded at Cambridge in 1948 with the physicist Richard H. Bolt. This company had performed its first tests in the planning of the auditorium and other public spaces of the United Nations building and in 1953 partnered with the architect Robert Newman and took the name Bolt, Beranek and Newman (BBN). It was essentially a research centre that aimed to expand to the fields of psychoacoustics and man-machine interaction.

Beranek knew Licklider well from their time at Harvard. He had remained in touch with him at MIT (where he had also transferred in 1947), and for good reason he singled him out as his "top candidate" to develop the key sectors. Indeed, he would have been hard pressed to find someone better than an experimental psychologist "interested most especially in how the brain works in conjunction with hearing, but also in speech and communication and human engineering."[29] Thus in 1957 Licklider joined BBN as head of the psychoacoustics, engineering psychology and information systems research departments, and also became vice president of the company.[30]

"Man-Computer Symbiosis"

Licklider – Beranek recalled – had been on staff only a few months when he told me, in fall 1957, that he wanted BBN to buy a digital computer for his group. When I pointed out that we already had a punched-card computer in the financial department and several analogue computers in the experimental psychology group, he replied that they did not interest him. He wanted a then state-of-the-art machine produced by the Royal-McBee Co., a subsidiary of Royal Typewriter. "What will it cost?" I asked. "Around $30,000", he replied, rather blandly, and noted that this price tag was a discount he had already negotiated. I exclaimed, "BBN has never spent anything approaching that amount on a single research apparatus. What are you going to do with it?" "I don't know," Lick responded "but if BBN is going to be an important company in the future, it must be in computers."[31]

28. William Aspray and Arthur Norberg, "An Interview with J.C.R. Licklider," 28 October 1988, University of Minnesota, CBI Collections, Oral History 150, http://conservancy.umn.edu/bitstream/107436/1/oh150jcl.pdf.

29. This is how Licklider defined himself in John A.N. Lee and Robert Rosin, eds., "The Project MAC Interviews," *IEEE Annals of the History of Computing*, 14, no. 2 (1992): pp. 15-16.

30. See Jordan Alperin, Alexander Brown, Jennifer Huang and Shastri Sandy, "Bolt, Beranek, and Newman Inc.: A Case History of Transition," December 2001, http://web.mit.edu/6.9333/www/Fall2001/BBN.pdf; Swets, "The ABC's of BBN."

31. Leo L. Beranek, "BBN's Earliest Days: Founding a Culture of Engineering Creativity," *IEEE Annals of the History of Computing*, 27, no. 2 (2005): p. 10.

In truth, Licklider knew full well what he would do with a digital computer. Even though he had not yet fully mastered the machines, he had already learned much about their features and possibilities from Wesley A. Clark. Clark was an electronics engineer at the Lincoln Laboratory who had played a fundamental role in the construction of the TX-2 – one of the first microcomputers and the very first to use a transistor – and subsequently made a significant contribution to the construction of Arpanet. It is no coincidence that Kenneth Olsen – president of the Digital Equipment Corporation (DEC) and also a Lincoln Laboratory alumnus – proposed in 1959 that Licklider and his staff test the prototype of his new PDP-1, another minicomputer.[32] And since Royal-McBee's machine had not had good results, following the test the BBN acquired in 1960 a PDP-1, on which Licklider experimented with a time-sharing system for the first time. Moreover, this system was none other than an attempt to put the ideas he had developed in previous years into practice. We should therefore consider what these ideas were and how he brought them to fruition.

Licklider's starting point had been the man-machine systems, which in a 1957 symposium of psychologists and engineers were defined as "a complex concatenation of men and machines performing a mixed sequence of manual and automatic operations entailing the real time handling and use of information in an environment characterized by multivariate feedback."[33] The systems considered covered all sorts of things (from an airplane and a combat information centre to a man with a pencil and a communication system), but it also included SAGE, and it was on an analysis of its characteristics and its limits that Licklider's reflections were based. Although these were openly set in the context of the competition between the USA and USSR and were often applied to military projects, they however had a different and much more general objective: the development of scientific research.

During the spring and summer of 1957, Licklider broke down his work time into parts, logged it, calculated its effect and reached the conclusion that a good 85% of his time was consumed by preliminary and support operations, and only the remaining 15% was dedicated to thinking.[34] This was the basis for a paper written a short while later for the National Academy of Sciences, which Chigusa Ishikawa Kita has rightfully traced to his experience with SAGE.[35] Although he made no explicit reference to SAGE, Licklider did play with the words of the title ("The Truly Sage System or Toward a Man-Machine System for Thinking"), alluding to the fact that SAGE was not "wise" enough to "improve the quality or efficiency of scientific and technical thinking."

32. Alongside Licklider, one person in particular who worked on the test was Edward Fredkin, a BBN engineer who also hailed from the Lincoln Laboratory.

33. Joseph C.R. Licklider, "Theoretical Aspects of Research on Man-Machine Systems," 31 October 1957 (Summary of a Symposium held, under the sponsorship of the US Air Force Office of Scientific Research at Endicott House, MIT, Dedham, MA, 30-31 May 1957), in Licklider Papers, Box 6, Folder "1957."

34. The experiment is described in Joseph C.R. Licklider, "Man-Computer Symbiosis," *IRE Transactions on Human Factors in Electronics*, HFE-1, no. 1 (1960): p. 6.

35. Kita, "J.C.R. Licklider's Vision for the IPTO," pp. 66-68.

Figure 11 – The DEC PDP-1 computer

Source: http://www.columbia.edu/acis/history/pdp1.jpg.

Given that "even highly creative scientists and engineers spend most of their time doing essentially clerical work," Licklider established the objective of a "man-machine thinking system." In order to achieve this system they would have had to use "the man for what he does best and the machinery for what it does best."[36] For each area of technological knowledge, he imagined various "thinking centres" equipped with digital computers and libraries containing books and magazines "adapted for rapid access to information." Operators would speak to the machine through microphones, would write on its monitor "with pencil or stylus," insert graphics and use teleprinters. Information retrieval and data processing were to be the primary, but not the only functions of the system:

> Perhaps one of these other functions is (or involves) discussion of technical questions with colleagues. One of the interesting possibilities opened up by the concept of a network of thinking centres is a technical discussion *within* the system. If several centres are connected together by high-capacity communication channels, we can imagine a telephone conversation, greatly augmented by access, at both ends of the line, to the facilities of the system. Or, we may imagine a conference facilitated by the fact that libraries of technical information, and also the advice of specialist consultants, are immediately available.[37]

36. Joseph C.R. Licklider, "The Truly Sage System or Toward a Man-Machine System for Thinking," 20 August 1957, 1-2, in Licklider Papers, Box 6, Folder "1957 (b)."
    37. *Ibid.*, p. 8.

As we can see, Licklider had something much greater than a man-machine system in mind. In addition to creating opportunities for debate between scholars, the network of thinking centres he imagined could in fifteen years produce a quantity of information "equal in extent to all the recorded technological literature of the past." Licklider did not address the technical aspects of the connection between various centres, but this is another reason to believe that he was arriving at the idea of a network of computers that started from a conception of the scientific community as a network. In addition, it is worth noting that every centre's computer was to be "time-shared among many users." As Chigusa I. Kita has pointed out, this is actually one of the first times that the concept of time sharing (which was already being used at SAGE, albeit with other meanings) was used with its current meaning. This is usually attributed to two documents from the year 1959: a memorandum by John McCarthy at MIT and a report by the Englishman Christopher Strachey at the UNESCO International Conference on Information Processing.[38]

"A fundamental factor influencing economic feasibility" wrote Licklider, "is simultaneous (rapid time-sharing) use of the machine computing and storage facilities by many people. But we could not expect to have more than a few people working at one time in the early stages." Only after being developed in a specific field could the system have had multiple applications outside the research area as well. Finally, the system was conceived

> to take advantage of the fact that the current and extrapolated capabilities of human brains and electronic data-processing systems are to large extent complementary. There is little reason to restrict either the man or the machine to what, at the outset, appears to be his zone. In fact, the problem of coupling between the man and the machine would be greatly simplified if the machine could be developed in part in man's image. It is desirable, therefore, to explore the possibilities of the field of research currently designated by the terms *artificial intelligence* and *self-organizing automata*. That study and the study of human thinking and perceiving should be mutually facilitating.[39]

The incipit of a 1958 presentation to the Committee on the Roles of Men in Future Air Force Systems was instead dedicated to a critique of artificial intelligence. Its title also anticipated Licklider's most famous work, which appeared in 1960: "Man-Computer Symbiosis." He expressed his reserve by drawing ironically on a science fiction scenario:

> The physicists, engineers, and mathematicians of the country had laboured for years to complete the ultimate digital computer. It was made of micro-miniature components and housed under a giant plastic dome in the space that once had been the courtyard of the Pentagon. The philosophers, theologians, psychologists, and elder statesmen of the

---

38. Kita, "J.C.R. Licklider's Vision for the IPTO," p. 68. See also J.A.N. Lee, "Time-Sharing at MIT: Introduction" and J.A.N. Lee, "Claims to the Term 'Time-Sharing,'" *IEEE Annals of the History of Computing*, 14, no. 1 (1992): pp. 13-17; John McCarthy, "Reminiscences on the History of Time-Sharing," *IEEE Annals of the History of Computing*, 14, no. 1 (1992): pp. 19-24, which includes McCarthy's 1959 memorandum; Hellige, "Leitbilder in der Genese von Time-Sharing Systemen."

39. Licklider, "The Truly Sage System," pp. 11-13.

nation had, after long and profound elaboration, selected the question to be addressed to the giant machine, and the question had been encoded for presentation. The leading public figures, representatives of industry, science, the arts, the military... all were assembled to witness the historic event. The President pressed the golden button. The wheels whirred, the lights flashed, the display panel came aglow, and the computer announced: "I am glad that you asked me that question."[40]

His prediction of a "dramatic failure of complete automation" rested on what this time was an explicit criticism of SAGE. Given that it had been conceived as a mostly automatic system, human operators had been utilized primarily to manage the activities that the machine could not do. As a result, a true man-computer symbiosis was undermined and the former was placed at the service of the latter.[41] In essence, Licklider believed that too much time would pass before artificial intelligence made it possible "for machines alone to do much thinking or problem solving." Thus in the meantime it was necessary to find a way to use "the fantastic – but in themselves insufficient – capabilities of computers to augment and facilitate human thinking and problem solving – and to put it on a fast enough time scale to make it useful in operational situations."[42]

In the 1960 essay, in which his vision is fully developed, Licklider took the middle ground between those who saw the computer as a "mechanical extension" of man[43] and artificial intelligence scholars. However, he did not fail to cite certain achievements by the latter, and he attributed them, both at the time and, as we will see, later, strategic significance. These achievements were mainly programmes that had the shared objective of teaching the computer to do something: to play chess, to solve complex problems by simulating the processes assumed by human beings (problem solving), to recognize and classify images, electronic signals, speech fragments, characters and so on (pattern recognition).[44] The contributions

40. Joseph C.R. Licklider, "Man-Computer Symbiosis," Part of the Oral Report of the 1958 NAS-ARDC Special Study, Presented on Behalf of the Committee on the Roles of Men in Future Air Systems, 20-21 November 1958, p. 1, in Licklider Papers, Box 6, Folder "1958." The other essay cited in the text is Licklider, "Man-Computer Symbiosis" (1960). Regarding his "fortune," see Tami K. Tomasello, "A Content Analysis of Citations to J.C.R. Licklider's 'Man-Computer Symbiosis,' 1960-2001: Diffusing the Intergalactic Network," The Florida State University, College of Communication, 2004, http://etd.lib.fsu.edu/theses_1/available/etd-04102004-214127/unrestricted/tkt_dissertation.pdf. See also Tami K. Tomasello, "J.C.R. Licklider and the Rise of Interactive and Networked Computing," in *Handbook of Research on Social Interaction Technologies and Collaboration Software: Concepts and Trends Volume 1*, ed. by Tatyana Dumova and Richard Fiordo, Hershey, PA – New York, Information Science Reference, 2010, pp. 1-10.

41. Licklider, "Man-Computer Symbiosis" (1958), pp. 2-3.

42. *Ibid.*, p. 4.

43. On this issue, Licklider cited John D. North, *The Rational Behavior of Mechanically Extended Man*, Wolverhampton, England, Boulton Paul Aircraft Ltd., 1954.

44. For Marvin Minsky "patterns are *classes* of signals or figures, not single figures. They are classes of figures which are grouped together because, for some purpose or other, they can be treated alike:" Woodrow W. Bledsoe, Jacek S. Bomba, Iben Browning, R. James Evey, Russell A. Kirsch, Richard L. Mattson, Minsky, Ulric Neisser and Oliver G. Selfridge, "Discussion of Problems in Pattern Recognition," in *Papers presented at the December 1-3, 1959, Eastern*

mentioned in "Man-Computer Symbiosis" included some of the many works by Allen Newell, John Clifford Shaw and Herbert A. Simon on problem solving.[45] On pattern recognition Licklider cited works by Wesley A. Clark (his guide to digital computers) and Belmont G. Farley, Gerald P. Dinneen and Oliver G. Selfridge.[46]

"It seems entirely possible" wrote Licklider, "that, in due course, electronic or chemical 'machines' will outdo the human brain in most of the functions we now consider exclusively within its province."[47] Therefore, it does not seem exactly correct to affirm, as has been done, that Licklider would have been against artificial intelligence nor that he would have opposed the complete automation that it sought.[48] This is an issue of the utmost interest, both because it connects to his option for time sharing and because as the head of IPTO Licklider allocated a significant portion of his funds to research development in this field, even going so far as to steer the direction that it took.[49]

Licklider had been in touch for some time with artificial intelligence exponents and in particular with the promoters of the Dartmouth College project, where the expression had been used for the first time. Besides the aforementioned Shannon; there was Minsky who had been one of his students at Harvard, and Rochester who had programmed a model for a neural network in the computer, drawing inspiration from a 1952 conference he gave on the psychologist Donald O. Hebb's theories. In his book *The Organization of the Behaviour* (1949), Hebb had argued that the brain responds to sensory impulses and adapts to external

Joint IRE-AIEE-ACM Computer Conference, New York, ACM, 1959, p. 234. For an overview, see Nils J. Nillson, *The Quest for Artificial Intelligence: A History of Ideas and Achievements*, Cambridge – New York, Cambridge University Press, 2010.

45. Allen Newell and John C. Shaw, "Programming the Logic Theory Machine," in *Papers presented at the February 26-28, 1957, Western Joint Computer Conference: Techniques for Reliability*, New York, ACM, 1957, pp. 230-240; Allen Newell, Herbert A. Simon and John C. Shaw, "Report on a General Problem Solving Program," in *Information Processing: Proceedings of the International Conference on Information Processing*, Paris, UNESCO, 1960. The conference was held in June 1959.

46. Wesley A. Clark and Belmont G. Farley, "Generalization of Pattern Recognition in a Self-Organizing System," in *Proceedings of the March 1-3, 1955, Western Joint Computer Conference*, New York, ACM, 1955, pp. 86-91; Gerald P. Dinneen, "Programming Pattern Recognition," in *Proceedings of the March 1-3, 1955, Western Joint Computer Conference*, New York, ACM, 1955, pp. 94-100; Selfridge, "Pandemonium: A Paradigm for Learning," in National Physical Laboratory, *Mechanisation of Thought Processes: Proceedings of a Symposium Held at the National Physical Laboratory on 24th, 25th, 26th and 27th November 1958*, vol. 1, London, Her Majesty's Stationery Service, 1959, pp. 511-531.

47. Licklider, "Man-Computer Symbiosis" (1960), p. 4.

48. Kita, "J.C.R. Licklider's Vision for the IPTO," pp. 68-69.

49. Regarding the subsequent controversies, see Mikel Olazaran, "A Sociological Study of the Official History of the Perceptron Controversy," *Social Studies of Science*, 26, no. 3 (1996): pp. 611-659 and Jon Guice, "Controversy and the State: Lord ARPA and Intelligent Computing," *Social Studies of Science*, 28, no. 1 (1998): pp. 103-138. See also Thomas C. Bartee, ed., *Expert Systems and Artificial Intelligence: Applications and Management*, Indianapolis, IN, H.M. Sams, 1988, ch. 8. This same text includes Joseph C.R. Licklider, "The Early Years: Founding IPTO," pp. 219-227.

reality, modifying its neural circuits with a mechanism for perception, learning and memorization.[50]

But it is perhaps in reference to McCarthy (at MIT from 1958 to 1961) that we can better understand the terms of the issue. Licklider recalled that he "was probably the source of most of the motivation and action" for BBN's time-sharing project, in which not coincidentally he involved both himself and Minsky as consultants. Certainly, he added, this project "was more just an exercise: because it was such a weak little computer, there was nothing really to time-share." McCarthy, on the other hand, had in mind a system with certain indispensable requisites, such as a million bit memory, and to Licklider at the time "that wasn't responsible thinking."[51]

In short, McCarthy's ideas seemed futuristic to Licklider, and he took the same attitude towards artificial intelligence. He was not opposed to it; on the contrary, he was somewhat favourable because – as he observed in a study performed in 1961 for the USAF entitled "The Cerebral Frontier" – it had a heuristic approach "leading to insight or discovery" as it intended "to lead to solutions or to new knowledge, whereas algorismic procedures are known, through definite proof, to achieve their proper goals."[52] In the same year, during one of the lectures on "Computers and the World of the Future" given on the occasion of MIT's centennial celebration, Licklider very explicitly confirmed that "the area of investigation that seems to me to offer the most direct path toward understanding of intellectual processes is the area called 'artificial intelligence,' the area concerned with the development of self-organizing and/or intelligent automata."[53]

Analyzing the relations between artificial intelligence, bionics and man-computer symbiosis, however, Licklider wrote: "It seems likely that there must be several years of hard work before there will be any truly symbiotic partnership between men and computers, and that there must be several further years of hard work before there will be any practically significant artificial intelligence."[54] In

50. Donald O. Hebb, *The Organization of Behavior: A Neuropsychological Theory*, New York, Wiley, 1949. On this issue, see M. Mitchell Waldrop, *Complexity: The Emerging Science at the Edge of Order and Chaos*, New York, Simon & Schuster, 1992, p. 157; Kita, "J.C.R. Licklider's Vision for the IPTO," p. 69.

51. "An Interview with J.C.R. Licklider." On the system of the BBN, see John McCarthy, Sheldon Boilen, Edward Fredkin and Joseph C.R. Licklider, "A Time-Sharing Debugging System for a Small Computer," in AFIPS, *Proceedings of the May 21-23, 1963, Spring Joint Computer Conference* (New York: ACM, 1963), pp. 51–57.

52. Joseph C.R. Licklider, "The Cerebral Frontier," p. 2, in Licklider Papers, Box 7, Folder "1962;" Joseph C.R. Licklider, "Studies in the Organization of Man-Machines Systems," December 1962, p. 10, in Licklider Papers, Folder "BBN Reports 1962."

53. Martin Greenberger, ed., *Computers and the World of the Future*, Cambridge, MA, MIT Press, 1962, p. 207. Licklider was, with Peter Elias, one of the discussants of the lecture by Alan J. Perlis on "The Computer in the University" (pp. 181-199).

54. Licklider, "The Cerebral Frontier," p. 10. Bionics was defined as the "integration of biological and technological ideas, problems, and capabilities" and specifically "the research in biology for nature's solutions to interesting and difficult problems and the application in technology of those solutions or of models or analogues of them" (*ibid.*, p. 2).

another written piece from a few years later, he once again clarified his point of view in the following terms:

> If valuable contributions can be made by "'artificial intelligences" of that date, there will be room for them, as well as the men to monitor them, in our basic schema. On the other hand, if it should turn out that the problems involved in developing significant artificial intelligence are extremely difficult, or that society rejects the whole idea of artificial intelligence as a defiance of God or a threat to man, then it will be good not to have counted on much help from software approaches that are not yet well enough understood to support extrapolation.[55]

Although Licklider's vision foresaw developments that existing technologies were not yet able to support, it was much more pragmatic. He intended to make use of artificial intelligence[56] in anticipation of its developments, although it was understood that his goal set him apart from it. This goal was a man-computer symbiosis that would have facilitated research in the field, but would have revolved around the human component. "Human hand and eye – he wrote in another 1961 essay – are much too slow to meet the need for record keeping in our major systems. Yet human judgment has not been replaced." Continuing, he wrote, "Brains are now the sole source of heuristics. The basic need is thus now to combine strategic guidance from the human brain with electronics' speed and mammoth memory."[57]

It was not a coincidence that he entitled the other aforementioned paper "The Cerebral Frontier:" it was the brain, the central organ "for planning and thinking, solving and deciding, perceiving and knowing, command and control" that distinguished men from "lower animals." "'Mind' is a fuzzy concept of outgrown philosophy. 'Intellect' is lifeless faculty of discarded psychology. The cerebrum, in contrast, is an active, vital organ: a living prototype for bionic investigation and a worthy partner for symbiotic interaction with the most advanced computing machine."[58] He also noted:

> In this field, a principal aim is to overcome the barriers caused by differences in language and in speed of operation that at the present time make it impossible for a commander or a scientist to work with a computer as he would with a colleague. It is to bring the great information storage and processing capabilities of modern computers under the moment-to-moment guidance of human brains, accepting such suggestions and hypotheses as the computer can provide, but relying mainly upon the human brains for planning, direction, and insight and mainly upon the machines for searching, calculating, simulating, and storing.[59]

55. Joseph C.R. Licklider, *Libraries of the Future*, Cambridge, MA, MIT Press, 1965, pp. 58-59.

56. This is clearly apparent in Joseph C.R. Licklider, "Artificial Intelligence, Military Intelligence, and Command and Control," in *Military Information Systems: The Design of Computer-Aided Systems for Command*, ed. by Edward Bennett, James Degan and Joseph Spiegel, New York, Praeger, 1964, pp. 118-133.

57. Joseph C.R. Licklider, "The System System," 3 November 1961, pp. 9, 14, in Licklider Papers, Box 6, Folder "1961." The essay is published in Edward M. Bennett, James Degan and Joseph Spiegel, eds, *Human Factors in Technology*, New York, McGraw-Hill, 1963.

58. Joseph C.R. Licklider, "The Cerebral Frontier," pp. 5-6.

59. *Ibid.*, pp. 3-4.

Although in this case a great deal of time was required for it to become operative, he believed that "once an effective system for real-time programming of a large, fast, time-sharing computer and for cooperative research (not 'team' research) by as many as ten advanced researchers is available, progress should be rapid." A "serious and intensive work on mechanized intelligence might lead to important advances in this area," he wrote, but "the most promising approach, in fact, involves a man-computer team."[60]

As we have already revealed, Licklider contributed to the development of a man-computer symbiosis conceived in this way by creating the prototype for a small time-shared system with five user stations at the BBN. In addition to McCarthy and Minsky, various researchers contributed to the project, some of whom had been with him at MIT, such as the psychologist Thomas M. Marill and the engineers Jerome I. Elkind and Edward Fredkin. The first programmes developed for the system made it clear the direction that Licklider intended to take. One of these programmes, which he tested with his adolescent daughters Tracy and Linda, was for the study of German, and was presented in 1961 at a conference on the "Application of Digital Computers to Automated Instruction." Another facilitated "a student's exploration of the relations between the symbolic and graphical forms of mathematical equations." A third helped to plan and carry out a series of treatments in hospitals.[61]

Libraries of the Future

As previously suggested with regards his "thinking centres", Licklider attributed particular significance to information retrieval and the processing of bibliographic materials. This was not merely wishful thinking on his part; indeed, from November 1961 at the BBN he led a study funded by the Council on Library Resources that sought to answer questions such as: "How can we formulate the tasks the library will face in the twenty-first century? What can the science of information handling do toward helping the library of the future perform its tasks in more effective ways?"[62] When Licklider left the BBN for the ARPA, the management of the project, which concluded in 1963, was taken over by John A. Swets, previously a psychology professor at MIT. However, it was Licklider who revealed the final results of the study in a volume entitled *Libraries of the Future*. Therefore, although not published until 1965, this work should also be considered

---

60. *Ibid.*, pp. 8, 14-15.

61. See Joseph C.R. Licklider and Welden E. Clark, "On-Line Man-Computer Communication," in *Proceedings of the May 1-3, 1962, Spring Joint Computer Conference*, New York, ACM, 1962, pp. 113-128 (the quote is on p. 116); Joseph C.R. Licklider, "Preliminary Experiments in Computer-Aided Teaching," in *Programmed Learning and Computer-Based Instruction*, ed. by John E. Coulson, New York, Wiley, 1962, pp. 217-239.

62. *Toward the Library of the 21st Century: A Report on Progress Made in a Program of Research Sponsored by the Council of Library Resources*, Cambridge, MA, Bolt Beranek and Newmann, March 1964, p. 2.

in order to understand the programmatic features established by Licklider at the IPTO between 1962 and 1964.

First of all, what had only been implied in previous writings was now stated explicitly: the interaction he was seeking was not just between man and computer, but also regarded the body of knowledge: "Though we shall use the convenient phrase, 'man-computer interaction,' it should be kept in mind that it is an abbreviation and that the body of knowledge is a coordinate partner of the men and the computers."[63] In addition, the libraries that Licklider advocated did not contain books: by "library" he and Marill – who in this study played an important role – meant a system "in which the primary function is to provide not documents but information."[64] Indeed, the printed page was considered incapable of allowing individuals to interact dynamically with the body of knowledge, and the book was to be replaced by "a device that will make it easy to transmit information without transporting material."

This meant that the libraries of the future would become "procognitive systems" which would "promote and facilitate the acquisition, organization and the use of knowledge."[65] The body of knowledge, estimated at 10^{15} bits (1,000 terabytes) and which by the year 2000 could have increased to $5 \cdot 10^{15}$, was represented as "strings of alphanumeric characters, and the associated diagrams, graphs, pictures, and so forth, that make up the documents that are preserved in recognized repositories." However this conceptual outline was deemed to be insufficient:

> Neuroanatomy and neurophysiology, together with human behavior, provide less definite, but nevertheless necessary, supplementary schemata that enrich the concept. These complex arrangements of neuronal elements and processes accept diverse stimuli, including spoken and printed sentences, and somehow process and store them in ways that support the drawing of inferences and the answering of questions; and though these responses are often imprecise, they are usually more appropriate to actual demands than mere reinstatement of past inputs could ever hope to be.[66]

On this basis, in reference to Noam Chomsky's transformational grammar,[67] Licklider and his collaborators clarified their idea of the body of knowledge, defining it as a set of entities, relations and properties connected by "multiple-argument relations" in a "relevance network," a relational network that was represented by the image shown in Figure 12.

"Some of that information" wrote Licklider, "resides in the syntactic structure; more of it would reside on the non-syntactic facets of the relations among the elements. Indeed there appear to be at least some thousands of significantly different relations among things."[68] Just as these networks – which were the

63. Licklider, *Libraries of the Future*, p. 90.

64. *Ibid.*, p. 153.

65. *Ibid.*, pp. 6, 21.

66. *Ibid.*, pp. 24-25.

67. Noam Chomsky, *Syntactic Structures*, Berlin – New York. Mouton de Gruyter, 2002 [1957].

68. Licklider, *Libraries of the Future*, p. 82.

Figure 12 – A Relevance Network

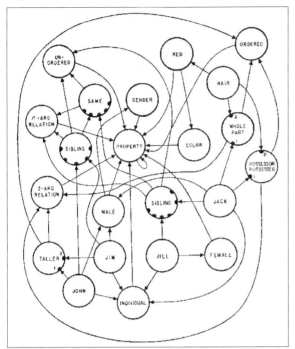

Source: Licklider, *Libraries of the Future*, p. 83.

specific focus of Marill's work – were conceived as semantic, so the studies to be performed on them would also be semantic, rather than syntactic.[69]

Licklider and his team's study, which was rightfully considered to be "surprisingly prescient" in light of subsequent developments in information retrieval and digital libraries, marked an important step forward with respect to previous "grand visions" of the organization of human knowledge.[70] Without going back as far as Diderot and D'Alembert's *Encyclopédie*,[71] his closest precedents were two works written by, respectively a biologist turned science fiction author and the engineer that had overseen the organization of research in the US during the Roosevelt administration.

69. *Ibid.*, pp. 154-156. See also Martin Campbell-Kelly and William Aspray, *Computer: A History of the Information Machine*, 2nd ed., Boulder, CO, Westview Press, 2004, ch. 12; Jay Hauben, "Vannevar Bush and JCR Licklider: Libraries of the Future 1945-1965," 2004, http://www.ais.org/~jrh/acn/acn15-2.articles/jhauben.pdf.

70. Bruce R. Schatz, "Information Retrieval in Digital Libraries: Bringing Search to the Net," *Science*, 275, no. 5298 (1997): pp. 327-328.

71. On this topic, see Hans Dieter Hellige, "Weltbibliothek, Universalenzyklopädie, Worldbrain: Zur Säkulardebatte über die Organisation des Weltwissens," *Technikgeschichte*, 67, no. 4 (2000): pp. 303-329, http://www.artec.uni-bremen.de/team/hellige/HDH-artec-Paper77.pdf.

The former was Herbert G. Wells, who in 1938 republished a contribution on "The Idea of a Permanent World Encyclopaedia", originally written for the *Encyclopédie Française* by Anatole De Monzie and Lucien Febvre, in an anthology with the telling title *World Brain*. The latter was Vannevar Bush, the author of a well-known article entitled "As We May Think" that was published in 1945 but originally conceived in the early 1930s.[72] Both works focused on the use of microfilm, which allowed entire libraries to be duplicated, archived in limited space and easily viewed.

> There is no practical obstacle – Wells wrote – whatever now to the creation of an efficient index to *all* human knowledge, ideas and achievements, to the creation, that is, of a complete planetary memory for all mankind. And not simply an index; the direct reproduction of the thing itself can be summoned to any properly prepared spot. A microfilm, coloured where necessary, occupying an inch or so of space and weighing little more than a letter, can be duplicated from the records and sent anywhere, and thrown enlarged upon the screen so that the student may study it in every detail. This in itself is a fact of tremendous significance. It foreshadows a real intellectual unification of our race. The whole human memory can be, and probably in a short time will be, made accessible to every individual.[73]

Bush in turn proposed a machine called Memex (Memory Extension), in which each individual could archive all of their books, records and communications, "mechanized so that it may be consulted with exceeding speed and flexibility. It is an enlarged intimate supplement to his memory." "The summation of human experience is being expanded at a prodigious rate" he wrote, "and the means we used for threading through the consequent maze to the momentarily important item is the same as was used in the days of square-rigged ships." Discussing hierarchical and indexed systems for information archival, he added:

> When data of any sort are placed in storage, they are filed alphabetically or numerically, and information is found (when it is) by tracing it down from subclass to subclass. It can be in only one place, unless duplicates are used; one has to have rules as to which path will locate it, and the rules are cumbersome. Having found one item, moreover, one has to emerge from the system and re-enter on a new path.
>
> The human mind does not work that way. It operates by association. With one item in its grasp, it snaps instantly to the next that is suggested by the association of thoughts, in accordance with some intricate web of trails carried by the cells of the brain. It has other characteristics, of course; trails that are not frequently followed are prone to fade, items are not fully permanent, memory is transitory. Yet the speed of action, the intricacy of trails, the detail of mental pictures, is awe-inspiring beyond all else in nature.
>
> Man cannot hope fully to duplicate this mental process artificially, but he certainly ought to be able to learn from it [...]. Selection by association, rather than indexing, may yet be mechanized.[74]

---

72. Ronald D. Houston and Glynn Harmon, "Vannevar Bush and Memex," *Annual Review of Information Science and Technology*, 41, no. 1 (2007): p. 57.

73. Herbert G. Wells, "The Idea of a Permanent World Encyclopedia," in H. G. Wells, *World Brain*, London, Adamantine Press, 1994 [1938], pp. 120-121.

74. Vannevar Bush, "As We May Think," *The Atlantic Monthly*, 176, no. 1, (July 1945): pp. 101-108. On this text and its "fortune", see James M. Nyce and Paul Kahn, eds., *From Memex to Hypertext. Vannevar Bush and the Mind's Machine*, Boston, Academic Press, 1991.

In essence, Bush had prefigured hypertext. The concept was formulated in 1965 by Theodor H. Nelson[75] and it is significant that the first functioning hypertext system was presented three years later at Stanford by Douglas C. Engelbart in the context of a project entitled "Human Intellect Augmentation Techniques," financed by Licklider's IPTO.[76] Licklider knew Bush if for no other reason than because he had chaired the debate for a lecture that he gave in 1961 during MIT's centennial celebration, and, indeed, the proceedings of these lectures represent a sort of summary of the research and cultural environment in which Licklider operated. On this occasion, moreover, Bush had joked about the comparison between automobile and computer that had been proposed by Rosenblith and endorsed by Licklider, according to which "cars have given us a mobility that far exceeds what evolution has provided us with; computers may constitute a comparable evolutionary step with respect to man's intellect." Bush commented "when you speak of rapport between men and machines and illustrate it by the automobile, I wonder how often you drive home in commuter traffic."[77] The fact remains that Bush was not cited in *Libraries of the Future*. He was however quoted in the introduction to the book written by Verner W. Clapp of the Council on Library Resources, as well as in Licklider's preface:

> Perhaps the main external influence that shaped the ideas of this book has its effect indirectly, through the community, for it was not until Carl Overhage noticed its omission from the References that I read Vannevar Bush's "As We May Think" […]. I had often heard about Memex and its "trails of references." I had hoped to demonstrate Symbiont to Dr. Bush as a small step in the direction in which he had pointed in his pioneer article. But I had not read the article. Now that I have read it, I should like to dedicate this book, however unworthy it may be, to Dr. Bush.[78]

75. Theodor H. Nelson, "A File Structure for The Complex, The Changing and the Indeterminate," in *ACM Annual Conference/Annual Meeting Archive, Proceedings of the 1965 20th National Conference*, New York, ACM, 1965, pp. 84-100.

76. See the final report in NARA, RG 330-71-A-1647, Carton 2, Folder "Stanford Research Inst. AO 808 (NASI – 7897)." The oN Line System (NLS) was presented by Engelbart in December 1968.

77. Greenberger, ed., *Computers and the World of the Future*, pp. 315, 318-319. Rosenblith and Shannon were the discussants of a lecture by John R. Pierce on "What Computers Should Be Doing."

78. Joseph C.R. Licklider, *Libraries of the Future*, pp. XII-XIII. Overhage developed the INTREX project at the Lincoln Laboratory to explore the possible characteristics of "review articles on-line, in which links are provided from the review article to the various documents reviewed:" Linda C. Smith, "'Memex' as an Image of Potentiality in Information Retrieval Research and Development," in *Proceedings of the 3rd Annual ACM Conference on Research in Information Retrieval*, Cambridge, Butterworth & Co., 1980, p. 356. An updated version of this essay is in Nyce and Kahn, eds., *From Memex to Hypertext*, p. 261. INTREX was considered "the most immediate outcome of Licklider's book:" Schatz, "Information Retrieval in Digital Libraries," p. 333. See Carl F.J. Overhage and Joyce R. Harman, eds., *INTREX: Report of a Planning Conference on Information Transfer Experiments, September 3, 1965*, Cambridge, MA – London, MIT Press, 1965, which includes four contributions by Licklider on pp. 147-155, 187-197, 215-218 and 235-236. The project continued in the following years with an IPTO contract: NARA, RG 69-A-4998, Box 2, Folder "Massachusetts Institute of Technology (ARPA Order 871)." Symbiont was part of the *Libraries of the Future* project and consisted in a

With this, "Memex has no networking or communication capability either with other information resources or with other users directly,"[79] so Bush's article was considered "more properly the seminal work on hypermedia systems for personal computers."[80] In contrast, Licklider's "procognitive" system was a network. He believed that once this system was developed it could have hundreds of user stations, and that "the main items of equipment that would be needed for group communication, not already discussed under the heading of man-computer communication, would be derivatives of the telephone and television."[81] However, in contrast to the relational networks that would organize the body of knowledge, this system had a hierarchical structure (see Figure 13).

Licklider and his team's attention was primarily focused on the nature of the system and the relations among its parts. The issue of the structure of the network that should have connected the various parts was not analyzed, and the team planned to make use of regular telephone lines.[82] One could deduce that, like the other protagonists of this story, Licklider, too, was unfamiliar with Baran's work. Although it had been sent for printing in August 1964 (in other words, just three months before he delivered *Libraries of the Future* to the editor), it is nonetheless impossible to confirm this with certainty. Indeed, his papers include two copies of Baran's memoranda, n. VI and n. XI. The latter is also a draft version, nearly identical to the final version but presumably written prior to the publication date. However there are no notes or other elements that allow us to understand when Licklider acquired them, much less when he read them.[83] At most it can be assumed therefore that he had not yet read them, otherwise he would have at least indicated as much.

This said, in a 1965 essay significantly entitled "The On-Line Intellectual Community," Licklider foresaw a scenario in which the network would allow users to have on their console the materials they needed along with the work that they were writing. All of this would be in a "dynamic" form, in other words modifiable during the course of work. Information retrieval and processing would take place "within the thought cycle," "not tomorrow or the next day" because "immediacy is especially important in constructive thinking." In addition, the computer's data processing and selection speed would increase the knowledge of scientific literature to an unprecedented degree, thus remedying the problem that "people read slowly." Above all, collaboration among various researchers would allow tasks that were too demanding for a single person to be handled by multiple

programme to archive, search and display documents. See Daniel G. Bobrow, Richard Y. Kain, Bertram Raphael and Joseph C.R. Licklider, "A Computer-Program System to Facilitate the Study of Technical Documents," *American Documentation*, 17, no. 4 (1966): pp. 186-189.

79. Linda C. Smith, "'Memex' as an Image," p. 358.

80. Schatz, "Information Retrieval in Digital Libraries," p. 327.

81. Licklider, *Libraries of the Future*, pp. 45, 101.

82. See also Thomas Marill, Daniel Edwards and Wallace Feurzeig, "DATA-DIAL: Two-Way Communication with Computers with Ordinary Dial Telephones," *Communications of the ACM*, 6, no. 10 (1963): pp. 622-624.

83. See Licklider Papers, Box 6, Folder "On Distributed Communications," U.S. Air Force Project RAND, ca. 1960s.

Figure 13 – A "Procognitive" System

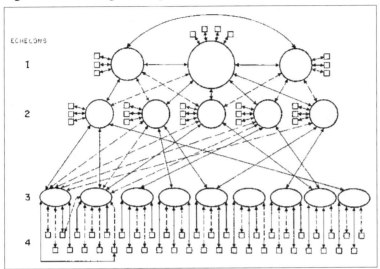

Source: Licklider, *Libraries of the Future*, p. 41.

individuals. "Simply by retrieving and using data or models or documents, people will generate 'trails' through the information base. These trails will bring about, at long last, a realization of Vannevar Bush's 'MEMEX.'"

Finally, in this text Licklider actually predicted the so-called Web 2.0 when he wrote: "Within the information network, there are several 'levels' of publication. In as much as the document is created within the system, a document is published, in a sense, as soon as it is given a tag that permits wide accessibility. In that informally published state, the document accumulates comments, criticisms, and appendages, put there by others who are interested in what it says." As such, although physically distant from one another, participants would collaborate "as effectively as if they were in a face-to-face conference."[84]

84. Joseph C.R. Licklider, "The On-Line Intellectual Community: Luncheon Address," in *Second National Symposium on Engineering Information. Theme: A Coordinated Engineering Information System, Proceedings of a Symposium Held in New York, N.Y. on October 27, 1965,* New York, The Engineers Joint Council, 1966, pp. 30, 32, 34-35.

3. The IPTO from Licklider to Taylor

An "Intergalactic Network"

When ARPA's director, Jack P. Ruina, appeared in 1962 for his annual hearing with the dedicated subcommittee of the House of Representatives, he spoke only very briefly of the agency's command and control projects, and only after a direct question from a representative.[1] In the report from May of the following year, he devoted more than three pages to explaining that this aspect of the agency's work focused on the software problem in human-machine interaction, specifically on the "languages and translators to bridge the gap between the way men think and the technical detail involved in the internal workings of the machines." Ruina also pointed out that ARPA was starting to work "on some of the extremely difficult computing and communication problems that arise when several machines are connected together in a network. Such combined computer nets," he added, "will very likely be necessary in future military command and control systems."[2]

One year later, Robert L. Sproull – a physicist from Cornell University who took Ruina's place in September 1963 – reported on ARPA's activities. On this occasion, the subcommittee learned that the office was no longer called Command and Control Research, but had become Information Processing Techniques, "in recognition that this research has implications of significance to other areas of Defence Department endeavour." Sproull also confirmed the features of the programme that had been outlined by his predecessor, noting that

> one of the next steps in this research will be the linking of an individual at MIT through the MIT computer to a computer at Carnegie Tech, Stanford, UCLA, or the System Development Corp., to permit the researcher at MIT to call forth programmes or information stored in these remote computers for use in solving his research problems. I wish to emphasize that this experimentation is in its infancy.[3]

1. See above, p. 56 and note 5.
2. DoD Appropriations for 1964, *Hearings Before the Subcommittee of the Committee on Appropriations, House of Representatives, Eighty-Eighth Congress, First Session*, Part 6. *Research, Development, Test, and Evaluation*, Washington, DC, US Government Printing Office, 1963, pp. 233-235.
3. DoD Appropriations for 1965, *Hearings Before the Subcommittee of the Committee on Appropriations, House of Representatives, Eighty-Eighth Congress, Second Session*, Part 4. *Secretary of Defense*, Washington, DC, US Government Printing Office, 1964, pp. 138-139.

Figure 14 – An image of SDC's AN/Q-32V computer

Source: http://ed-thelen.org/comp-hist/q32_1-.jpg.

The image created by these reports faithfully mirrors Licklider's organization of the office. As he himself explained years later, his "really wasn't a command and control programme. It was an interactive computing programme."[4] The contract that had already been funded at the Santa Monica Systems Development Corporation was thus used "as a vehicle to seek out the leading edge of the computer community" with a "decreasing emphasis on the SDC work and increasing support for academic 'centres of excellence,' notably MIT and other institutions in the Boston area."[5] Indeed, from the beginning, Licklider restructured SDC's programme so that the computer it had inherited from SAGE (an enormous AN/FSQ-32V built specifically by IBM) was readapted for time-sharing, and used the programme to involve groups of scholars who were already working in the field.

Moreover, the SDC did not have the expertise necessary to carry out this conversion, and thus a contract was drawn up with Information International Inc. – a small company founded by Edward Fredkin, who had worked with Licklider at the BBN – and one of the architects of the mini-computer DEC PDP-1, Benjamin M. Gurley. These individuals were chosen because

4. Barber Associates, *The Advanced Research Project Agency*, p. V-51, which cites an interview with Licklider from 15 April 1974.

5. Ibid., V-53. SDC's funding decreased from 6 to 2 million dollars in 1964 in the face of a budget increase at IPTO of 9 to 13 million dollars.

of the approximately dozen people who have been leaders in pushing the time-sharing concept, two are at Carnegie Tech receiving support on another ARPA programme, but will able to provide some consultation. The rest are at universities or non-profit laboratories and are essentially not available to spend the amount of time required of the programme leader. In view of the competency of Information International with respect to computer time-sharing and the unavailability of others with comparable talent, Information International is essentially the only group able to perform the outlined work.[6]

At the same time, however, Licklider left immediately to meet those "dozen people" and put them to work on a project that he defined as "a system of contracts designed to advance the technology of time-sharing and close human-machine cooperation in information processing."[7] A network of research centres thus formed around the IPTO that in addition to the SDC and the Carnegie Institute of Technology included the Universities of California at Los Angeles and Berkeley, the Stanford Research Institute (SRI), McCarthy's Artificial Intelligence Group (also in Stanford) and the RAND Corporation. Unsurprisingly, "the centrepiece"[8] of this network was the Massachusetts Institute of Technology. This community therefore was centred on two main entities: the SDC on the West Coast, around which an academic "California network group" acquired greater importance,[9] and MIT on the East Coast.

Rather than limiting himself to funding some of the pre-existing time-sharing projects, Licklider took advantage of ARPA's contractual power and the wide margin of discretion that enabled him to insert these projects into a single integrated programme, within which he assumed a strong organizational and directional role. It was no coincidence that, as well as the University of Michigan, McCarthy also presented one of the projects for the production of new time-shared systems that were proposed to the agency but ultimately rejected. MacCarthy's group received funding to develop a programming language for use in the SDC's system.[10]

Meetings were immediately organized to promote the exchange and dissemination of knowledge among the groups participating in the project. The first took place in November 1962 at the SDC and others soon followed. In April 1963, in preparation for one of these meetings, Licklider sent a memorandum to his contractors addressed jokingly to the "Members and Affiliates of the Intergalactic Computer Network." This document is often cited because of its heading, but in truth it illustrates both the direction in which its author was moving and the

6. ARPA, "Program Proposal (Information International) Command and Control," n.d. (but 1962), in NARA, RG 330-69-A-4998, Box 2, Folder "Information International, Inc. (ARPA Order 422)" (2).

7. Licklider to Robert C.F. Bartels, 30 September 1963, in NARA, RG 330-73-A-2108, Carton 1, Folder "Michigan, Univ. of."

8. Barber Associates, *The Advanced Research Project Agency*, p. V-51.

9. The expression, coined by Licklider, is quoted in Norberg and O'Neill, *Transforming Computer Technology*, p. 93.

10. See Norberg and O'Neill, *Transforming Computer Technology*, pp. 102-103. For this part, unless otherwise indicated, see ch. 2 of this text, specifically from p. 91 onwards. The University of Michigan was subsequently funded, but in the behavioral sciences sector: NARA, RG 330-73-A-2108, Carton 1, Folder "Michigan, Univ. of."

nature of the problems the network was facing, although Licklider was aware that these were still "things that I feel intuitively, not things that I perceive in clear structure."[11] The text's primary points included one on work methods, which purportedly would have been much more fruitful if everyone shared, discussed and modified their projects, aspirations and struggles *in itinere*. Another important issue was the compatibility of the language used for programming, debugging and verification in each of the systems under development,[12] which seemed much more complex for the management of a network of computers.

> Consider the situation in which several different centers are netted together, each center being highly individualistic and having its own special language and its own special way of doing things. Is it not desirable, or even necessary for all the centers to agree upon some language or, at least, upon some conventions for asking such questions as "What language do you speak?" At this extreme, the problem is essentially the one discussed by science fiction writers: "how do you get communications started among totally uncorrelated 'sapient' beings?"[13]

Having raised what he would shortly come to term "the knotty problem of standardization"[14], and aware that the project would have required software and hardware instruments that were impossible to procure in a reasonable amount of time, Licklider noted:

> It will possibly turn out, I realize, that only on rare occasions do most or all of the computers in the overall system operate together in an integrated network. It seems to me to be interesting and important, nevertheless, to develop a capability for integrated network operation. If such a network as I envisage nebulously could be brought into operation, we would have at least four large computers, perhaps six or eight small computers, and a great assortment of disc files and magnetic tape units – not to mention the remote consoles and teletype stations – all churning away. It seems easiest to approach this matter from the individual user's point of view – to see what he would like to have, what he might like to do, and then to try to figure out how to make a system within which his requirements can be met.[15]

At that time, even a network of just four large computers was significant and this was in fact the number of Arpanet's nodes when it began working six

11. Joseph C.R. Licklider, "Memorandum for Members and Affiliates of the Intergalactic Computer Network," 25 April 1963. At various times the original, kept in NARA, RG 330-69-A-4998, Box 3, was listed as missing; additional copies are in Licklider Papers, Box 3, Folder "Correspondence 1958-1969" and Box 7, Folder "1963." For online material, see http://www.packet.cc/files/memo.html. In addition to members of the centres cited above, the recipients included Glen J. Culler of Thompson Ramo Woolridge Inc., who along with Burton D. Fried, presented in 1963 an interactive system for mathematic calculation: Glen J. Culler and Burton D. Fried, "An On-Line Computing Center for Scientific Problems," 11 January 1963, http://www.dtic.mil/cgi-bin/GetTRDoc?AD=AD296532&Location=U2&doc=GetTRDoc.pdf; Glen J. Culler and Burton D. Fried, "An On-Line Computing Center," July 1963, http://www.dtic.mil/cgi-bin/GetTRDoc?AD=AD414564&Location=U2&doc=GetTRDoc.pdf.
12. Among those that Licklider made explicit reference to, besides FORTRAN, ALGOL and IPL-V (due to Newell, Simon and Shaw), there were also JOVIAL (developed at the SDC by Jules I. Schwartz) and LISP (the language that McCarthy worked on).
13. Licklider, "Memorandum for Members and Affiliates."
14. Licklider to Robert C.F. Bartels, 2 October 1963.
15. Licklider, "Memorandum for Members and Affiliates."

years later. However, another important passage of the above excerpt is where, after imagining the network's machines as "churning away", Licklider asserts that in order to control and develop the system, it would have been preferable to adopt the perspective of the single users and their needs and expectations. Indeed, this perspective would also characterize the Arpanet project and ensured that the network developed "from the demand side." This approach allowed for the project's success and established the fundamental characteristics that define it to this day.

As Licklider wrote more clearly in another contribution from 1964 "the main requirement [...] is for a vigorous, interactive intellectual community capable of nurturing the system during its formulative years. Large-scale multistation computation systems will have to be developed mainly by their users."[16] This structure – along with, *ça va sans dire*, IPTO's ample funds – met the necessities of the universities and research centres active in the sector that not only required machines, computer utilities, operative systems and appropriate languages, but also had a need to experiment and compare their ideas. [17]

Time-Sharing at the IPTO

On this basis, work proceeded swiftly beginning at MIT, in whose Computation Centre – according to elaborations from McCarthy, Herbert M. Teager, Jack B. Dennis and others – Fernando J. Corbató had created an initial experimental version of Compatible Time-Sharing System (CTSS) in 1961.[18] In addition, a new project was developed following Licklider's discussion in October 1962 with Robert M. Fano about what would become Project MAC. Significantly, the acronym stood for both Multiple-Access Computing and Machine-Aided Cognition. Within a year, the programme – which Minsky and the Artificial Intelligence Laboratory also participated in – produced a functional system based on a second version of CTSS, with a central IBM 7094 computer, which was connected to 24 remote stations on the institute's campus, which increased to 40 in 1964.[19]

16. Licklider, "Artificial Intelligence, Military Intelligence, and Command and Control," p. 128.

17. See Atsushi Akera, *Calculating a Natural World: Scientists, Engineers, and Computers During the Rise of the U.S. Cold War Research*, Cambridge, MA, MIT Press, 2007, pp. 313-314. Although he supports the argument that IPTO had a "major influence on the development of computer time sharing and networking," Akera tempers Norberg and O'Neill's interpretation, revealing "a separate set of motivations that emerged from the expanding demand for academic computing facilities."

18. See Fernando J. Corbató, Marjorie M. Daggett and Robert C. Daley, "An Experimental Time-Sharing System," Spring Joint Computer Conference Paper, 3 May 1962, now in Per Brinch Hansen, ed., *Classic Operating Systems: From Batch Processing to Distributed Systems*, New York, Springer, 2001, pp. 117-137.

19. Fano, "The MAC System: A Progress Report." Here the author thanked Licklider, "whose technical vision and contagious enthusiasm as Assistant Director of ARPA were responsible for the initiation of Project MAC." See *Ibid.*, ch. 1, pp. 54-55. On time-sharing at MIT and the University of Michigan, see also Akera, *Calculating a Natural World*, ch. 9.

Meanwhile, on Licklider's request, the staff of Jules I. Schwartz also realized a time-shared system at the SDC during the first six months of 1963.[20] In turn, the contract signed in June of the same year between the IPTO and UCLA's Western Data Processing Center – then under the direction of George W. Brown and R. Clay Sprowls – was explicitly intended for the study of computer network problems and time-sharing. A few months later, a report by Sprowls mentioned 11 universities and schools connected to the system.[21] IPTO was also simultaneously funding a project for a time-shared system at the University of California at Berkeley, within the greater context of Project Genie, which was first led by Harry D. Huskey and then by Edward A. Feigenbaum and David C. Evans.[22] Numerous people participated in the venture – based from 1964 on a SDS 930 computer subsequently modified for this purpose – including L. Peter Deutsch, Butler W. Lampson, W. Wayne Lichtenberger and Melvin W. Pirtle.[23]

The Carnegie Institute of Technology, which in August 1962 proposed a project to IPTO in the information-processing sector, also received funding.[24] A system was also created here in 1964 with 12 remote teletypes on the campus[25] but in this case the study primarily focused on "programming languages, the theory of programming, artificial intelligence, the interpretation of natural languages, man-computer interaction, and the design of machines."[26] In addition to Allen Newell, Alan J. Perlis and Herbert A. Simon, the group also included the cognitive psychologist Bert F. Green Jr., who in 1961 had created a programme at the

20. See Jules I. Schwartz, Edward G. Coffman and Clark Weissman, "A General-Purpose Time-Sharing System," in *Proceedings of the April 21-23, 1964, Spring Joint Computer Conference*, New York, ACM, 1964, pp. 397-411.

21. R. Clay Sprowls, Report to ARPA, 3 October 1963, in NARA, RG 330-71-A-1647, Carton 2, untitled Folder (UCLA, SD 184 contract). This is Program Plan n. 93 from 5 April 1963 entitled "Computer Network and Time-Sharing Research," now at http://blogs.archives.gov/ndc/wp-content/uploads/2011/07/ARPA-Order-Internet.pdf.

22. See "Remote Stations & Programs for Computer Network," Program Plan n. 95, 5 April 1963, *ibid.*

23. See Butler W. Lampson, Wayne W. Lichtenberger and Melvin W. Pirtle, "A User Machine in A Time-Sharing System," *Proceedings of the IEEE*, 54, no. 12 (1966): pp. 1766-1774. See also Thierry Bardini, *Bootstrapping: Douglas Engelbart, Coevolution, and the Origins of Personal Computing*, Stanford, Stanford University Press, 2000, pp. 23-27. According to Robert W. Taylor's memoir, moreover, the project was initially undertaken "simply to help Licklider monitor the progress at System Development Corporation to try to see what they could do with timesharing on this large computer, this AFSQ32 machine:" William Aspray, "An Interview with Robert Taylor" conducted 28 February 1989, University of Minnesota, CBI Collections, Oral History 154, http://conservancy.umn.edu/bitstream/107666/1/oh154rt.pdf.

24. See "A Proposal from Carnegie Institute of Technology to the Advanced Research Project Agency for Funds to do Basic Research in Information Processing," 13 August 1962, in Carnegie Mellon University, Herbert A. Simon Collection, Box 7, http://ptfs.library.cmu.edu/awweb/main.jsp?flag=browse&smd=1&awdid=1 (accessed 30 November 2012).

25. "Center for the Study of Information Processing," The Carnegie Technical Institute, *Faculty Bulletin*, 7 October 1964, http://ptfs.library.cmu.edu/awweb/main.jsp?flag=browse&smd=1&awdid=1 (accessed 30 November 2012).

26. "A Proposal from Carnegie Institute of Technology to the Advanced Research Project Agency," p. 26.

Lincoln Laboratory to allow computers to respond to questions posed to them in "ordinary English."[27]

In previous years the Carnegie Tech group (as it was called) had worked in strict collaboration with the RAND Corporation, whose Computer Sciences Department also joined the IPTO network. From 1961 under the management of Willis H. Ware – who had been one of Baran's professors – the department had developed the Johnniac Open Shop System (JOSS) project under the initiative of John Clifford Shaw. The project started with 10 remote consoles in January 1964, following experimentation with an "austere version" the previous year.[28] It was not, however, JOSS that was funded, but rather only a graphic interface – the RAND Tablet – created by Thomas O. Ellis and in use from September 1963.[29]

In February 1963, funding was assigned to the Stanford Research Institute for Douglas C. Engelbart's "Augmenting Human Intellect" project, which already boasted funding from the Air Force Office of Scientific Research, and from 1964 could also count on more significant financial resources from NASA. But ARPA's contribution to his programme was modest, which may seem surprising given the similarities present between Licklider's human-computer symbiosis and Engelbart's vision[30]. Engelbart himself noted this many years later: "I was standing at the door with this 1962 report and a proposal. I had met Licklider before and heard about him setting up a programme, and I thought, 'Oh boy, with all the things he's saying he wants to do, how can he refuse me?'"[31]

It is worth therefore pausing for a moment on this matter, bearing in mind too the role Engelbart would later play in this story. By "augmenting human intellect," he meant "increasing the capability of a man to approach a complex problem situation, to gain comprehensions to suit his particular needs, and to derive solutions to problems." Influenced primarily by Bush, but at least in part also by Licklider, Engelbart imagined the human-machine relationship as a synergy "between human problem-solver and computer 'clerk.'"[32]

27. Bert F. Green, Jr., Alice K. Wolf, Carol Chomsky and Kenneth Laughery, "Baseball: An Automatic Question Answerer," in *Computers and Thought*, ed. by Edward A. Feigenbaum and Julian Feldman, New York, McGraw-Hill, 1963, pp. 207-216.

28. John C. Shaw, "JOSS: A Designer's View of an Experimental On-Line Computing System," The RAND Corporation, P-2922, August 1964, http://www.rand.org/pubs/papers/P2922.html. Various other documents relative to JOSS are available for consultation at http://www.rand.org/. See also above, pp. 47-48.

29. See Malcolm R. Davis and Thomas O. Ellis, "The RAND Tablet: A Man-Machine Graphical Communication Device," The RAND Corporation, Memorandum RM-4122-ARPA, August 1964, http://www.rand.org/pubs/research_memoranda/RM4122.html. IPTO also funded a graphic input language called GRAIL at RAND in 1964.

30. Engelbart's texts can be consulted at http://sloan.stanford.edu/mousesite/EngelbartPapers/FindingAid.html.

31. Douglas C. Engelbart, "Interview 2," conducted by Judy Adams and Henry Lowood, 14 January 1987, http://www-sul.stanford.edu/depts/hasrg/histsci/ssvoral/engelbart/engfmst2-ntb.html.

32. Douglas C. Engelbart, "Augmenting Human Intellect: A Conceptual Framework," October 1962, http://sloan.stanford.edu/mousesite/EngelbartPapers/B5_F18_ConceptFrameworkInd.html.

Thierry Bardini placed great emphasis (in contrast to Chigusa I. Kita) on the role of artificial intelligence in Licklider's programmes, and he argued that his setup could not have been more distant from that of Engelbart. In his concept of symbiosis, he observed, a cybernetic "mechanist bias" was implicit, according to which "the human participant could and should be seen as a machine." In its communication with humans, Engelbart considered the computer to be a mere instrument, whereas for Licklider it was a "mechanical 'partner in interaction,'" an "'artificial' colleague."[33]

As well as their similarities, there are clear differences between the two projects, but these do not explain IPTO's limited funding of Engelbart's project, nor is Licklider's support for artificial intelligence enthusiasts inconsistent with their relative differences in approach. On this point, Thierry Bardini's observations are particularly pertinent:

> Engelbart's criticism of the way people become subservient to a big technological system like a steamship or locomotive, instead of being given their autonomy by a technological innovation such as the automobile. The paradox of time-sharing, according to this rationale, is that it provided less "personal access," access to meet a personal task, because it was supposed to provide more access to individual users.[34]

In fact, Engelbart above all had in mind a personal workstation. For the moment, moreover, his project did not foresee operational repercussions. Dividing the existing works into two categories based "upon the possibilities of using a computer in real-time working association with a human to improve his working effectiveness," Engelbart placed the project (along with Bush and Licklider's "Man-Computer Symbiosis") in the category that "presents speculations and possibilities but does not include reporting of significant experimental results."[35] In the second category, in addition to MIT's CTSS, JOSS, and the texts of other authors, Engelbart also included an earlier contribution by Licklider and Welden E. Clark that intended to illustrate the applications of the human-computer symbiosis in various fields. After making a net distinction between human and machine capabilities, the two authors deemed "the conventional computer-centre mode of operation" inadequate, and identified the first steps of time-sharing "in hardware form" as an opportunity for obtaining effective online human-computer communication.[36]

It would therefore appear that SRI's marginality among IPTO's contractors essentially depended on the operative character of Licklider's project, and specifically on the fact that time-sharing was one of his priorities, while it was not for Engelbart. In addition, Engelbart's centre did not have a computer that could support a time-shared system and Licklider – who already bore the heavy legacy of SDC – had no intention of taking on the very high costs that this would entail.

As a result, the partners who already possessed time-shared systems or machines that supported them were given preference, while the SRI group was

33. Bardini, *Bootstrapping*, pp. 27-28.
34. *Ibid.*, pp. 31-32.
35. Engelbart, "Augmenting Human Intellect."
36. Licklider and Clark, "On-Line Man-Computer Communication," pp. 113-114.

asked to develop programming language for the Santa Monica AN/FSQ-32V[37] (for which John H. Wensley, among others, took responsibility). Thus, although statements made long after events should always be taken with a grain of salt, the explanation that Licklider gave in 1988 is very plausible: "we needed to have time-sharing systems before we could do man computer interaction research."[38] These words are in fact consistent with what he said in 1963 at a NATO symposium:

> There are two general approaches to solution of the speed-cost mismatch problem. One is to construct a large number of small, inexpensive computers. Small, inexpensive computers are extremely attractive, and this approach is active. However, at present and for some time into the future, a small, inexpensive computer is necessarily a computer with a small memory. More and more, we are finding that large memory is an essential prerequisite for effective man-computer interactions of many types. Moreover, we are sensing that the truly important thing is not interaction between one man and a computer, but interaction between several or many men and a computer. The approach based on small, inexpensive machines does not lead to that goal.[39]

Having experimented with time-sharing on a minicomputer when he was at the BBN, Licklider knew all of this in hindsight, and it is not a coincidence that the PDP-1 were used by the IPTO community as satellite-machines with accessory functions. It is true that the subsequent development of individual workstations and personal computers (to which Engelbart made a significant contribution) would lead to a decline in the sharing of large machines, but at that time, the problem with memory was the deciding factor. Indeed, this was so true for Licklider that he believed the expression "time-sharing" inadequately reflected the terms of the issue that he and his collaborators were facing. Back in January 1963 he had confirmed the need "to provide an arrangement that will make the computer remember what it was doing for each non-current user, so that, when it is turned on again, or when he needs attention, the computer can take up where it left off, without loss of data or direction."[40] Then, a year later, he added:

> The reason for speaking of "memory sharing" instead of "time sharing" is that, as many of us have recognized, it is the sharing of memory, more than the sharing of processor or of time itself, that is fundamental. Time-sharing is presently, indeed, the most practicable technique with which to achieve memory sharing, and it may achieve some additional advantages through the sharing of other computer subsystems as well, but it is nevertheless merely a technique. Memory sharing, on the other hand, is a fundamental advance toward coordination and mutually facilitory interaction among the efforts of many people, working together either on particular tasks or in the general intellectual endeavor of mankind.[41]

37. See also Charles P. Bourne and Trudy Bellardo Hahn, *A History of Online Information Services, 1963-1976*, Cambridge, MA, MIT Press, 2003, pp. 14-15.
38. Aspray and Norberg, "An Interview with J.C.R. Licklider."
39. Joseph C.R. Licklider, "Problems in Man-Computer Communications," in *Communication Processes, Proceedings of a Symposium Held in Washington, 1963*, ed. by Frank A. Geldard, Oxford, Pergamon Press, 1965, p. 260.
40. Licklider, "Computer Integrated Community," MS, p. 5, in Licklider Papers, Box 7, Folder "1963." A hand written note by the author specifies that this is a "JCRL Speech given at NSF on 1/22/63."
41. Id., "Address: Command of Procedures," ds., 1-2, in Licklider Papers, Box 7, Folder "1964." Dated "late '63 or early '64," the work was sent to Fubini with this hand-written note:

It was not for excessive caution that during a hearing at the House of
Representatives Sproull felt the need to stress that IPTO's experiment was still
"in its infancy." For example, while SDC's system was connected to Project
MAC's CTSS by teleprinter in 1963,[42] another contemporary attempt to connect
it to SRI, made at Licklider's request, was not successful.[43] Although the history
of scientific and technological innovation is always marked by failures, the truth
is that, as we have already noted, his team lacked the hardware and software
supports that allowed him to put his ideas quickly into practice.

Graphics and "Dynamic Modeling"

When Licklider left ARPA in July 1964 to become a consultant for IBM's
Thomas J. Watson Research Centre, the area of IPTO activity that continued to
be characterized by a wide gap between theoretical elaborations and concrete
applications was the very one that represented its ultimate goal: the creation
of a long distance network. Indeed, in April 1965 Sproull told the House of
Representatives that a computer network system was still being defined. When
he noted that "we can foresee the day when such computer networks will
automatically distribute computation and information to diverse users,"[44] the
director of ARPA was actually expressing a conviction that was anything but
unfounded, but nonetheless on an operative level there was still much to be done.
A short while later Licklider outlined four problems "that stand in the way of
realization of the on-line intellectual community: 1) getting text into computer-
processible form, 2) providing wide-band switchable communication channels, 3)
providing economical yet adequate graphical displays and, 4) developing a good
interaction language." Regarding the second point he said:

> At the present time, wide-band switchable communication channels are not widely
> available through common carriers, and the available narrower band or non-switchable
> channels place undesirable restrictions upon the flexibility and capability of information
> networks. It seems desirable to set up, in an experimental way and at an early date, a pilot
> network with wide-band switchable channels.[45]

"Gene: the marked part is relevant to your insistence that 'time sharing' is not a good term to
describe what most of the people who use the term actually mean when they use it. Lick."
42. See Sidney G. Reed, Richard H. Van Atta and Seymour J. Deitchman, "DARPA
Technical Accomplishments: An Historical Review of Selected DARPA Projects," vol. 1, IDA
Paper P-2192, Alexandria, VA, Institute for Defense Analyses, 1990, 19-11, www.darpa.mil/
WorkArea/DownloadAsset.aspx?id=2678.
43. See Douglas Engelbart, "The Augmented Knowledge Workshop," in John R. White
and Kathi Anderson, eds., *Proceedings of the ACM Conference on The History of Personal
Workstations*, pp. 65, 77.
44. DoD Appropriations for 1966, *Hearings Before the Subcommittee of the Committee
on Appropriations, House of Representatives, Eighty-Ninth Congress, First Session*, Part 5.
Research, Development, Test, and Evaluation, Washington, DC, US Government Printing
Office, 1965, p. 536.
45. Licklider, "The On-Line Intellectual Community," p. 36.

Figure 15 – Licklider with a "light pen" at a DEC monitor

Source: http://webmuseum.mit.edu/grabimg.php?wm=1&kv=130243.

Significant progress had instead been made in the development of interactive computing, in the strict sense of the term. Without entering into complex technical issues about programming languages, some words should be devoted to graphical displays. In addition to the RAND Tablet, another graphic interface had been realized at SDC, and in July 1964 Project MAC gained a "multiple display system for computer-aided design," with a terminal called KLUDGE.[46] Already in 1963, Licklider clearly explained how crucial these mechanisms were:

> In the conventional computer centre, the physical interface between the man who formulates the problem and the computer that solves it is, almost literally, the plate-glass wall that lets him look at the computer but not touch it. Actually, he communicates not with the computer but with computer programmers, or coders, or keypunch operators, and with the receptionist who gives him the inch-thick sheet of "printouts" and the decks of punched cards when he returns to pick up the results of the run. In the kind of man-computer interaction about which we are talking here, however, the situation is quite different. The physical interface is the "console."
>
> At the present time, the console is usually just a typewriter or teletypewriter. In a few instances, however, the console is truly a console: a desk with a computer-operated electric typewriter, a cathode-ray-tube screen for dynamic display, a "light pen" with which the operator can designate significant locations on the screen and (aided by the computer)

46. Van Atta, Reed and Deitchman, "DARPA Technical Accomplishments," vol. 2, "An Historical Review of Selected DARPA Projects," IDA Paper P-2429, Alexandria, VA, Institute for Defense Analyses, 1991, pp. 13-4 – 13-5, http://www.darpa.mil/WorkArea/DownloadAsset. aspx?id=2679. See also Norberg and O'Neill, *Transforming Computer Technology*, pp. 122-128.

write and draw, and miscellaneous buttons, switches and lights. The consoles with which I am familiar leave much room for creative invention and development.[47]

However, Licklider had not cited his group's projects as proof that the cathode ray tube screen and the light pen would allow for a more flexible man-computer communication than that carried out by a keyboard. Instead, as an example he had used the works that had recently been carried out on the Lincoln Laboratory's TX-2 by Ivan E. Sutherland and Timothy E. Johnson,[48] which to this day are considered milestones in the history of computer graphics. The result of a PhD dissertation completed under Shannon's supervision, Sketchpad (as Sutherland's programme was called) traced polygons and circumferences with a light pen on video and allowed human and machine "to converse rapidly through the medium of drawings."[49] Johnson, in turn, had completed his doctorate degree by rendering the same figures tridimensional and making them turn on each axis, to observe them simultaneously from multiple points of view.[50]

Licklider attributed a critical function to these interfaces, in the belief that "the concept of man-computer interaction virtually demands [...] a multiconsole system in which the consoles are not just typewriters but truly consoles,"[51] and with an online intellectual community in mind that was far greater than that of the programmers and without boundaries. "In my picture, the console is essentially the desk which has become an active thing," he said in 1965, once again citing Sketchpad to clarify his idea of a simulation:

> different enough from conventional computer-programme simulation, particularly in making extensive use of dynamic displays, that I shall refer to it by another name – *dynamic modeling*. The dynamic-modeling service facilitates one's expression, one's formulation of ideas, allows one to develop his formulations in a progressive way that involves trial and error and play back his ideas in graphic form and study them to find implications and consequences that otherwise would be hidden.[52]

47. Licklider, "Problems in Man-Computer Communications," p. 263.

48. *Ibid.*, p. 264.

49. Ivan E. Sutherland, "Sketchpad: A Man-Machine Graphical Communication System," in AFIPS, *Proceedings of the May 21-23, 1963, Spring Joint Computer Conference*, p. 329. The thesis, submitted in January 1963, is at http://dspace.mit.edu/handle/1721.1/14979; the video of Sketchpad's demonstration can be viewed on YouTube.

50. Timothy E. Johnson, "Sketchpad III: Three Dimensional Graphical Communication with a Digital Computer," May 1963, http://dspace.mit.edu/handle/1721.1/11559; Timothy E. Johnson, "Sketchpad III: A Computer Program for Drawing in Three Dimensions," in AFIPS, *Proceedings of the May 21-23, 1963, Spring Joint Computer Conference*, pp. 347-352.

51. Joseph C.R. Licklider, "Man-Computer Partnership," *International Science and Technology*, 41 (May 1965): p. 23. Not long before, he wrote: "It seems to me to be worthwhile to start early to encourage the use of the term, 'console,' and to discourage the use of the term, 'terminal.' The reason is that the 'terminal' is truly a terminal only if one restricts his attention to the physical system, whereas the spirit of man-computer interaction requires that one look upon the users as a part of the system. In fact, each user is likely to think of himself as a very central part of the system." (Licklider, "Memo to R.J. Potter," Dec. 11, 1964, in Licklider Papers, Box 3, Folder "IBM, Memos from JCRL, 1964").

52. Licklider, "The On-Line Intellectual Community," p. 30.

Licklider had more thoroughly explained what he meant the year before in a symposium on auditory and visual perception, where he had presented a paper titled "Dynamic Modeling," which – as usual – merged human-machine interaction and cognitive psychology in a unified and thus more productive vision. Before discussing this paper, however, it is necessary to first provide a quick summary of its precedents, beginning with Licklider's studies in the 1950s on the perception of sound frequencies in which he cited the work of Donald O. Hebb. According to Hebb, the visual experience is the result of learning and is based on the processing of models that reflect only some aspects of reality.[53]

In the same period, Licklider performed three studies on the use of sound for analgesic purposes, two of which he carried out in cooperation with a dentist, Wallace J. Gardner.[54] The third, "On Psychophysiological Models," appeared in the proceedings of a 1959 symposium on sensorial communication, although the author had redrafted the final text because his original presentation had used generic terms that many participants had not clearly understood. As he recalled "In that talk I summarized experimental data on information-processing capabilities of human beings and described a model for categorizing patterns of stimulation. The data were intended to set boundary conditions on the communicative capabilities of the over-all human organism."[55] In any case, Licklider made three important observations in the printed version of the text, which Robert M. Fano summarized as follows:

> The first one is that a model, while a tentative and oversimplified representation of reality, organizes and interrelates the experimental evidence in a concise way that is easy to understand and remember. The second observation is that one can validate a model by observing its behaviour, when simulated on a digital or analogue computer, and comparing it with qualitative as well as quantitative evidence. The third point is that a model can be a valuable stepping stone in planning further experiments and in identifying the experimental data to be obtained.[56]

On this basis, in 1964 Licklider explained that he saw dynamic modelling as "a meld of mathematical modeling, computer-programme simulation, dynamic display, and on-line interaction between human modellers and computers."

---

53. See above, pp. 68-69 and note 50; Licklider, "A Duplex Theory of Pitch Perception;" Licklider, "Three Auditory Theories;" Hebb, *The Organization of Behavior*; Donald O. Hebb, "A Neuropsychological Theory," in *Psychology, a Study of a Science Volume 1*, ed. by Sigmund Koch, New York, McGraw-Hill, 1959, pp. 622-643. See also Alain De Cheveigné, "Pitch Perception Models," in *Pitch*, ed. by Christopher Plack, Richard Fay, Andrew Oxenham and Arthur Popper, New York, Springer, 2005, pp. 169-233.

54. Wallace J. Gardner and Joseph C.R. Licklider, "Auditory Analgesia in Dental Operations," *Journal of the American Dental Association*, 59 (1959): pp. 1144-1149; Wallace J. Gardner, Joseph C.R. Licklider and Alex Z. Weisz, "Suppression of Pain by Sound," *Science*, 132, no. 3418 (1960): pp. 32-33.

55. Joseph C.R. Licklider, "On Psychophysiological Models," in *Sensory Communication: Contributions to the Symposium on Principles of Sensory Communication, July 19 – August 1, 1959, Endicott House, M.I.T.*, ed. by Walter A. Rosenblith, New York – London, MIT Press – Wiley, 1961, p. 49.

56. Fano, "Joseph Carl Robnett Licklider," p. 10.

In his view, it was a method capable of "handling problems and processes of the complexity that is encountered at every hand in the psychophysiology of cognition."[57] Significantly, the first dynamic models he observed had been fine-tuned in 1957 by a team from the Lincoln Laboratory and MIT and addressed "the dynamic behaviour of assemblies of schematized neurons of the kind discussed by Donald Hebb in his *Organization of Behaviour.*"[58] As well as Belmont G. Farley, John T. Gilmore and Lawrence S. Frishkopf, their authors also included Wesley A. Clark.

Two years earlier, Clark and Farley had presented a paper at the Western Joint Computer Conference on "pattern recognition in a self-organizing system,"[59] and it is no less significant that in the early 1960s the psychologist Leonard M. Uhr also dedicated himself to this topic.[60] During his management of IPTO, Licklider, in agreement with Miller, assigned funding to Uhr to work in the area of behavioral sciences on a number of projects at the University of Michigan on the modelling of cognitive processes.[61] However, according to Licklider, applications by Sutherland, Johnson and others (including Lawrence G. Roberts)[62] were also dynamic models, as they were not limited to the visualization of objects. Indeed, their "intellectual power" could have been even greater:

57. Joseph C.R. Licklider, "Dynamic Modeling," in *Models for the Perception of Speech and Visual Form: Proceedings of a Symposium Sponsored by the Data Sciences Laboratory, Air Force Cambridge Research Laboratories, Boston, Massachusetts, November 11-14, 1964*, ed. by Weiant Wathen-Dunn, Cambridge, MA, MIT Press, 1967, pp. 11-12. See also Joseph C.R. Licklider, "Interactive Dynamic Modeling," in *Prospects for Simulation and Simulators of Dynamic Systems*, ed. by George Shapiro and Milton Rogers, New York – London, Spartan Books – Macmillan, 1967, p. 281: "A 'dynamic' model is a model that performs, a model in which physical parts move or abstract quantities vary. Such a model usually reacts to, or interacts with, a simulated environment. An 'interactive' model, as I shall use the term, is a model that interacts with its modeler."

58. Licklider, "Dynamic Modeling," p. 17. See Belmont G. Farley, Wesley A. Clark Jr., John T. Gilmore Jr. and Lawrence S. Frishkopf, "Computer Techniques for the Study of Patterns in the Electroencephalogram," Lincoln Lab. Tech. Rep. n. 165, 1957, http://dspace.mit.edu/handle/1721.1/4482.

59. Clark and Farley, "Generalization of Pattern Recognition in a Self-Organizing System."

60. See Leonard M. Uhr, ed., *Pattern recognition: Theory, Experiment, Computer Simulations, and Dynamic Models of Form Perception and Discovery*, New York, John Wiley & Sons, 1966; Leonard M. Uhr and Charles Vossler, "A Pattern Recognition Program that Generates, Evaluates, and Adjusts its Own Operators," in *Papers Presented at the May 9-11, 1961, Western Joint IRE-AIEE-ACM Computer Conference*, New York, ACM, 1961, pp. 555-569; Rebecca C. Prather and Leonard M. Uhr, "Discovery and Learning Techinques for Pattern Recognition," in *Proceedings of the 1964 19th ACM National Conference*, New York, ACM, 1964, pp. D2.2-1 – D2.10.

61. See NARA, RG 330-73-A-2108, Carton 1, Folder "Michigan, Univ. of, AO716, DA-49-083 OSA-3050."

62. Lawrence G. Roberts, "Machine Perception of Three-Dimensional Solids," Lincoln Lab. Tech. Rep. n. 315, 1963. Published in James T. Tippett, David A. Borkowitz, Lewis C. Clapp, Charles J. Koester and Alexander Vanderburgh Jr., eds., *Optical and Electro-Optical Information Processing*, Cambridge, MA, MIT Press, 1965; consultable at: http://www.packet.cc/files/mach-per-3D-solids.html.

in dealing with abstractions [...] to register directly through perception, and people seem to grasp complex, dynamic things much more readily when they see them happen than when they have to reconstruct such processes mentally from a succession of messages that define, but do not dynamically depict, the processes. Complex, abstract processes there is no way to see directly [*sic*]. Dynamic modeling may have great value, therefore, in converting such abstractions to concrete form through dynamic display.[63]

Researchers working in a computer network would also be able to collaborate remotely, to the point of substituting "the running of a model for mere talk about it."

From Sutherland to Taylor

It is unsurprising, therefore, that IPTO's director (who only received a console connected to California in his Pentagon office during his final days of employment there)[64] chose the brilliant Sutherland, at the time only 27 years old, to be his successor. Once they had resolved the problem of Sutherland's rank (he was only a First Lieutenant at the National Security Agency, while as director of IPTO he was entitled (if only *pro tempore*) to a higher title), the young designee took office in July 1964 and remained in post until June 1966. Although Sutherland kept the general structure established by his predecessor, he placed greater emphasis not only on graphics but also on hardware architectures.[65]

Both areas were likely to fulfil military needs in the not too distant future, and it is possible that the US's growing involvement in the Vietnam War pushed Sutherland in this direction, although we cannot be certain of this. Indeed, on the one hand, his impact on ARPA was felt "both in terms of its research programmes and more indirectly, but profoundly, in terms of the relative de-emphasis of advanced R&D in DoD, and the growing negative relationship between ARPA's university base of research and the needs and interests of military R&D."[66] On the other hand, "the gradually increasing emphasis on defence relevance which had begun to effect the other research-oriented offices appears not to have affected IPT to nearly the same extent. Broad-based computer research simply was accepted as relevant on its face."[67]

In this framework, and leaving to one side the results of IPTO various activities between 1964 and 1966, it is sufficient to state that Sutherland's overall

63. Licklider, "Dynamic Modeling," p. 19.
64. Aspray and Norberg, "An Interview with J.C.R. Licklider."
65. These projects included a 1965 contract with the University of Washington at St. Louis, and a 1966 contract with the University of Illinois at Urbana. The first contract (which was undertaken by researchers working for Wesley A. Clark, who in the meantime had left MIT) aimed to create a macromodular system: "a set of relatively simple, easily inter-connected modules from which working systems can be readily assembled for evaluation and study," Wesley A. Clark, "Macromodular Computer Systems," in *Proceedings of the April 18-20, 1967, Spring Joint Computer Conference*, New York, ACM, 1967, p. 335. The second contract dealt with a supercomputer known as ILLIAC IV (on the question of ILLIAC IV see below, pp. 118-120).
66. Van Atta, Deitchman and Reed, "DARPA Technical Accomplishments," vol. 3, p. III-4.
67. Barber Associates, *The Advanced Research Project Agency*, p. VII-32.

contribution was positive, although not at all levels. He encountered a "major failure," as he defined it, in his attempt to carry through an idea, first floated by Licklider, for a network connecting UCLA's three large computers. According to Sutherland, "it was not something that they wanted. It wasn't a programme that they were interested in from a technical point of view, nor was it something that they would reap enormous economic benefits from, although there were some."[68] For his interlocutors, instead, the initiative was not successful because it lacked sufficient funds. The fact remains that the project, which began in February 1965,[69] after little more than a year was "redirected to permit individuals to submit separate proposals for submission to ARPA" and "these actions effectively close out the proposed large scale Network Project, leaving the ARPA contract divided into two independent but possibly mutually cooperating projects."[70] The result was that UCLA's team ended up concentrating "on more basic studies on modelling and measurement of networks of computers."[71]

In the meantime, as we have seen, Sutherland and a number of his partners participated in the seminar on time-sharing promoted by Davies in November 1965 in England.[72] He had built on the "mismatch between time-sharing and the telephone network" that had been discussed on the occasion to focus his ideas about the network and packet switching.[73] There is however no trace of these ideas in subsequent writings by researchers working on IPTO's projects, not even in those by Lawrence G. Roberts, who at the time of his transfer to Great Britain had just started to experiment with Thomas M. Marill on a telephone connection between the Lincoln Laboratory's TX-2 and the SDC's AN/FSQ-32V.

As we will see, Marill and Roberts' work resumed in 1966 and led to important results. However, as Roberts and Barry D. Wessler wrote in 1970, the experiment was undertaken primarily "to test the philosophy" of a network connection. Since the telephone lines left much to be desired and were prohibitively expensive, "after the Lincoln-SDC network experiments, it was clear that a completely new communications service was required in order to make an effective, useful resource-sharing computer network."[74] Ultimately, when Sutherland left his position in June 1966 to go first to Harvard and then to the University of Utah

68. William Aspray, "An Interview with Ivan Sutherland" conducted 1 May 1989, University of Minnesota, CBI Collections, Oral History 171, http://conservancy.umn.edu/bitstream/107642/1/oh171lis.pdf.

69. "Proposal to the Advanced Research Projects Agency," 2 February 1965, in NARA, RG 330-71-A-1647, Carton 2, Untitled Folder (UCLA, SD 184 contract).

70. The citations in the text are taken from a report by R. Clay Sprowls dated 11 July 1966, in NARA, RG 330-71-A-1647, Carton 2, Untitled Folder (UCLA, SD 184 contract).

71. Gerald Estrin, "Final Technical Report to Advanced Research Projects Agency," 4 March 1970, p. 2, in NARA, RG 330-71-A-1647, Carton 2, Untitled Folder (UCLA, SD 184 contract).

72. *Ibid.*, p. 59.

73. Campbell-Kelly, "Oral history interview with Donald W. Davies."

74. Lawrence G. Roberts and Barry D. Wessler, "Computer Network Development to Achieve Resource Sharing," in AFIPS, *Proceedings of the May 5-7, 1970, Spring Joint Computer Conference*, New York, ACM, 1970, p. 543.

(which thanks in part to his influence would become the cornerstone for research in computer graphics sponsored by IPTO), some steps to make Licklider's vision a reality had been taken, but a long distance network was yet to come.

From June 1966 to March 1969, the office was headed by Robert W. Taylor, a 34-year-old psychologist who had taken a very similar path to that of Licklider. He had studied psychoacoustics and the function of the nervous system at the University of Texas at Austin, and like Licklider he had conducted his research in a defence laboratory "on hearing and how the human nervous system can localize sound and things like that, and masking of signal by noise."[75]

Subsequently Taylor had worked for a company specialized in flight simulation design, after which he joined the Office of Advanced Research and Technology at NASA. In addition to the areas of work with which he had been entrusted (manned flight control systems and flight displays), Taylor also created another area in the simulation technology field, and it was he who got the agency to fund Engelbart. In 1965 he transferred to IPTO, joining Sutherland most likely on the recommendation of Licklider, who already knew him. For his part, Taylor, who like Licklider had cultivated an increasing interest in computer research, had been profoundly influenced not only by his research on psychoacoustics, but also and above all by his vision of interactive computing. "The reason I moved from the NASA position," he recounted in 1989, "is fundamentally because over time, I became heartily subscribed to the Licklider vision of interactive computing. The 1960 man-computer symbiosis paper [...] had had a large impact on me."[76]

Indeed, it was with ample references to this essay that Taylor opened and concluded a piece from November 1966, in which he wrote "today the question is no longer whether we should bring interactive computing to the sciences, engineering, law, publishing, libraries, the government, economics, banking and finance, manufacturing, management, and education – but how."[77] It was on this basis that in early 1966, prior to formally taking on responsibility for IPTO, Taylor put onto the agenda a project for a network that integrated the groups formed around the IPTO-funded time-shared systems into a single "meta-community".

As Taylor remembers it, his adhesion to Licklider's idea of creating a network was reinforced by the fact that there were three teleprinters in his office at IPTO connected to three computers at MIT, the SDC and Berkeley, each of which worked differently from the others. "Well this is silly," he thought, "I should be able to access any of these systems from a single terminal."[78] Moreover, when in February 1966 he went to the director of ARPA to propose the idea of starting up the project for what would become Arpanet, it only took

75. Paul McJones, "Oral History of Robert (Bob) W. Taylor," interviewed 10-11 October 2008, Computer History Museum, http://archive.computerhistory.org/resources/access/text/2013/05/102702015-05-01-acc.pdf.

76. Aspray, "An Interview with Robert Taylor."

77. Robert W. Taylor, "Man-Computer Input-Output Techinques," *IEEE Transactions on Human Factors in Electronics*, HFE-8, no. 1 (1967): 1. The date indicated in the text refers to when the manuscript was turned in to the magazine.

78. McJones, "Oral History of Robert (Bob) W. Taylor."

15 minutes to obtain his agreement. Despite this, it was only in early 1967 that a plan began to take shape.

It is important to clarify certain points about these recollections. The first regards the immediate acceptance of what was a simple declaration of intent, all the more so because only a few months before, in June 1965, a new director, Charles M. Herzfeld, previously a professor of Physics at the University of Maryland, had replaced Sproull. It is thus not surprising that he accepted Taylor's proposal without hesitation, because before taking over the directorship of ARPA he had served as Deputy Director since 1961. In this role, he had been responsible for IPTO, and therefore he had been a participant from the beginning in its activities and objectives.

Another aspect that may not seem obvious is the total lack of formal decision-making procedures at ARPA, and the resulting speed and discretional nature of its director's choices. Also in this case confirmation of can be found in coeval sources. Indeed, in his 1967 hearing with the House of Representatives, Herzfeld asserted in no uncertain terms: "if we decide that something has to get done and Mr. Beard assures me that the money is available and that we would not be breaking regulations by doing so, we can sign an ARPA order and get it out into the field in an hour, if necessary. There is no other organization in Washington that I know that can do that."[79]

It is more difficult to understand why the actual project launch was delayed for almost a year, despite the fact that in the first half of 1966 various meetings were organized to discuss it.[80] Taylor recalled that the majority of individuals consulted did not seem "enamored with the idea," and he added that in his view "some of the people saw it initially as an opportunity for someone else to come in and use their cycles."[81] In other words, one could say that the failure of Sutherland's previous attempt and the halting of the UCLA network project had not been the result of isolated opinions. Taylor's recollections coincide with Roberts', who in 1967 met with the same problems when it was his turn to launch the project. "The universities," he said, "in general did not want to share their computers with anybody. They wanted to buy their own machines and hide in the corner."[82] Anyone who has attended any university in the world knows that these attitudes are not limited to computers or to the America of the 1960s, but this was not the reason for the delay; in fact, this time, the initiative was not stopped.

The extreme difficulty that ARPA was facing at the time is the more likely reason why Taylor's idea did not immediately become a working project. According

79. DoD Appropriations for 1968, *Hearings Before the Subcommittee of the Committee on Appropriations, House of Representatives, Ninetieth Congress, First Session*, Part 3. *Research, Development, Test, and Evaluation*, Washington, DC, US Government Printing Office, 1967, p. 191. Russell W. Beard was Appointed Director of the agency's Program Management.

80. This is discussed in a letter from Schwartz to Herzfeld dated 6 June 1966, in NARA, RG 330-71-A-1647, Carton 1, Folder "System Development Corporation," which mentions among its participants, in addition to the SDC, the University of California at Berkeley and the BBN.

81. Aspray, "An Interview with Robert Taylor."

82. Norberg, "An Interview with Lawrence G. Roberts."

to Richard J. Barber Associates, in mid-1966 the agency "was in immense trouble" because of the deteriorating rapport between the Department of Defence and the scientific community, especially the university community, where protests against the Vietnam War had become ever more frequent. Indeed, it accused ARPA of tolerating an "academic" atmosphere, of expecting operational independence with no strings attached, of clashing with the armed forces and undertaking projects "for their own sake." McNamara and his right-hand man, Cyrus R. Vance, even considered closing ARPA, and if this did not ultimately occur, it is thanks to the support given to the agency by John S. Foster, the director of the Defence Research and Engineering Office at the Department.[83]

Nonetheless, not even this hypothesis provides a sufficient explanation for the delay. Indeed, on the one hand, the Defence's priorities limited projects at ARPA that were not connected to the Vietnam War. This led to a decrease in its overall funding, but did not affect IPTO's budget, which rose 35.7% between 1965 and 1966, and only saw a slight reduction of 5.3% in 1967, before beginning to grow again the following year.[84] On the other hand, and above all, the agency faced the most difficult period after Herzfeld's departure in mid-1967.[85] This was precisely the time of the network project's consolidation and prior to the arrival of a new director, Eberhard Rechtin, an electronics engineer who had studied at the California Institute of Technology. Although the delay could essentially be attributed to this crisis, the reason why the initiative was able to get underway before things improved remains to be seen.

Reflecting many years later on the failure of his attempt and wondering "what it took to make networking happen in ARPA," Sutherland responded that "first of all, there was Larry Roberts."[86] Leaving aside the clarity of hindsight, this observation captures an important point that cannot be overlooked: neither he nor his successor had an expert among their staff who was able to plan and oversee such a venture. For Taylor, who was not a computer scientist, the problem was decisive. It is also unsurprising that the 29-year-old Roberts embodied the most suitable programme manager. Roberts had worked side by side with Sutherland at MIT, where in 1963 he had earned a PhD in Electronic Engineering with a dissertation on the "Machine Perception of Three-Dimensional Solids,"[87] on which he based the work included by Licklider among his examples of dynamic modelling. Moreover, Roberts, along with Marill, had just experimented with the connection between the Lincoln Laboratory and the SDC that we previously discussed. Although he was hesitant to abandon his research,[88] he declined multiple

83. Barber Associates, *The Advanced Research Project Agency*, p. VIII-3-6.

84. *Ibid.*, tables VI-1, VII-1, VIII-1 and IX-1.

85. *Ibid.*, pp. VII-37 – VII-40.

86. Aspray, "An Interview with Ivan Sutherland."

87. Roberts' thesis – available for consultation at http://dspace.mit.edu/handle/1721.1/11589 – was "a cross between math[ematics] and computers [...], founded in psychology and math," Norberg, "An Interview with Lawrence G. Roberts."

88. See Lawrence G. Roberts, "A Graphical Service System with Variable Syntax," *Communications of the ACM*, 9, no. 3 (1966): pp. 173-175; Lawrence G. Roberts, "The Lincoln

requests by Taylor that he transfer to ARPA, and in order to ultimately convince him, Herzfeld had to put pressure on Roberts' superiors. By then it was nearly the end of 1966, and thus it was only in January of the following year that he began working at IPTO.

Like others who had preceded him at the agency, Roberts, too, was heavily influenced by Licklider's vision, which he saw as inspiring his own interest in computer networking.[89] However, other considerations weighed in favour of the creation of a network with respect to developments in time-sharing. These must be explained if for no other reason than because Taylor recalled only two individuals who guaranteed their support: Licklider, who had been its primary cheerleader, and Wesley A. Clark, who in contrast had been very critical of time-sharing, because he thought it to be inefficient and costly.[90] It is no coincidence that in previous years, first at MIT and later at Washington University at St. Louis, Clark and his team had devoted themselves to the construction of LINC, a small machine for biomedical research that was a forbearer to the personal computer.[91] It is thus necessary to ask whether the network project was the logical evolution of time-sharing, or whether it was born out of a desire to exceed its limits.

In previous years, time-shared systems had become quite common even outside of universities and research centres, but problems as well as successes plagued their history: recurrent malfunctions, problems with overload, the extreme complexity of the system's software and rejected or missing objectives.[92] One setback – particularly significant, as it took place at MIT – was Project MAC's new Multics system. The project, started in 1964 by a team led by Corbató and presented at the 1965 Fall Joint Computer Conference,[93] was supposed to be completed within one year, but ended up taking much longer. Various criticisms tempered initial enthusiasm for the project, once again drawing attention to the imbalance between the results that were obtained and the elevated costs of large time-shared systems. As an alternative to these systems, new smaller machines were being imagined, also because their calculating power was becoming increasingly less expensive.

These limits were made even worse by the incommunicability of the various systems and the widespread "proprietary" attitudes, which meant that the strong

WAND," in AFIPS, *Proceedings of the November 7-10, 1966, Fall Joint Computer Conference*, pp. 223-227.

89. Roberts, "The ARPANET and Computer Networks," pp. 143-144.

90. Aspray, "An Interview with Robert Taylor."

91. See Wesley A. Clark, "The LINC was Early and Small," in *Proceedings of the ACM Conference on The History of Personal Workstations*, ed. by John R. White and Kathi Anderson, New York, ACM, 1986, pp. 133-155.

92. On this topic see Norberg and O'Neill, *Transforming Computer Technology*, pp. 106-112 and, on MIT, Akera, *Calculating a Natural World*, pp. 332-335. On commercial systems, see Martin Campbell-Kelly and Daniel D. Garcia-Swartz, "Economic Perspectives on the History of the Computer Time-Sharing Industry, 1965-1985," *IEEE Annals of the History of Computing*, 30, no. 1 (2008): pp. 16-36.

93. The papers presented at the conference, along with other materials, are consultable at http://www.multicians.org/papers.html.

development of time-sharing transformed into an increase in costs and programming work. Indeed, Licklider himself, according to what Schwartz reported in 1968, "stated informally that he was surprised and pleased by the number of current time-sharing systems, but [...] disappointed at the lack of coherence in them."[94] On this matter, moreover, he had already clearly expressed himself in May 1967 in a memorandum for IBM, writing:

> One of ARPA's main aims in fostering work on or toward a computer network, I think, is to exploit first the network project and later the network itself as inducers of coherence [...]. Without some correlating or unifying factor, such as the network, the several contractors are likely in some instances to duplicate one another's efforts to an embarrassing extent and in other instances to wander off in different directions – and thus not produce a good over-all product. Working toward – and later within – the network, on the other hand, the contractors will be more likely to make their parts (especially software) complement one another and fit together to make a result of great and obvious value.[95]

Having shortly afterwards resumed teaching at MIT, where in 1968 he became head of Project MAC, Licklider was also disappointed by Multics' human-machine communication procedures. As he wrote in 1970, on his return he felt that these procedures were "rather far removed from the fast-response graphic interaction of which my dreams were made and that the 'on-line community' was not so much a community of users as an in-group of computer programmers."[96] The opinions of the very person most responsible for the development of time-sharing would be sufficient to conclude that the network project was a logical evolution of time-sharing, and, not contradictorily, a way to correct its defects.

This was also confirmed by numerous testaments from the direct protagonists of the venture, starting with the presentation given in 1967 by ARPA's director at the House of Representatives. After recalling the results of the research carried out in this field by IPTO, and their effect on the computer production industry, at the same time very important and exceptionally quick, Herzfeld announced that the agency was beginning to implement a computer network that would have interconnected various laboratories:

> Today, a computer programme written for one machine will usually not be accepted by another machine. A network of time-sharing systems will permit two major capabilities not now available: (1) the ability to use computer programmes on-line from some other centre in the network, and (2) the ability to specialize hardware and software at a centre for economic advantage. This will eliminate the need for duplicate programming efforts within the network.[97]

---

94. Jules I. Schwartz, "Interactive Systems: Promises, Present and Future," in *Proceedings of the December 9-11, 1968, Fall Joint Computer Conference Part 1*, New York, ACM, 1968, p. 91.

95. Joseph C.R. Licklider, "Memorandum to A.H. Eschenfelder," 3 May 1967, in Licklider Papers, Box 3, Folder "IBM, Memos from JCRL 1967."

96. Licklider, "The Future of Project MAC," 1970, quoted in Norberg and O'Neill, *Transforming Computer Technology*, p. 111.

97. DoD Appropriations for 1968, *Hearings Before the Subcommittee of the Committee on Appropriations, House of Representatives, Ninetieth Congress, First Session*, Part 3, pp. 185-186.

Roberts was even clearer in a 1967 report in which perhaps for the first time he used the term "ARPA Net." The possibility of sharing data and programmes instead of copying and re-writing them every time would bring about enormous savings, without taking into account that "a network would foster the 'community' use of computers. Cooperative programming would be stimulated, and in particular fields or disciplines it will be possible to achieve a 'critical mass' of talent by allowing geographically separated people to work effectively in interaction with a system."[98] The following year he wrote:

> Just as time-shared computer systems have permitted groups of hundreds of individual users to share hardware and software resources with one another, networks connecting dozens of such systems will permit resource sharing between thousands of users. Each system, by virtue of being time-shared, can offer any of its services to another computer system on demand.[99]

Other participants of the project would later reaffirm as much in even more explicit terms: in 1970 C. Stephen Carr, Stephen D. Crocker and Vinton G. Cerf wrote that the first studies on time-sharing "have had a considerable influence on the design of the network. In some sense, the ARPA network of time-sharing computers is a natural extension of earlier time-sharing concepts."[100]

98. Roberts, "Multiple Computer Networks and Intercomputer Communication," pp. 3.1-3.2.
99. Lawrence G. Roberts, "Resource Sharing Computer Networks," ARPA Program Plan n. 723, 3 June 1968, now at http://www.archive.org/details/ResourceSharingComputerNetworks.
100. C. Stephen Carr, Stephen D. Crocker and Vinton G. Cerf, "HOST-HOST Communication Protocol in the ARPA Network," in AFIPS, *Proceedings of the May 5-7, 1970, Spring Joint Computer Conference*, p. 589.

4. Roberts and the Others: Building the Network

Closing the Circle

When he started to work at ARPA in early 1967, Roberts did not begin from square one. The experimental connection between the Lincoln Laboratory and the SDC that he had previously established together with Marill had produced some important results. This success confirmed that a network was the most appropriate instrument for solving the problem of computer incompatibility. In any case, the alternative option of adopting standard hardware and software would have been extremely expensive, even simply homogenizing those systems under IPTO's control. Ultimately, it would have been impossible to impose these standards on the market. Instead, in a network, "a user of any cooperating installation would have access to programmes running at other cooperating installations, even though the programmes were written in different languages for different computers." In this way, everyone would work together to resolve common problems. Marill and Roberts also convinced themselves that there was no need to treat "satellite" and network computers any differently:

> Small time-shared computers will be found to be efficiently utilized when employed only as communication equipment for relaying the users' requests to some larger remote machine on which the substantive work is done. Such smaller installations might then be considered to be "retail outlets" for the "wholesale computer power" provided by the giant machines.

During the course of experimentation, an essential communication instrument was prepared: a protocol containing all the rules that two network nodes needed to respect in order to ensure the successful exchange of data. Indeed, Marill and Roberts defined their message protocol as "a uniform agreed-upon manner of exchanging messages between two computers in the network." The authors felt that the use of a standard protocol should be encouraged but not imposed: "since the motivation for the network is to overcome the problems of computer incompatibility without enforcing standardization, it would not do to require adherence to a standard protocol as a prerequisite of membership in the network."[1]

1. Marill and Roberts, "Toward a Cooperative Network of Time-Shared Computers," pp. 426, 428.

On this basis, Roberts, like Taylor before him, began his work by promoting a series of meetings with IPTO contractors. He was met with no less resistance, but in his case the consolidated *modus operandi* of the office – founded on the involvement of potential users and the comparison of their ideas – ultimately worked to his advantage. Indeed, at the end of one meeting among the various group managers held on 9-11 April 1967 at the University of Michigan, Ann Arbor, an idea took centre stage that would turn out to be fundamental. The idea belonged to Wesley A. Clark, who had not worked on the network project before and who many years later in 1990 explained his train of thought in the following way:

> I just suddenly realized the fairly obvious thing that they had an n-squared (n^2) interaction problem within computer nodes, and that that was the wrong way to go about it. It would be hard to fund and control, and everything else. And so, the idea was to simply define the network to be something self-contained without those n nodes... without those n ARPA-supported big computers [...]. They weren't part of the network, the network was everything from there in, and that should be around a single, common message-handling instrument of some kind, so that the design of that instrument and all of the lines were under central control – ARPA central control. They could fund it, get projects started to design the parts, define its finest characteristics and so forth.[2]

In other words, identical minicomputers – whose function pre-dated that of modern-day routers – would perform software integration, instead of carrying out the process inside each machine, as had been the plan up to that point. This was a decisive idea that – not coincidentally – the IPTO community immediately adopted as its own. One month later, during a meeting on 18 May, Clark's minicomputers were baptized Interface Message Processors (IMPs).[3] Roberts summarized this and other acquisitions from those meetings, as well as the early developments of the project, in a report prepared in June 1967 for the ACM symposium, which was scheduled for the month of October. The IMPs were to have uniform hardware and software to simplify the creation and management of a "message switching network." Each of them would connect to a host, meaning one of the existing time-shared machines, while the network would connect all the other IMPs. Two images included in Roberts' text illustrate, respectively, the network's structure and its geographical configuration, as it was imagined at that time, with 35 computers and 16 different localities (Figures 16 and 17).

The project's objectives were indicated in the load sharing (that is, in the sending of programmes and data to other machines to balance out the load), and in the sharing of one, the other or both, if they were installed in a remote computer. The network was also used for transmitting interpersonal messages. Other issues discussed in the Ann Arbor meeting had to do with the technical features and

2. Judy O'Neill, "An Interview with Wesley Clark" conducted 3 May 1990, University of Minnesota, CBI Collections, Oral History 195, http://conservancy.umn.edu/bitstream/107217/1/oh195wc.pdf.

3. On 6 June 1967, Licklider wrote to Daniel Bobrow and William Sutherland: "The ARPA network circle meeting of May 18, 1967, decided [...] to adopt the Interface Message Processor concept," (available at http://www.archive.org/details/AModifiedBnfNotationForDescribingNetworkMessages).

Figure 16 – Use of Interface Message Processors (IMPS)

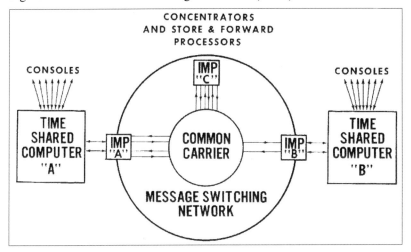

Source: Roberts, "Multiple Computer Networks and Intercomputer Communication," p. 3.5.

Figure 17 – ARPA's Network

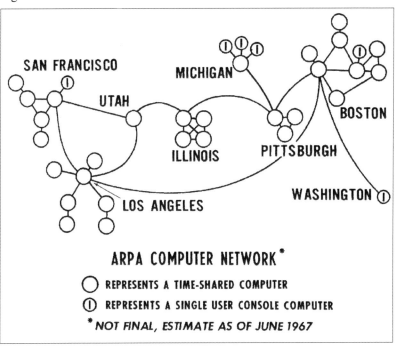

Source: Roberts, "Multiple Computer Networks and Intercomputer Communication," p. 3.6.

the speed of the telephone line that would connect the IMPs. Following the meeting, work began on developing an initial communication protocol, and an ARPA Computer Network Working Group was created. Elmer B. Shapiro, an expert in communication networks from SRI who had previously worked for Bell Telephone Laboratories, managed the group. Group activity, however, intensified only following another event that would prove to be even more important: the ACM symposium, held from 1-4 October in Gatlinburg, Tennessee.

It was here, as already mentioned,[4] that Roger A. Scantlebury presented a report on the work done by Davies and his team at the NPL. Among the solutions proposed were the interface computers imagined by the English to connect slow terminals to the network without reducing its overall speed; however, this was not the solution that enriched the "state of the art" that the IPTO group had attained. Indeed, these machines were not conceived as network nodes, but rather as interfaces for the single user terminals. To a certain extent, they reflected those proposed by Clark, they had different functions and they did not resolve the problem with host incompatibility. On the other hand, a decisive contribution to the network's development came from packet switching, which took up a great deal of space in Scantlebury's report and was capable of dramatically reducing both costs and waiting times in the transmission of messages. Indeed, multiple users could share the same line, because the line was busy during the packet's transmission for only a very brief moment to seem imperceptible.

However, in 1978, Roberts recognized the speedier lines to be the primary difference between the NPL and IPTO projects, as well as the former's greater contribution to the latter, writing that the report he had described at Gatlinburg "consisted of a packet switching network."[5] In truth the text, despite affirming that "it has proven necessary to hold a line which is being used intermittently" to obtain the response times requested for an interactive work,[6] does not mention the division of messages into packets. In the absence of coeval sources attesting that Roberts and his partners had figured this out on their own, it can be deduced that the packet switching idea actually came from the other side of the Atlantic. This also appears to be confirmed in a memo written by Engelbart following a meeting held at ARPA a few days after the symposium on 9-10 October 1967, which states that "the notion of packet (an entity of 1000 bits maximum) was introduced, where a given message could be composed of many packets."[7]

Roberts and his collaborators became aware of Baran's memoranda thanks to the report by Davies' group. Indeed, the first of these memoranda was mentioned

4. See above, p. 51.

5. Lawrence G. Roberts, "The Evolution of Packet Switching," *Proceedings of the IEEE*, 66, no. 11 (1978): p. 1308. Subsequently, he generously recognized the impact of Davies and Baran's work: Roberts, "The ARPANET and Computer Networks," p. 147. See also the meticulous reconstruction in Davies, "An Historical Study of the Beginnings of Packet-Switching," pp. 158-161.

6. Roberts, "Multiple Computer Networks and Intercomputer Communication," p. 3.3.

7. The minutes can be consulted at http://sloan.stanford.edu/mousesite/EngelbartPaper/B1_F20_CompuMtg.html.

as "the most relevant previous work" on networks, and Baran became again the referent for the procedures for routing the packets, which he defined as "hot potato routing."[8]

A Collaborative Project

At this point IPTO's staff had everything they needed to guarantee a real increase in quality. The fact that they were fully aware of this is demonstrated by the importance that they immediately attributed to Baran's work: the same month of October was not yet over and he had already been involved in the Arpanet project. It is true that Baran was only a consultant, but Barry W. Boehm participated intensively at the Network Working Group. Boehm also worked at the RAND Corporation, and in 1966, he performed a study with Robert L. Mobley on routing techniques. This study was inspired by Baran's work, in particular his second memorandum, which he wrote in collaboration with Boehm's wife, Sharla Perrine Boehm.[9]

During the first meeting in which Baran participated on October 31, 1967, the group discussed certain aspects of the "routing doctrine," as well as how to define IMP characteristics.[10] Numerous meetings were subsequently dedicated to this objective, and between 1967 and 1968 nearly 50 individuals, many of them team leaders, attended the meetings with varying frequency. It is perhaps because so many people were present that an informal and limited coordinating body formed within the work group comprised of Shapiro, Boehm, Kleinrock and Gordon Buck from the University of California at Santa Barbara, as well as Roberts and Barry D. Wessler from IPTO.[11]

SRI played a central role in this phase: in December 1967, they received a contract for "A Study of Computer Network Parameters."[12] A draft report of the work they had done was due by January 1968, but just before the deadline, Shapiro informed

8. Davies, Bartlett, Scantlebury and Wilkinson, "A Digital Communication Network for Computers Giving Rapid Response at Remote Terminals," pp. 2.1-2.2.

9. See Barry W. Boehm and Robert Mobley, "Adaptive Routing Techniques for Distributed Communications Systems," The RAND Corporation, Research Memorandum RM-4781, 1966, http://http://www.rand.org/pubs/research_memoranda/RM4781.html; Barry W. Boehm, "An Early Application Generator and Other Recollections," [1997] in *Software Engineering: Barry W. Boehm's Lifetime Contributions to Software Development, Management, and Research*, ed. by Richard W. Selby, Hoboken, NJ, IEEE Computer Society – John Wiley & Sons, 2007, p. 66.

10. Boehm, Kleinrock, Shapiro and Keith W. Uncapher participated in the meeting, which was held at RAND. The meeting's minutes, sent by Kleinrock to Roberts on 3 November 1967, can be found in NARA, RG 330-71-A-647, Carton 1, Folder "Arpa Computer Network Working Group."

11. These recipients appear most frequently in Shapiro's letters, which can be found in NARA, RG 330-71-A-647, Carton 1, Folder "Arpa Computer Network Working Group." Later on, Glen J. Culler replaced Buck.

12. The conclusive report, prepared by Shapiro in December 1968, is in NARA, RG 330-71-A-647, Carton 1, Folder "Stanford Research Inst. Arpa Order 1137 – DAHC04 68 C 0017," and also in Peter H. Salus, ed., *The Arpanet Sourcebook: The Unpublished Foundations of the Internet*, Charlottesville, VA, Peer-To-Peer Communications, 2008, pp. 103-176.

Roberts that they still had much to do, and subsequently it was moved to 1 April.[13] In the following months, the group dedicated itself to the examination of common problems, and members of the various offices involved in the project held periodic consultations among themselves.[14] The first nodes of the network were pinpointed at the University of California, Los Angeles and Santa Barbara, the University of Utah, Salt Lake City and in the SRI. On this basis, on July 29, 1968, the US Army Research Office sent a Request for Quotation on ARPA's behalf to 140 potential bidders for the realization of the IMPs. The request included a document from the agency outlining the specific techniques of the 19 requested machines, and it was also decided that the first four techniques would have to be installed by whoever was granted the contract.[15] Under the circumstances, Roberts further explained the project's goals:

> The development of this distributed communication system will not only provide the communications capability required for the ARPA computer research facilities, but will also be a unique prototype of future communication systems. Additionally, this network will provide an opportunity to demonstrate a form of communications organization recommended in a distributed digital network study by the RAND Corporation.[16]

Out of the twelve agencies that presented proposals, four were chosen: the BBN, Bunker Ramo, Jacobi Systems and Raytheon. Following further consultations and examination, these were then cut down to two. In the end, the BBN beat Raytheon to win the contract on 2 January 1969.[17] According to Taylor, the choice took into account "BBN's culture and the people in it, and the [fact that the] people who would be involved in carrying out this work are very similar to the people in the ARPA culture and the other places that we fund from IPTO."[18] They were not so much entrepreneurs as they were academics, and for the most part, they already knew many of the researchers working on the project, as they came from the same backgrounds, specifically from MIT.[19]

13. Correspondence between Elmer B. Shapiro and Lawrence G. Roberts, January 19, 1968, in NARA, RG 330-71-A-647, Carton 1, Folder "Stanford Research Inst. Arpa Order 1137 – DAHC04 68 C 0017."

14. Correspondence between E. Shapiro and B. Boehm, G. Culler, Kleinrock, L. Roberts and B. Wessler, February 15, 1968, in NARA, RG 330-71-A-647, Carton 1, Folder "Stanford Research Inst. Arpa Order 1137 – DAHC04 68 C 0017."

15. A copy of the request and the document is at http://www.cs.utexas.edu.users/chris/DIGITAL_ARCHIVE/ARPANET/RFQ-ARPA-IMP.pdf (accessed 30 November 2012). Fourteen of the planned nineteen nodes were universities: Berkeley, Carnegie Mellon, Dartmouth, Harvard, Illinois, the Lincoln Laboratory, Michigan, MIT Project MAC, Stanford, SRI, Utah, UCSB, UCLA and Washington. The others were the BBN, the Bell Telephone Laboratories, RAND, SDC and ARPA. In total, 30 computers and 21 different models were installed in these locations.

16. Lawrence G. Roberts, "Memorandum for the Director, Program Management," June 21, 1968, can be consulted at http://www.archive.org/details/InteractiveComputerNetwork-CommunicationSystem.

17. See Norberg and O'Neill, *Transforming Computer Technology*, pp. 167-168. Hafner and Lyon, *Where Wizards Stay Up Late*, p. 80, provide slightly different information.

18. McJones, "Oral History of Robert (Bob) W. Taylor."

19. The staff that conducted the DEC project, where it was chosen, also had similar characteristics: in addition to the director Marill, C. Gordon Bell and Hallam G. Murray

Indeed, Frank Heart, who directed the staff in charge of drafting and carrying out the project, had worked with Forrester to create the Whirlwind computer, and he had been at the Lincoln Laboratory until 1966. William R. Crowther and David C. Walden, who were in charge of software development, had also been at the Lincoln Laboratory, as had Severo M. Ornstein, who had worked with Clark at Washington University and handled the fine tuning of the hardware. Finally, Robert E. Kahn, who coordinated various aspects of the work, had joined BBN after working as an assistant professor at MIT.[20]

While the selection of the agency to create the IMPs forged ahead, the community continued its research in the second half of 1968, making or acting upon some significant choices. These included the decision to assign the function of Network Measurement Centre to Kleinrock's group at UCLA, with the task of monitoring the network's speed and capacity. The theoretical models, the simulations and the analytical tools elaborated by the group would prove to be essential to ensuring that Arpanet performed adequately.[21] Another relevant decision could be traced back to the Ann Arbor meeting, in which the group decided to create a Network Information Centre (NIC). As Roberts wrote in June 1968,

> in order for people to utilize the envisioned computer network effectively, it will be necessary to provide extremely good documentation on what programs and files are available throughout the net. This information should be available on-line to any individual in the network. It should be possible for him to add new program descriptions, edit previous descriptions, retrieve relevant information based on keyword searches and affix comments to program descriptions which he has used. To achieve this goal, Stanford Research Institute has been tasked with developing such a facility. This is an extension of the capability already achieved at SRI and is in progress in order that it may become available concurrently with the network.[22]

In actual fact, and by no coincidence, it was Engelbart who had offered to develop the facility. The NIC would offer the feedback "of a wider class of knowledge workers"[23] to the system he had developed with his staff: a collection of texts that were structured and codified in paragraphs and subparagraphs,

had studied at MIT. The proposal can be viewed at http://www.archive.org/details/InterfaceMassageProcessorsForTheArpaComputerNetwork.

20. Other group members included Ben Barker, Bernie Cosell, Jim Geisman, Hawley Rising, Truett Thach and Marty Thrope.

21. For a list of the documents produced by the centre, see DARPA, "A History of the Arpanet: The First Decade," 1 April 1981, III-41 – III-44, www.darpa.mil/WorkArea/DownloadAsset.aspx?id=2677 (this is the Completion Report n. 4799 from the BBN, that was drawn up on 4 January 1978 by Frank Heart, Alex McKenzie, John McQuillan and David Walden). See in particular Kleinrock, "Analytic and Simulation Methods in Computer Network Design," in AFIPS, *Proceedings of the May 5-7, 1970, Spring Joint Computer Conference*, pp. 569-579; Leonard Kleinrock and William E. Naylor, "On Measured Behavior of the ARPA Network," in AFIPS, *Proceedings of the May 6-10, 1974, National Computer Conference and Exposition*, New York, ACM, 1974, pp. 767-780.

22. Roberts, "Resource Sharing Computer Networks."

23. Engelbart, Richard W. Watson and James C. Norton, "The Augmented Knowledge Workshop," in AFIPS, *Proceedings of the June 4-8, 1973, National Computer Conference and Exposition* (New York: ACM, 1973), 16-17.

indexed and connected by links with advanced editing and information retrieval procedures. It was called oN Line System (NLS), and it was presented to the public on 9 December 1968 in a famous presentation at the AFIPS conference held in San Francisco. It made use of a mouse invented by Engelbart in collaboration with William K. English, and it was the first hyper-textual system ever to be created and tested.[24]

As has been observed, unironically it was precisely the development and initial functioning of the network that revealed NLS' limits and sent it into crisis.[25] However, in the immediate aftermath the structure of Engelbart's project and NIC's fine-tuning made an important contribution to the consolidation of a work ethos founded on sharing and mutual exchange that was the foundation of Arpanet's construction. Indeed, a documentary base was made accessible to various groups, and a newsletter and a "first mail and 'Journal' system as part of an explicit pursuit of a 'Dialogue Support System'" were created. However, NLS was online only within the SRI system and while waiting for the network to get off the ground information was transmitted to the other centres by mailing them microfilms.[26]

In addition, the practice that was perhaps most exemplary of the IPTO community's *modus operandi* was also closely connected to the NIC. This practice, Requests for Comments (RFC), began in April 1969 on the initiative of a UCLA graduate student, Stephen D. Crocker, and others who had been students of Estrin and Kleinrock. It consisted of messages sent to other members of the community to seek opinions, discuss problems and make proposals. The first request, sent on 7 April by Crocker, raised a series of questions regarding software and communication between hosts, and proposed some technical solutions to access NLS.[27] He received an answer from William Duvall at SRI, and shortly afterwards, the RFC were published in the Journal of the NIC. From the third note on, the participants began referring to themselves as the Network Working Group, and Crocker – who was the group's chairman – wrote that it "seemed" to be comprised by him and Gerard Deloche (UCLA), Duvall and Jeff Rulifson (SRI) and C. Stephen Carr (Utah). But, he added, "membership is not closed." The RFC's text makes the informal nature of the initiative clear:

> The content of a NWG note may be any thought, suggestion, etc. related to the HOST software or other aspect of the network. Notes are encouraged to be timely rather than polished. Philosophical positions without examples or other specifics, specific suggestions

24. See Doug Engelbart and William K. English, "A Research Center for Augmenting Human Intellect," in AFIPS, *Proceedings of the December 9-11, 1968, Fall Joint Computer Conference Part 1,* New York, ACM, 1968, pp. 395-410. A video of the demonstration can be viewed at http://sloan.stanford.edu/mousesite/1968Demo.html.

25. See Bardini, *Bootstrapping,* pp. 147 and 182-187.

26. See "NIC Newsletter," 16 January 1969, in NARA, RG 330-71-A-647, Carton 1, Folder "Arpa Computer Network Working Group," available at http://ia600406.us.archive.org/9/items/NoTitle/NIC16J69/; Doug Engelbart, "The Augmented Knowledge Worskhop," in *Proceedings of the ACM Conference on the History of Personal Workstations,* New York, ACM, 1986, p. 79.

27. Stephen D. Crocker, "Host Software," RFC 1, 7 April 1969. All of the RFC are archived at http://www.rfc-editor.org/.

or implementation techniques without introductory or background explication, and explicit questions without any attempted answers are all acceptable. The minimum length for a NWG note is one sentence.

These standards (or lack of them) are stated explicitly for two reasons. First, there is a tendency to view a written statement as ipso facto authoritative, and we hope to promote the exchange and discussion of considerably less than authoritative ideas. Second, there is a natural hesitancy to publish something unpolished, and we hope to ease this inhibition.[28]

In 1969, 26 RFCs were sent and the group grew. The most active members were Crocker, Deloche and Vinton G. Cerf who like Jonathan Postel (who would become its editor) was also a student at UCLA. Early on, the circulation of the news was slow and limited because the network was still not operative, "so," Crocker recalled, "we wrote our visions for the future on paper and sent them around via the postal service."[29] It was only later, when Arpanet became a reality and a File Transfer Protocol (FTP) had been put into place that it was possible to send them quickly. Meanwhile, in 1970 the RFCs grew to reach 58, thus becoming the main seat for the collegial elaboration of a protocol for host-to-host communication, which was not among the BBN's tasks. As some of the protagonists wrote in 2009

the effect of the RFCs was to create a positive feedback loop, with ideas or proposals presented in one RFC triggering another RFC with additional ideas, and so on. When some consensus (or a least a consistent set of ideas) had come together a specification document would be prepared. Such a specification would then be used as the base for implementations by the various research teams.[30]

This evolutionary and distributive means of proceeding was inherited by the Internet and is common to this day; in June 2013 the RFCs reached 6,964.[31] Early on, to exceed the limited circulation of news, an attempt was also made to surpass the boundaries of the IPTO community with a programmatic dissemination of the results as they were obtained. Roberts wrote in June 1968 that the external transfer of new network technologies should take place "through the open scientific and technical literature" and using "common carriers or other commercial organizations concerned with data transfer and dissemination."

It was a slow process, but necessary and effective, as the extension of time-sharing from universities to private industry had proved. It would also be possible to connect to network structures such as the Office of Educational Regional Laboratories, other institutions supported by the National Science Foundation, and various groups financed by the National Institutes of Health. Finally, over the

28. Stephen D. Crocker, "Documentation Conventions," RFC 3, April 1969.

29. Stephen D. Crocker, "How the Internet Got Its Rules," *The New York Times*, 6 April 2009. Elizabeth J. Feinler, "Reflecting on 30 Years of RFCs," in RFC 2555, 7 April 1999, wrote: "RFC 1 was, I believe, a paper document. RFC 2 was produced online via the SRI NLS system and was entered into the online SRI NLS Journal. However, it was probably mailed to each recipient via snail mail by the NIC." Feinler became manager of the NIC in 1972.

30. Barry M. Leiner, Vinton G. Cerf, David D. Clark, Robert E. Kahn, Kleinrock, Daniel C. Lynch, Jonathan Postel, Lawrence G. Roberts and Stephen Wolff, "A Brief History of the Internet," *Computer Communication Review*, 39, no. 5 (2009): p. 28.

31. See http://www.rfc-editor.org/rfc-index2.html.

long term, the same management of the IMPs could be transferred to a common carrier that provided a "digital message service directly to the individual users on a tariff basis," thus allowing ARPA "to terminate its system responsibility."[32]

Obviously, Roberts had made sure to announce that the results of their work would also be transmitted to the command and control military centres, and he had emphasized the IPTO's "close working relationship" with the Department of Defence. However, ARPA's strategy had other priorities, and the agency's outlook for the future centred on the decision to prioritize the base research developed in universities and other research centres. It is no coincidence that during a report to the Senate on 10 June 1969, the agency's director, Eberhard Rechtin, responded with a laconic "no" to Senator Stephen M. Young, who had asked him "Is any of this work performed in Department of Defence installations?"[33] Rechtin wrote in his report:

> The network is constructed to make it possible for conversations between computers to take place at an extremely high data rate. If this concept can be demonstrated as feasible, it could make a factor of 10 to 100 difference in effective computer capacity per dollar among the users. The ARPA network will connect universities engaged in computer sciences research, the final DoD application would connect Defence installations.[34]

The Birth and Early Development of the Network

Meanwhile, in March 1969, Taylor, exhausted from missions that he had carried out in Vietnam on ARPA's behalf, had left IPTO to join Sutherland and Evans at the University of Utah. The following year Taylor transferred to Xerox PARC, a research centre that the Xerox Corporation had recently founded in Palo Alto. Roberts took over office management and in order to respect the schedule, work on realizing the IMPs had continued at a brisk pace. The selected computer was Honeywell's DDP-516 minicomputer, with which the BBN stipulated a subcontract specifying that necessary modifications would take place according to the team's instructions. A protocol to connect the IMPs in a packet-switching store-and-forward network and a routing algorithm for choosing the quickest routes within the network were developed alongside the fine-tuning of the hardware.

Even though the IMP network was the only one to be planned, from the perspective of the final product the network was configured as if it were a subnet, with the single but fundamental function of allowing multiple machines to communicate automatically. Indeed, Arpanet would also include the hosts and it would be a human-computer network: the users, unaware of the mechanisms in the IMPs' sub-network, would connect with each other from the terminals of their respective hosts. An interface would be provided for each of the hosts, but

---

32. Roberts, "Resource Sharing Computer Networks."

33. DoD Appropriations for 1970, *Hearings Before the Subcommittee of the Committee on Appropriations, United States Senate, Ninety-First Congress, First Session on H.R. 15090*, Part 1, Washington, DC, US Government Printing Office, 1969, p. 442.

34. *Ibid.*, p. 433.

Figure 18 – Frank Heart and the Honeywell DDP-516 IMP

Source: http://www.walden-family.com/dave/archive/frank-and-imp.jpg.

since some centres already had more than one machine the IMPs were designed only to be used for up to four of them. A great deal of work was dedicated not only to checking for and correcting errors, but also and above all to the system's reliability. To guarantee this, reset procedures were put into place in the event that the network or one of the IMPs were to freeze.[35]

Predictably, the processing of the IMP-host and host-host protocols was particularly laborious. The number of versions that needed to be created was dependent on the number of computer models installed in the various offices. For example, in the first four nodes alone there were as many machines with different operating systems: an SDS Sigma 7 at UCLA, an XDS 940 at SRI, an IBM 360/75 at UCSB and a DEC PDP-10 at the University of Utah. The significant involvement of the teams of each office was thus indispensable. To facilitate this involvement,

35. See the BBN Reports n. 1763 (January 1969) and n. 1783 (April 1969) in Salus, *The Arpanet Sourcebook*, pp. 363-443, 445-460. More generally see Frank E. Heart, Robert E. Kahn, Severo M. Ornstein, William R. Crowther and David C. Walden, "The Interface Message Processor for the ARPA Computer Network," in AFIPS, *Proceedings of the May 5-7, 1970, Spring Joint Computer Conference*, pp. 551-567.

in May 1969 the BBN distributed its Report n. 1822, a wide-reaching paper by Kahn that illustrated in detail the specifications for connecting a host to an IMP.[36] On this basis, the Network Working Group increased its activity with meetings and RFC exchanges, but the work proceeded with subsequent approximations while the installation of the IMPs went ahead. It was only in 1970 that a Network Control Programme with protocols for a host-host connection accessible from the terminals of time-shared systems (Telnet) and for data transmission (FTP) was actually completed.[37]

The first DDP-516 was installed at UCLA on 30 August 1969. It was connected to its host by way of an interface hardware created by the student Mike Wingfield. The second IMP, delivered to the SRI on 1 October of the same year, used a programme created by Duvall, and was used to experiment a connection between the first two nodes of the network. Other procedures were subsequently applied to the third and fourth IMPs, which were installed in November at UCSB and in December at the University of Utah. Communication took place through designated telephone lines at 50 kilobits per second, which was much faster than an ordinary line, and for which specific contracts had been drawn up with AT&T and with other companies for certain sections of the lines.[38]

As Figure 19 shows, Arpanet's structure in late 1969 was still very simple, so much so that only four of the six theoretically possible connections were activated, with the SRI's node in Menlo Park serving as a channel between Salt Lake City, Santa Barbara and Los Angeles. Installing two more lines would not have been impossible, but with the connection of many other nodes, a high redundancy network such as the one imagined by Baran would have become extremely expensive, as the number of telephone lines would have grown exponentially. It was therefore necessary to single out the circuits that allowed costs and communication time to be optimized among the many possible combinations, keeping in mind the traffic of the various nodes and avoiding problems with congestion.

The task of defining the topology of the network was entrusted to a small company, the Network Analysis Corporation, recently founded by Howard Frank, previously a professor of Electronic Engineering at Berkeley.[39] His work, together and in connection with that of the BBN and Kleinrock's team, steered Arpanet's growth to ensuring the highest level of reliability.[40] As a result, the

36. As in other cases, the document was periodically updated during 1976: BBN Report n. 1822, "Interface Message Processor: Specifications for the Interconnection of a Host and an IMP," January 1976 revision, http://bitsavers.informatik.uni-stuttgart.de/pdf/bbn/imp/BBN1822_Jan1976.pdf.

37. See Carr, Crocker and Cerf, "HOST-HOST Communication Protocol in the ARPA Network," pp. 591-595.

38. DARPA, "A History of the Arpanet: The First Decade," p. II-10.

39. See Howard Frank, Ivan T. Frisch and Wushow Chou, "Topological Considerations in the Design of the ARPA Computer Network," in AFIPS, *Proceedings of the May 5-7, 1970, Spring Joint Computer Conference*, New York, ACM, 1972, pp. 581-587.

40. See Howard Frank, Robert E. Kahn and Leonard Kleinrock, "Computer Communication Network Design: Experience with Theory and Practice," in AFIPS, *Proceedings of the May 16-18, 1972, Spring Joint Computer Conference*, New York, ACM, 1972, pp. 255-270.

Figure 19 – The initial configuration of Arpanet

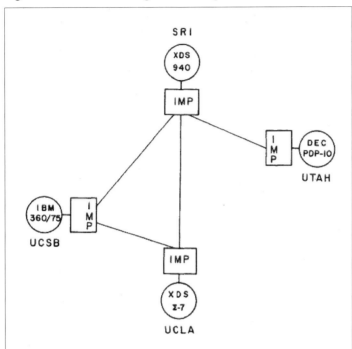

Source: Carr, Crocker and Cerf, "HOST-HOST Communication Protocol in the ARPA Network," p. 590.

network spread rapidly, growing from 4 to 9 nodes in June 1970, to 13 the following December, 18 in September 1971, 25 in March 1972 and 29 in August of the following year. A new Terminal Interface Processor (TIP) that had been tested at the BBN in 1971 facilitated this growth. The terminal used a Honeywell DDP-316 minicomputer and joined the functions of an IMP and a host, placing numerous terminals in direct communication with each other while increasing the network's speed. Figure 20 demonstrates how four clusters were configured at the time, two on the West Coast and two on the East Coast, connected by cross-country telephone lines.

As Roberts and Wessler explained, the network's development saw two distinct phases. The first was of an experimental nature and concluded in 1971 with the connection of 13 centres that were involved to various degrees in constructing Arpanet. Everyone was committed to computer research and worked especially in the fields of time-sharing, graphics and artificial intelligence.[41] During this period, a community that comprised, according to the authors, about 2,000 people used

41. The group included UCLA, SRI, UCSB, the University of Utah, RAND, SDC, MIT, BBN, Harvard University, Stanford University, Carnegie Mellon University, the Lincoln Laboratory and the University of Illinois. The connections grew to 14 in 1971 when a second

Figure 20 – Arpanet in August 1972

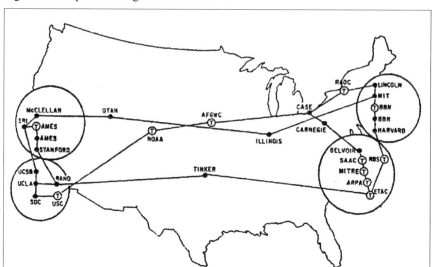

Source: DARPA, "A History of the Arpanet: The First Decade," p. III-82.

the network to develop and test it, to connect with the NIC and to share both software resources and "the educational experience of using a wider variety of systems than previously possible."[42]

However, ARPA's programme was further reaching and more ambitious: it amounted to a project of national interest that went beyond computer science to be a resource that could be used in other fields. It was no surprise that Roberts and Wessler stated that in the second phase they would work with three different research sectors funded by ARPA: Behavioural Science, Climate Dynamics and Seismology. In these sectors, the use of the network would be "oriented more toward the distribution and sharing of stored data, and in the latter two fields the use of the ILLIAC IV at the University of Illinois."[43] Figure 21, which depicts the growth in Arpanet's nodes from December 1969 to August 1972, demonstrates the clear distinction between the two phases. It illustrates how after September 1971 the nodes specifically dedicated to computer science did not change, while those from different fields increased significantly.

Roberts and Wessler made no reference to the connection of military sites, yet these comprised 7 (not including ARPA itself) of the 27 institutions connected to Arpanet in August 1972. In June 1969, Rechtin discussed the attachment of

experimental link was installed at the BBN to test the new Terminal Interface Processor. At this time NASA's Ames Research Center also had two connections.

42. Roberts and Wessler, "Computer Network Development to Achieve Resource Sharing," p. 548.

43. *Ibid.*

Figure 21 – The network's development, 1969-1972

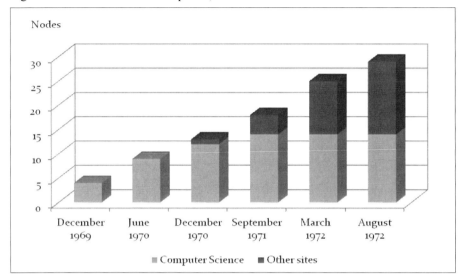

Source: our elaboration from DARPA, "A History of the Arpanet: The First Decade," pp. III-77 – III-82, III-89. The distinction between sites dedicated primarily to research in field of computer research and other sites has been inferred from other sources.

the Department of Defence's installations as the "final DoD application." Had its time thus come or had it been cut short with respect to predictions? To clarify this point we must reconsider the political-institutional context within which the early development of the Net was unfolding.

Research and Politics during the Vietnam Years

An amendment that was proposed in late 1969 by the democratic senator Mike Mansfield, and accepted in the Military Procurement Authorization Act of 1970, proscribed that "none of the funds authorized to be appropriated by this act may be used to carry out any research project or study unless such project or study has a direct and apparent relationship to a specific military function or operation."[44] This law was but one sign of many indicating the difficult situation that the Vietnam War's development had created for the Defence Department. It had exposed the Department to the crossfire of the growing hostility in Congress and the antiwar protests, which were increasingly common on American university campuses.

44. William G. Bell, ed., "Department of the Army Historical Summary: Fiscal Year 1970", Washington, DC, Center of Military History, United States Army, 1973, p. 123, http://www.history.army.mil/books/DAHSUM/1970/chIX.htm#n1.

The policy to "Vietnamize" the war pursued by the new Republican president Richard M. Nixon, who had taken office in January 1969, certainly did not ease tensions.[45] Indeed, autumn 1969 was a period of large demonstrations that continued and only intensified in subsequent years, during which American de-escalation was accompanied by massive bombing of the Indo-Chinese peninsula, especially Cambodia. In truth, the Mansfield amendment was not strictly enforced and its effects were limited. This was in part because the following 1971 Act adopted a more moderate formula: "an increase in Government support of basic scientific research is necessary to preserve and strengthen the sound technological base essential both to protection of the national security and the solution of unmet domestic needs."[46]

A large part of this support was nonetheless attributed to the National Science Foundation, and federal funds diminished as a result of the country's difficult economic-financial situation, which in 1971 pushed the USA to put an end to the gold dollar standard system, enacted in 1944 at the Bretton Woods conference. In any case, in the areas of mathematics and computer sciences, basic research was not affected.[47] Only the Department of Defence reduced its support, placing greater emphasis on applied research, and both the Mansfield amendment and the student movements contributed to this. As has been observed,

> there was an unintended symmetry between these two developments. The Mansfield Amendment deprived universities of the most congenial kinds of support from the DoD, those unrelated to military purposes. Student protesters excised the least congenial forms of research, those which were most immediately linked to military ends.[48]

ARPA was in any case one of the Department structures least affected by these changes, even though it "felt compelled to develop entirely new layers of paper relevance justification requirements and has appeared to move toward shorter-term programs with more direct military applications."[49] Indeed, in the three-year period from 1970 to 1972, the agency's funds increased 6% in comparison to 1969. As for IPTO, the increase of its budget was more than double (13.3%) and was almost entirely spent on the two most difficult projects of the period: Arpanet and

45. See Andrew L. Johns, *Vietnam's Second Front: Domestic Politics, the Republican Party, and the War*, Lexington, University Press of Kentucky, 2010; Jeffrey P. Kimball, "Richard M. Nixon and the Vietnam War," in *The Columbia History of the Vietnam War*, ed. by David L. Anderson, New York, Columbia University Press, 2011, p. 217-244.

46. Barber Associates, *The Advanced Research Project Agency*, pp. VIII-19 - VIII-20.

47. Compared to 1969 the average values of the period 1970 to 1972 indicate a 3.2% increase in base research and a 19.4% decrease in applied research: Kenneth Flamm, *Targeting the Computer: Government Support and International Competition*, Washington, DC, Brookings Institution, 1977, p. 245.

48. Roger L. Geiger, *Research and Relevant Knowledge: American Research Universities Since World War II*, 2nd ed., New Brunswick, NJ, Transaction Publishers, 2009, p. 241. The Pentagon's support for academic research decreased from 279 million dollars in 1969 to 184 million 5 years later. See also Bruce L.R. Smith and Joseph J. Karlesky, *The State of Academic Science: The Universities in the Nation's Research Effort*, New York, Change Magazine Press, 1977, p. 35.

49. Barber Associates, *The Advanced Research Project Agency*, p. VIII-20; Flamm, *Targeting the Computer*, p. 88 note 122.

the ILLIAC IV supercomputer, which was under construction at the University of Illinois, Urbana. It is significant, however, that this increase did not receive any response in the budget chapters. Officially, IPTO's funds decreased and in 1971-1972 a sizeable budget was instead assigned to an item of a new institution called Distributed Information Systems (DIS). The sub-section Distributed Networks, whose allowance increased from 3.3 million dollars in 1970 to 7.3 million in 1972, was also transferred to DIS.[50]

On 20 April 1971, ARPA's new director, Stephen J. Lukasik – a physicist who had come to the agency in 1966 from the Stevens Institute of Technology in Hoboken, New Jersey, just after Rechtin – explained to the Senate commission that these new developments reflected "a continuing ARPA movement from basic research in this area to the exploratory development phases." He cited the network as a good example of that transition and added, "in fiscal year 1971 this program was transferred to DIS and development initiated to bring this new capability to service readiness. By the end of fiscal year 1972 several joint service tests should be underway on the network in the areas of logistics and command and control."[51] The fact remains, moreover, that management of the projects categorized under Distributed Information Systems was also attributed to IPTO. Therefore, what Lukasik stated in 1991 was plausible; that is, the decision to institute it "was a little bit [...] tactical" to avoid a decrease in the agency's budget.[52] Essentially, ARPA attempted to adapt to the new context of the early 1970s and maintained a low profile, in part because its possibilities remained uncertain.

According to some, the agency's relocation to Rosslyn highlighted its precarious state, even though the new office was also in Arlington, Virginia and was only two and a half miles away from the previous one in the Pentagon. On the contrary, a more stable arrangement was made in March 1972, when a directive from the Department of Defence separated ARPA from Defence Research and Engineering's management, placing it under the direct control of the offices of the Secretary of Defence. The agency's name subsequently became DARPA, and sometimes the additional D for Defence was understood as a sign of a desire to underline its military purposes. In truth, however, no further significant changes took place. The fact remains that in any case, those who intervened after the Mansfield amendment were anything but insignificant, and they allow us to better understand the early development of Arpanet.

In August 1972 only two academic nodes had been added to those that were connected in the first phase: Case Western Reserve University and the University

50. DoD Appropriations for Fiscal Year 1972, *Hearings Before a Subcommittee of the Committee on Appropriations, United States Senate, Ninety-Second Congress, First Session,* Washington, DC, US Government Printing Office, 1971, pp. 646-647. The IPTO went from 23.5 million dollars in 1970 to 16.2 million in 1971 and to 14.3 million in 1972. 10.5 million dollars in 1971 and 17.2 million in 1972 were assigned to the Distributed Information Systems.

51. *Ibid.,* pp. 648, 698.

52. Judy O'Neill, "An Interview with Stephen Lukasik" conducted 17 October 1991, University of Minnesota, CBI Collections, Oral History 232, http://conservancy.umn.edu/bitstream/107446/1/oh232sl.pdf.

of Southern California. Both were involved in programmes funded by ARPA for the security of time-shared systems and the network,[53] as was the National Bureau of Standards, which was also connected in the same year.[54] The US Air Force and the MITRE Corporation also participated in these programmes. Connected to Arpanet from 1971, the latter was also the head of various command and control projects. Among the other new nodes, three of them were directly involved with the ILLIAC IV.

ILLIAC IV was a computer with 64 parallel operating processors, which should have made it fifty times faster than the normal machines of the period.[55] Due to its calculating power, it was capable of processing an enormous quantity of data, including those related to climatological and oceanic studies, meteorological forecasts and the effect of underground nuclear explosions, "all of which have a major significance to the Defence Department."[56] It is thus not surprising that in 1972 the National Oceanic and Atmospheric Administration (NOAA) was connected to Arpanet, even though it was taking longer than predicted to get ILLIAC IV off the ground. It is also no coincidence that already in 1971 NASA's Ames Research Centre joined the network: as well as the fact that it was NASA that sent the NOAA's meteorological satellites into orbit, the Centre performed sophisticated calculations of fluid mechanics for the planning of aerospace vehicles, towards which the new supercomputer could make an important contribution.[57]

It might seem less obvious that a second network connection was installed at the Ames Research Centre in 1972, if it were not for the fact it was decided to transfer ILLIAC IV here. In the early months of 1970, when protests against the Vietnam War were reaching their peak, the University of Illinois' campus was shaken by a wave of protests against the programme. Thousands of students mobilized when they learned that the computer would be used for two thirds of the time by ARPA ("an agency deeply involved in counterinsurgency operations")

---

53. IPTO set up a task force for these problems in 1967, see Willis H. Ware, "Security Controls for Computer Systems (U): Report of Defense Science Board Task Force on Computer Security," 11 February 1970, http://csrc.nist.gov/publications/history/ware70.pdf.

54. A number of Trojan horses were already identified at the time: James P. Anderson, "Computer Security Technology Planning Study," October 1972, p. 62, http://csrc.nist.gov/publications/history/ande72.pdf. See also Adam L. Young, "Trojan Horse Programs," in *Handbook of Information Security Volume 3: Threats, Vulnerabilites, Prevention, Detection and Management Contents*, ed. by Hossein Bigdoli, Hoboken, NJ, Wiley, 2006, p. 107-118.

55. See Wendell J. Bouknight, Stewart A. Denenberg, David E. McIntire, J. Michael Randal, Amed H. Sameh and Daniel L. Slotnick, "The Illiac IV System," *Proceedings of the IEEE*, 60, no. 4 (1972): pp. 369-388; R. Michael Hord, *The Illiac IV: The First Supercomputer*, Rockville, MD, Computer Science Press, 1982.

56. DoD Appropriations for 1971, *Hearings Before the Subcommittee of the Committee on Appropriations, House of Representatives, Ninety-First Congress, Second Session*, Part 5, Washington, DC, US Government Printing Office, 1970, p. 1047; DoD Appropriations for Fiscal Year 1972, *Hearings Before a Subcommittee of the Committee on Appropriations*, p. 653.

57. See the annual reports by the centre's director in *The Astrogram*, 1 March 1973, http://history.arc.nasa.gov/Astrogram/astrogram_1973_3.pdf and 1 March 1974, http://history.arc.nasa.gov/Astrogram/astrogram_1974_3.pdf.

Figure 22 – An image of ILLIAC IV

Source: http://www.nasa.gov/images/content/704944main_48i_mwm_boyd_mark_4_full.jpg.

and for the development of "more sophisticated nuclear weaponry."[58] After these disturbances the agency decided to relocate the ILLIAC IV at the Ames Research Centre as soon as it was operational. The campus newspaper attributed this development to the protests in previous months.[59] Lukasik denied it, citing considerations relative to the costs and efficiency of the programme, but it is clear that the situation created problems for ARPA and weighed on the relationship between the Department of Defence and the universities.[60]

58. "Defeat Illiac Center Proposal," *The Daily Illini*, 6 March 1970. The newspaper articles on the "Illiac Controversy" are viewable at http://www.library.illinois.edu/dnc/Default/Skins/ UIUC/Client.asp?Skin=UIUC&AppName=2&AW=1370507112413. On this issue, see Patrick D. Kennedy, "Reactions Against the Vietnam War and Military-Related Targets on Campus: The University of Illinois as a Case Study, 1965-1972," *Illinois Historical Journal*, 84, no. 2 (1991): pp. 101-118; David Bell, "The Battle for the University: The Vietnam-Era Student Movement at Universities in Central Illinois," 2004, p. 16-23, http://ia700208.us.archive.org/7/ items/battleforunivers00bell/battleforunivers00bell.pdf.

59. "Defense Department Reviews Decision to Install Illiac Here," *The Daily Illini*, 15 May 1970.

60. See Barber Associates, *The Advanced Research Project Agency*, pp. VIII-62 – VIII-67, which devotes ample space to the "Illiac controversy," considering it "an illustration of the sad state of DoD-university relations in the late 1960s and the problems posed for ARPA by these developments."

Indeed, some of the military structures that had been connected to the network in 1972, mostly from the aviation sector, were involved in the ILLIAC IV project: the Environmental Technical Application Centre, the Seismic Array Analysis Centre and the Air Force Global Weather Centre. Completing the picture were two USAF bases (Tinker in Oklahoma and McLellan in California), Fort Belvoir (the seat of a military engineering school) and the Rome Air Development Centre, which was a partner of MIT and Harvard University in a project in the behavioural sciences sector funded by ARPA.

There is no need to state that these structures were involved in military activities. They also shared strategically significant programmes with various civil centres connected to Arpanet in its second phase of development. At the same time, however, their objectives were not solely military. It can be assumed that the attempts made during the period to accelerate the "final DoD application", which Rechtin had spoken about, were the upshot of the new context that had emerged following the Mansfield amendment. The emphasis that Lukasik placed on the passage from basic research to exploratory development responded to the need to justify to the Department of Defence and the US Congress the development of IPTO's projects, which were the least oriented towards military objectives among of those pursued by ARPA. In any case, Arpanet was never the target of criticism in the same way as ILLIAC IV. This does not mean, however, that the Department of Defence did not use it for operations that were capable of provoking protests, as an incident during these years attests.

In January 1970, a young ex-military intelligence official, Christopher H. Pyle, revealed to the press that in 1967 the army had gathered information on the so-called civil disturbances of those years, monitoring no less than 100,000 dissidents, most of whom were involved in civil rights and anti-Vietnam war movements.[61] The news caused uproar, the first amendment was invoked[62] and a Senate sub-committee for constitutional rights headed by the democrat Sam J. Ervin Jr. investigated the activities. From the outset, military authorities promised that databases on civilians (some of which were computerized) had been destroyed, but the investigation revealed that, although many records no longer existed, "many others undoubtedly have been hidden away."[63]

61. Christopher H. Pyle, "CONUS Intelligence: The Army Watches Civilian Politics," *Washington Monthly*, January 1970, pp. 4-16. CONUS stood for Continental US. See also Christopher H. Pyle, "CONUS Revisited: The Army Covers Up," *Washington Monthly*, July 1970, pp. 49-58; Christopher H. Pyle, *Military Surveillance of Civilian Politics, 1967-1970*, New York, Garland, 1986; Joan M. Jensen, *Army Surveillance in America, 1775-1980*, New Haven – London, Yale University Press, 1991, pp. 241-247.

62. "Congress shall make no law respecting an establishment of religion, or prohibiting the free exercise thereof; or abridging the freedom of speech, or of the press; or the right of the people peaceably to assemble, and to petition the Government for a redress of grievances," Constitution of the United States, Bill of Rights, http://www.archives.gov/exhibits/charters/bill_of_rights_transcript.html.

63. "Army Surveillance of Civilians, A Documentary Analysis by the Staff of the Subcommittee on Constitutional Rights, Committee on the Judiciary, United States Senate", Washington, DC, US Government Printing Office, 1972, p. VI, http://bkofsecrets.files.wordpress.com/2009/06/armyciviliansurveillance.pdf.

Some years later it was discovered that in January 1972 the digital portion of those documents had been moved from the mainframe of the Fort Holabird US Army Investigative Records Repository to another office, passing through the Massachusetts Institute of Technology "via a Defence Department computer network."[64] Investigations led by the MIT student newspaper, "The Tech," played a fundamental role in this discovery. In 1975, the paper made explicit reference to Arpanet and affirmed that the documents had been moved first to the Lincoln Laboratory and then to the Natick Army Research Centre.[65] However, the administration and the military authorities' reticence never allowed the full truth to come out. In April 1974, the chairman of the Defence Investigative Review Council, David O. Cooke, assured the Senate sub-committee on constitutional rights that all files on civilians had been destroyed. However, he must not have been very convincing, since Ervin replied "I must say your statement is about the most interesting literature I have read since I read Jules Verne's 'Twenty Thousand Leagues Under the Sea.'"[66]

Following approval of the Privacy Act in the same year, on 3 June 1975 Cooke was once again called to testify, this time in front of a sub-committee of the House of Representatives. Pressed by deputies Bella Savitzky Abzug and Andrew Maguire with a barrage of questions intended to reveal if, how and where the civil files had been moved, Cooke presented information about Arpanet, but for the rest mostly defended himself by replying "I don't know" and "I am not sure." In all instances, he added, if those documents had not been destroyed it was "through inadvertence or other reasons." As can be inferred from the minutes, moreover, Cooke's task was facilitated by the fact that his interlocutors only had a very vague idea about what a computer network consisted in.[67]

In the sub-committee's 1973 conclusive report, Ervin had invoked the "Orwellian nightmare of a government always watching, and, armed with the knowledge of its citizens' thoughts and ambitions, silencing their adverse views with real or presumed threats of reprisals, in a vision which has haunted twentieth-century."[68] Despite this, the press never picked up Arpanet's role in the event. Why was this?

64. "Supplemetary Detailed Staff Reports on Intelligence Activities and the Rights of Americans," Book III, "Final Report of the Select Committee to Study Governmental Operations with Respect to Intelligence Activities United States Senate," 23 April 1976, http://www.icdc.com/~paulwolf/cointelpro/churchfinalreportIIIk.htm.

65. Norman Sandler and Mike McNamee, "Computers Carried Army Files; MIT Investigation Underway," *The Tech*, 11 April 1975. The newspaper is consultable at http://tech.mit.edu/browse.html.

66. "Military Surveillance. Hearings Before the Subcommittee on Constitutional Rights of the Committee on the Judiciary United States Senate, Ninety-Third Congress, Second Session on S. 2318," Washington, DC, US Government Printing Office, 1974, pp. 103, 116, http://ia600303.us.archive.org/4/items/militarysurveill00unit/militarysurveill00unit.pdf.

67. "Implementation of the Privacy Act of 1974: Data Banks, Hearing Before a Subcommittee of the Committee on Government Operations, House of Representative, Ninety-Fourth Congress, First Session, June 3, 1975," Washington, DC, US Government Printing Office, 1975, pp. 52-70, http://babel.hathitrust.org/cgi/pt?id=purl.32754075436844;page=root ;seq=2;view=1up;size=100;orient=0.

68. "Military Surveillance of Civilian Politics. A Report of the Subcommittee on Constitutional Rights, Committee on the Judiciary, United States Senate," Washington, DC,

In all likelihood, it was in part because of two other events that attracted the attention of the mass media and to a certain extent distracted the public opinion from the investigation of the military surveillance of civilians. The first event was the Pentagon Papers, a monumental report on America's involvement in Vietnam commissioned by McNamara at the Defence Department in 1967, excerpts of which were shared in 1971 by one of its authors to *The New York Times*. The publication of the papers not only revealed unknown aspects of the American intervention in Indo-China to the general public, but also illustrated how the government had lied to the country on many occasions. These revelations had a major impact on the democrats in particular, who were in power during the central years of the war. Nixon attempted to both use the papers to his advantage and to stop them, but the Supreme Court declared the publication of the documents legitimate. The Pentagon Papers episode, which is often cited as an antecedent to the Wikileaks scandal,[69] and the uproar that followed were closely connected to the other incident that overlapped with the civil disturbances issue: Watergate.[70] The scandal broke in 1972 and led two years later to Nixon's resignation as president of the United States.[71]

However, although this all contributed to placing the issue of military surveillance of civilians on the back burner, this was also the result of the fact that most people knew nothing of the network's existence, and even those who were aware of it did not know how it worked or its potential. On the contrary, this is the likely reason why Arpanet was protected from controversy and protests such as those seen for ILLIAC IV.[72]

Email

Even in scientific circles there was little knowledge of the network. It appears that the efforts of Roberts and others to spread the word about the results they had obtained by granting interviews and giving presentations at conventions had not

US Government Printing Office, 1973, p. 118, http://students.washing ton.edu/trevorg/pdfs/Domestic%20Intelligence/Military%20Surveillance%20of%20Civilian%20Politics%201973.pdf (accessed 2 February 2012).

69. For a comparison of the two cases, see Patricia L. Bellia, "WikiLeaks and the Institutional Framework for National Security Disclosures," *The Yale Law Journal*, 121, no. 6 (2012): pp. 1448-1526.

70. See David Rudenstine, *The Day the Presses Stopped: A History of the Pentagon Papers Case*, Berkeley – Los Angeles, University of California Press, 1996.

71. See Keith W. Olson, *Watergate: The Presidential Scandal That Shocked America*, Lawrence, University Press of Kansas, 2003.

72. It is less clear if and to what extent members of the community were aware of the issues, besides those who transferred the military files to the Lincoln Laboratory. It is significant, however, that the Harvard jurist Arthur Miller, author of a book with a preface written by Ervin, thanked Licklider for his help untangling the technical aspects of the problem: Arthur R. Miller *The Assault on Privacy: Computers, Data Banks, and Dossiers*, Ann Arbor, University of Michigan Press, 1971, also at http://www.archive.org/details/assaultonprivacy00mill.

entirely paid off. Ultimately, it was a public demonstration organized in Washington in October 1972 for the first International Conference on Computer Communication that brought Arpanet out of its "semi-clandestine" status. Robert E. Kahn worked on the event for an entire year in collaboration with Albert Vezza, a member of Project MAC's staff, and the two of them also involved Cerf, Postel and Robert M. Metcalfe from MIT, as well as numerous other members of the IPTO community. Kahn wrote that "the theme of the demonstration will be on the value of computer communication networks, emphasizing topics such as data base retrieval, combined use of several machines, real-time data access, interactive cooperation, simulation systems, simplified hard copy techniques, and so forth."[73]

A network node and various terminals were installed at the Washington Hilton Hotel, which was crowded with hundreds of scientists, technicians and managers from the field, and the equipment was used to stage 19 different "scenarios." Some of these were sure to have an impact on the media, such as the one in which two programmes prompted an automatic conversation between a psychiatrist and a patient, both virtual. The first programme was on a BBN machine, the second was at Stanford's artificial intelligence laboratory, and the data passed through UCLA's host.[74] The demonstration was a huge success and represented a turning point in the network's development, because it was the premise for growth that was no longer limited to ARPA's military, institutional or academic contractors. Less than two years later the network's nodes had grown to 48, and it is significant that some of these were private, such as Culler-Harrison Inc., Systems Control Inc., Tymshare Inc., Univac and the Xerox Corporation.[75] It is equally important, on the other hand, that some of the companies agencies were connected in various ways to the research experiences of the IPTO community. For example, Glen J. Culler founded Culler-Harrison Inc. in 1969, and Taylor had gone to work at Xerox PARC.

However, one innovation in particular contributed to making 1972 a turning point in the history of the network: email, which was destined to radically modify the network's very conception.[76] Email was not entirely new because procedures

73. Robert Kahn, "Demonstration at International Computer Communications Conference," RFC 371, July 12, 1972. See also Lawrence G. Roberts and Robert E. Kahn, "Special Project: Participating Demonstrations of a Multi-Purpose Network Linking Dissimilar Computers and Terminals," in *Computer Communications: Impacts and Implications. The First International Conference on Computer Communication, Washington, D.C., October 24-26, 1972*, ed. by Stanley Winkler, New York, ACM, 1972, pp. 40-42.

74. The conversation was published in Vinton G. Cerf, "PARRY Encouters the DOCTOR," RFC 439, 21 January 1973. An enjoyable reenactment of the event is in Hafner and Lyon, *Where Wizards Stay Up Late*, p. 177.

75. "Network Hosts and Associates," June 1974, in Licklider Papers, Box 3, Folder "Arpanet Directory, NIC 22979, June 1974." DARPA, "A History of the Arpanet: The First Decade," III-89 counts only 46 nodes.

76. On the development of email, see Ian R. Hardy, "The Evolution of ARPANET Email," History Thesis Paper, University of California at Berkeley, Spring 1966, http://www.livinginternet.com/References/Ian%20Hardy%20Email%20Thesis.txt and C. Partridge, "Technical Development of Internet Email," *IEEE Annals of the History of Computing*, 30,

for sending messages from one user to another already existed in the single time-shared systems of the 1960s. Nevertheless, it was the entry of such procedures into the network and the developments that followed that led to a great transformation in the history of communications.

The need to create a mailbox protocol on Arpanet was raised in July 1971 in an RFC by Richard W. Watson from Engelbart's group. It would have allowed the NIC to send and receive messages "without having to know the details of path name conventions and file system commands at each site."[77] Perhaps stimulated by this RFC and others that followed,[78] at the end of the same year, a young BBN engineer, Ray Tomlinson, incorporated a protocol for the transmission of files into a local mail programme and used it to send himself a test message through the network. SNDMSG ("send message" – this was the name of Tomlinson's programme) was first mentioned in July 1972 in an RFC that emphasized "networks have great though unexploited potential for inter-personal communication."[79] In this and subsequent RFCs, SNDMSG appears alongside various other informative services without any kind of distinction, which could seem surprising for two reasons in particular.

First of all, Tomlinson had introduced an important innovation, using the @ symbol to separate the user's name from the host's name. In addition to having limited circulation within single local systems, messages until then had not been sent to recipients, but rather deposited in the central computer's memory, from which they could be accessed. Similarly, it was not possible to send a direct response. With SNDMSG's address method, email became interactive, as it allowed for an unmediated connection between sender and recipient that was also individual, because the messages were sent to the single user of a specific host. The second reason for surprise was the exceptional size and speed of email's success, despite the fact that the use of SNDMSG was limited by the variety of the operating systems that existed in the various hosts and the relative languages. Tomlinson's programme worked on TENEX, which was a widely used operating system, and its fortune was at least in part dependent on this. However, again in 1974, for example, it was noted that "the fact that the Multics line-kill character is the at-sign (@) caused grief in reading mail from TENEX users."[80]

Despite this, in less than two years email became the most widely used application on Arpanet. Although we do not have statistical data from the period to document this, every testimony agrees on this point. In 2011, Lukasik mentioned a 1974 study by the MITRE Corporation, according to which email accounted

no. 2 (2008): pp. 3-29. Unless otherwise indicated, in the following pages we refer to these publications in our discussion of the technical aspects.

77. Watson, "A Mail Box Protocol," RFC 196, 20 July 1971.

78. Throughout the year Watson developed the theme, as did Alex McKenzie, Bob Braden, Eric Harslem, John Heafner, John Melvin, Bob Sundberg and Jim White in RFCs 221 on 25 August, 224 on 14 September and 278 on 17 November.

79. John Pickens, "Evaluation of Arpanet Services," RFC 369, 25 July 1972.

80. Kenneth Pogran and Nancy Neigus, "Response to RFC 607, 'Comment on the File Transfer Protocol,'" RFC 614, January 1974.

Figure 23 –Arpanet traffic, 1972-1973

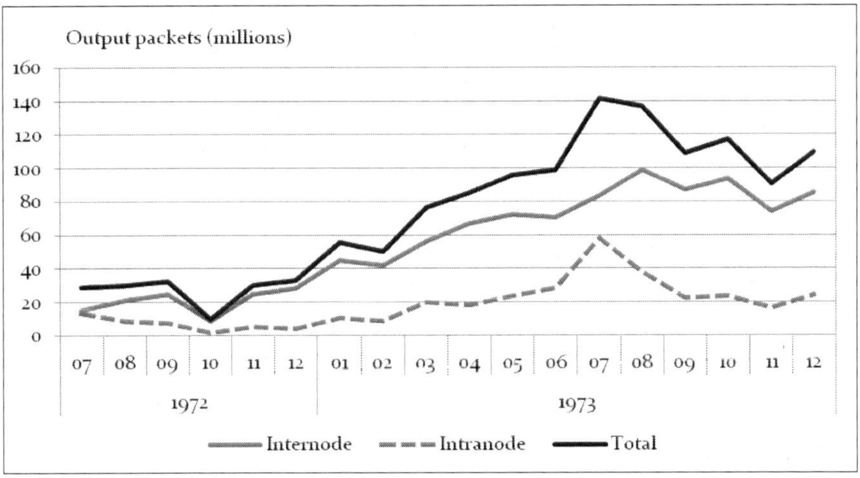

Source: Our elaborations from RFCs 378, 391, 400, 413, 422, 443, 455, 482, 497, 509, 522, 538, 556, 566, 579, 586, 601 and 612.

for 75% of network traffic.[81] As Figure 23 illustrates, from July 1972 to the end of 1973, Arpanet grew 278.4%, eventually levelling off at around 110 million packets a month. It can thus be deduced that in December 1973 more than 80 million packets were carrying email messages.

In order to explain this apparent contradiction, it must be stated that although SNDMSG was rather rudimentary software, it was integrated and perfected over the years. As was the custom, its development was a collective effort that saw the contribution from many members of the Arpanet community. Since a utility to facilitate the reading of the messages did not exist, a programme called READMSG was created, which first Roberts and then Barry D. Wessler worked to improve in 1972. Two graduate students from the University of Southern California, Marty Yonke and John J. Vittal further developed their work in 1973 and 1974, enhancing and integrating the procedures for sending, receiving and managing emails into a single software package. The result, MSG, became the most widely used email programme and remained so for a number of years.

During this early period numerous other "mail systems" were created. In 1979, David Farber counted 26 of them, noting that many "were not formal projects (in the sense of explicitly sponsored research), but things that 'just happened.'"[82] The development of email was naturally connected with the development of the File

81. Stephen J. Lukasik, "Why the Arpanet Was Built," *Annals of the History of Computing*, 33, no.3 (2011): p. 14.
82. Jon Postel, "Summary of Computer Mail Services Meeting Held at BBN on 10 January 1979," RFC 808, 1 March 1982.

Transfer Protocol, in which specific commands for sorting email were inserted,[83] and it was only in November 1977 that an "official" standard was defined.[84]

Another reason for the minimal emphasis on the news of Tomlinson's innovation is the fact that email was introduced and developed on the autonomous initiative of Arpanet's users, but it was not among its institutional goals. In 1967, Roberts had actually written that "in addition to computational network activities, a network can be used to handle interpersonal message transmissions." However immediately afterwards, although he conceded that "this type of service can also be used for educational services and conference activities," Roberts stated that "it is not an important motivation for a network of scientific computers."[85]

However, opposing the bottom-up spontaneous initiative of the users to the activities planned by the network's managers, as has often been done, would give the impression that email's history is much more black and white than is actually the case. This is proven by the fact that IPTO's director was among those who developed its procedures, despite what he had affirmed years before. Moreover, it was his immediate superior, Lukasik, who asked him to do it. Lukasik was impressed by email and began to use it regularly in 1972, but it was precisely for this reason that he needed an instrument to order and manage it more effectively. The fact that ARPA's director used email for his communication urged managers from the agency's various offices to do the same, and this also played a significant part in email's fortune.

The fact remains, as Licklider and Albert Vezza wrote in 1978, that up to that point "in the developmental history of the Arpanet, electronic message service was a sleeper," but "it soon became obvious that the Arpanet was becoming a human-communication medium with very important advantages over normal US mail and over telephone calls." In addition to speed, its advantages included the possibility to "write tersely and type imperfectly, even to an older person in a superior position and even to a person one did not know very well, and the recipient took no offense." Email also made it possible to "proceed immediately to the point without having to engage in small talk first," and it was not necessary that both the sender and the recipient were available at the same time.[86] Indeed email brought about a very important social change in interpersonal communication methods, and rapidly established itself as the primary reason for using the Net. As Licklider wrote in 1974, it was one of its "greatest near term attractions,"[87] because it met a need that was widely felt by its users.

83. See RFCs 385 on 18 August 1972, 561 on 5 September 1973, 680 on 30 April 1975, attributed to Abhay K. Bhushan, Kenneth Pogran, Ray Tomlinson, Jim White, Theodore H. Myer and D. Austin Henderson.

84. David H. Crocker, John J. Vittal, Kenneth Pogran and D. Austin Henderson Jr., "Standard for the Format of ARPA Network Text Messages," RFC 733, 21 November 1977.

85. Roberts, "Multiple Computer Networks and Intercomputer Communication," p. 3.1.

86. Joseph C.R. Licklider and Albert Vezza, "Applications of Information Networks," *Proceedings of the IEEE*, 66, no. 11 (1978): p. 1331.

87. Joseph C.R. Licklider, "Potential of Networking for Research and Education," p. 11, in Licklider Papers, Box 10, Folder "1974." The work was published in Martin Greenberger, Julius Aronofsky, James L. McKenney and William F. Massy, *Networks for Research and*

"The Computer as a Communication Device:" Networks and Mental Models

Although the advent of email marked a turning point in Arpanet's history, this was not because direct communication between human beings had been extraneous to Licklider and his successors' organization of the project up until this point. Of course, the concept of human-computer symbiosis would be sufficient to explain the importance that IPTO's founder attributed to the interaction between human, machine and – through the machine – the body of knowledge, as well as the instruments to access and process it. However, from 1957, Licklider had included the possibility of a discussion between colleagues, in the form of a telephone conversation or conference, as one of the various functions of his thinking centres.[88]

His elaborations had certainly not stopped in the first half of the 1960s. First, he had reproposed the idea for a "face-to-face conference" among geographically distant individuals in a 1965 essay on "The On-Line Intellectual Community."[89] In a paper written two years later for the Carnegie Commission for Educational Television, Licklider had advocated television "as a medium for two-way communication," and envisioned teleconferences "in which the participants remain in their homes or offices yet, with the aid of teletype, telephone, and television, work together in close interaction."[90]

The most significant work on this topic is undoubtedly "The Computer as a Communication Device," which he published with Taylor in 1968, while work was underway to create the network. The authors predicted "in a few years, men will be able to communicate more effectively through a machine than face to face," but right from the start they deliberately placed people at the centre of attention. Licklider and Taylor distinguished themselves from the typical way in which engineers interpreted communication, which was simply about "transferring information from one point to another in codes and signals." They noted:

> But to communicate is more than to send and to receive [...]. We believe that communicators have to do something nontrivial with the information they send and receive. And we believe that we are entering a technological age in which we will be able to interact with the richness of living information – not merely in the passive way that we have become accustomed to using books and libraries, but as active participants in an ongoing process, bringing something to it through our interaction with it, and not simply receiving something from it by our connection to it [...].
>
> Many communications engineers, too, are presently excited about the application of digital computers to communication. However, the function they want computers to implement is the switching function [...]. The switching function is important but it is not the one we

Education: Sharing Computer and Information Resources Nationwide, Cambridge, MA, MIT Press, 1974.

88. Licklider, "The Truly Sage System or Toward a Man-Machine System for Thinking," pp. 77-78.

89. Licklider, "The On-Line Intellectual Community," p. 34.

90. Licklider, "Televistas: Looking Ahead Through Side Windows," pp. 201, 223, http://web.mit.edu/~schultze/www/Licklider-Televistas-Carnegie-1967.pdf (accessed 30 November 2012)

have in mind when we say that the computer can revolutionize communication. We are stressing the modeling function, not the switching function."[91]

The switching function was the primary task that the computer network developed by IPTO, and most particularly the subnet of IMPs, would have to perform. The concept was called store and forward, and it consisted of saving the incoming message and distributing it to another receiver without changing its content. Licklider and Taylor on the other hand emphasized what they referred to as the modelling function. A model, they explained, "is a conceptual structure of abstractions formulated initially in the mind of one of the persons who would communicate." If the mental models of two people were too different, there could be no communication, but if a "common framework" existed between them, then a cooperative model would be possible: "if the two mental models were structurally dissimilar, then the achievement of communication would be signalled by structural changes in one of the models, or both of them."[92] Naturally, as Licklider and Taylor continued to note in 1968, "the meeting of many interacting minds is a more complicated process. Suggestions and recommendations may be elicited from all sides. The interplay may produce, not just a solution to a problem, but a new set of rules for solving problems. That, of course, is the essence of creative interaction." Through the network, in particular, the groups that had already formed around single time-shared systems would be transformed into a "super-community" comprised of many communities "not of common location, but of *common interest*."[93]

The interactive communication that each group would develop with its online community, consisting "of short spurts of dialogue" that would not use telegrams or telephone calls, would be mediated by its OLIVER. This acronym stood for On-Line Interactive Vicarious Expediter and Responder and it designated a series of programmes and data to which many minor and routine operations would be delegated, without requiring the user's attention:

> At your command, your OLIVER will take notes (or refrain from taking notes) on what you do, what you read, what you buy and where you buy it. It will know who your friends are, your mere acquaintances. It will know your value structure, who is prestigious in your eyes, for whom you will do what with what priority, and who can have access to which of your personal files [...]. Some parts of your OLIVER program will be common with parts of other people's OLIVERS; other parts will be custom-made for you, or by you, or will have developed idiosyncrasies through "learning" based on its experience in your service.
> Available within the network will be functions and services to which you subscribe on a regular basis and others that you call for when you need them. In the former group will be investment guidance, tax counselling, selective dissemination of information in your field of specialization, announcement of cultural, sport, and entertainment events that fit your interests, etc. In the latter group will be dictionaries, encyclopaedias, indexes, catalogues,

91. Joseph C.R. Licklider. and Robert W. Taylor, "The Computer as a Communication Device," *Science and Technology*, no. 76 (April 1968), now in "In Memoriam: J.C.R. Licklider, 1915-1990," Palo Alto, CA, Digital Systems Research Center, 7 August 1990, pp. 20, 28, ftp:/ gatekeeper.research.compaq.com/pub/DEC/SRC/research-reports/SRC-061.pdf.

92. *Ibid.*, pp. 22, 24.

93. *Ibid.*, pp. 24, 32, 38.

editing programs, teaching programs, testing programs, programming systems, data bases, and – most important – communication, display, and modeling programs.[94]

There is no need to dwell on the function of social networks or more generally on the so-called web 2.0 to highlight the authors' capacity to anticipate future developments. It is however necessary that we contextualize their ideas – in order also to better understand the meaning of the article – by connecting them to Licklider's previous reflections, of which they were the logical development.

The authors wrote that they chose the acronym OLIVER, in honour of Oliver G. Selfridge, "originator of the concept." A student of Wiener's and scholar of neural networks and artificial intelligence, Selfridge had worked in the Lincoln Laboratory since 1951, and in the 1960s he was the associate director of Project MAC. In 1955, his paper on "Pattern Recognition and Modern Computers" appeared in the acts of the Western Join Computer Conference, below that of Clark and Farley cited above.[95] As Selfridge explained, pattern recognition meant "the extraction of the significant features from a background of irrelevant detail." Simulating this on a computer was of interest to Selfridge both because machines were still not able to do it as well as the human brain, and for the purpose of studying other questions, such as the learning process. He had essentially tried "to specify one way in which certain visual patters can be recognized by the computer, and in which the computer may improve its recognition by learning."[96]

In 1958, after attending the Dartmouth College conference on artificial intelligence, Selfridge had developed these lines of research in a report given at a National Physical Laboratory convention, and this is most likely the piece (also cited in "Man-Computer Symbiosis") to which Licklider and Taylor referred. Inspired by the seventeenth-century poem *Paradise Lost* by John Milton, it was entitled "Pandemonium: A Paradigm for Learning," and it proposed the model for a neural network system for the perception of Morse code and the letters of the alphabet based on the recognition of their most basic components. Each component was recognized by a low level "demon," whose signal was selected by a higher level "demon," and so on.[97]

Perhaps the most innovative aspect of Licklider and Taylor's essay was the application of the mental model concept to a communication mediated by complex procedures such as those of human-machine systems and, above all, of the network being built at the time. The way in which they conceived of interpersonal communication was actually just the logical development of ideas that Licklider had already clearly expressed way back in 1950, when he had participated in the debate following Shannon's presentation at the Macy Conference that year. After he spoke, a psychologist from the University of Michigan, Donald Marquis, had commented with the quip that "the best communication occurs if you say what the

94. *Ibid.*, pp. 34, 38-39.
95. See Oiver G. Selfridge, "Pattern Recognition and Modern Computers," in *Proceedings of the March 1-3, 1955, Western Joint Computer Conference*, ch. 2, p. 81 and note 47; ch. 3, p. 114 and note 58.
96. *Ibid.*, pp. 91, 93.
97. Selfridge, "Pandemonium."

listener expects you to say." Licklider had responded that actually an "optimum degree of correlation between the talker and the listener" was a halfway point: "if the correlation is zero, the listener has no expectations and understands nothing. If the correlation is unity, he doesn't need to listen."[98]

By using the mental model concept, Licklider and Taylor were taking a significant step forward because their work anticipated the full development of modern theories of mental models, which occurred in the 1970s. The Scottish physiologist and psychologist Kenneth J.W. Craik first proposed the concept in 1943 in a book on the nature of explanation. For model, the author intended "any physical or chemical system which has similar relation-structure to that of the process it imitates."

> If the organism carries a "small-scale model" of external reality and of its own possible actions within its head, it is able to try out various alternatives, conclude which is the best of them, react to future situations before they arise, utilize the knowledge of past events in dealing with the present and the future, and in every way to react in a much fuller, safer, and more competent manner to the emergencies which face it.[99]

Craik was not thinking of models that "pictorially" resembled reality, in contrast to what various precursors of mental model theories had done, in particular Charles Sanders Pierce, who Philip N. Johnson-Laird had considered their "intellectual grandfather." Licklider had never made explicit reference to Pierce, but among those precursors was also his professor, Wolfgang Köhler, according to whom "vision creates an isomorphism between brain fields and the world."[100]

As it was almost entirely without citations, "The Computer as a Communication Device" did not reference this work. However, the fact that its authors had set themselves squarely within that genealogy is entirely evident. Indeed, Craik's book had had a significant influence on cybernetics and had been cited many times by those promoting Dartmouth College's artificial intelligence project.[101] Together with a meeting on the theory of information held at MIT in 1956, the project was recognized by many scholars, including George A. Miller, as a founding moment in the so-called cognitive revolution.[102] Finally, the aforementioned studies by

98. Von Foerster, Mead and Teuber, *Cybernetics*, p. 141. See also Dupuy, *Aux origines des sciences cognitives*, p. 128.

99. Kenneth J.W. Craik, *The Nature of Explanation*, Cambridge: Cambridge University Press, 1943, pp. 51, 61.

100. See Philip N. Johnson-Laird, "The History of Mental Models," in *Psychology of Reasoning: Theoretical and Historical Perspectives*, ed. by Ken Manktelow and Man Cheung Chung, New York, Psychology Press, 2004, pp. 181-182; Wolgang Köhler, *The Place of Value in a World of Facts*, New York, Liveright, 1938.

101. See McCarthy, Minsky, Rochester and Shannon, "A Proposal for the Dartmouth Summer Research Project on Artificial Intelligence." Craik was also cited by Minsky, "Matter, Mind and Models," MIT Project MAC, Artificial Intelligence Memo n. 77, MAC-M-230, March 1965, http://dspace.mit.edu/bitstream/handle/1721.1/6119/AIM-077.pdf?sequence=2.

102. See George A. Miller, "The Cognitive Revolution: A Historical Perspective," *Trends in Cognitive Science*, 7, no. 3 (2003): p. 142. More generally see Bernard J. Baars, *The Cognitive Revolution in Psychology*, New York – London: The Guilford Press, 1986. According to George Mandler, the term "revolution" is instead inappropriate: "there were no cataclysmic events, the

Licklider on sound perception, psychophysiological models and dynamic models were also influenced by the same approach.[103]

Compared to these studies, the authors were now shifting the focus of their attention from the human-machine relationship to a direct communication between human beings mediated and sustained by the computer and by the network, recognizing therein a new kind of collective development of knowledge. As to something that could have predicted email, the authors made no reference,[104] but the perspective they were emphasizing went well beyond applications of that kind. Licklider explicitly reiterated as much in 1973, after confirming that to take advantage of the computer's abilities "in formulative thinking" it was essentially necessary to change the expression "'one builds a model in his mind' to 'one builds a model in his computer:'"

> Human communication is not merely sending messages back and forth. It is a joint activity of two or more people – thinking together, solving problems together, making decisions together. More basically, it is modeling together – creating, exploring, comparing, modifying, adjusting, and evaluating models together. Just as modeling is the essential process in thinking, problem solving, and [...] decision making, modeling is the essential process in human communication.[105]

What remains of all this in the documentation produced by those who built the network? In truth, there is not much. In the RFCs, for example, the expression 'dynamic modelling' is only used to indicate the membership structure of some participants, and it is no coincidence that it refers to MIT, specifically to the "PDP-10 at Project MAC, affectionately known as the Dynamic Modeling System."[106] More generally, in their coeval work, traces of the multidisciplinary and anticipating structure that characterized IPTO's early years of activity are nearly non-existent, and can only be found in Engelbart's contributions. Had they gone from poetry to prose, so to speak? In part, yes – also because what Licklider and Taylor referred to as switching function was obviously fundamental to the realization and functioning of Arpanet.

However, despite this, the two perspectives were not as distant as they may initially appear. Indeed, also during this phase Licklider participated in the IPTO

change occurred slowly in different subfields over some 10 to 15 years, there was no identifiable flashpoint or leader, and there were no Jacobins," George Mandler, "Origins of the Cognitive (R)Evolution," *Journal of History of the Behavioral Sciences*, 38, no. 4 (2002): p. 339.

103. See above, pp. 91-92.

104. References to email were made in Joseph C.R. Licklider, "Communication and Computers," in *Communication, Language, and Meaning: Psychological Perspectives*, ed. by George A. Miller, New York, Basic Books, 1973, p. 206 and in Licklider, "Potential of Networking for Research and Education." In the first case, the author refers to the procedures for sending messages preceding Tomlinson's innovation.

105. Licklider, "Communication and Computers," pp. 198-199, 205.

106. Vezza, "MIT-DMS on Vacation," RFC 419, 12 December 1972. A research group by this name had been formed by Licklider in 1968 "to simplify human-computer interaction through visual interfaces," Simon L. Garfinkel, *Architects of the Information Society: Thirty-Five Years of the Laboratory of Computer Science at MIT,* (edited by Hal Abelson, preface by Michael L. Dertouzos), Cambridge, MA, MIT Press, 1999, p. 44.

community's work,[107] and he certainly did not fail to exercise his influence on its youngest members, who had joined the project in the network's planning phase. This may also explain why many of them claimed to be situated in a sort of genealogy that started with Linklider and led to Roberts.

As for Roberts, he also hailed from the same multidisciplinary cultural environment whose main centre was in the Lincoln Laboratory. In the first half of the 1960s, especially, he had worked intensely on pattern recognition, assuming the same reference points as Licklider and not without explicit references to psychophysiological theories.[108] It was perhaps no coincidence that when he presented Arpanet to the outside world in 1971, Roberts compared computer-to-computer communication with people-to-people communication through telegraphs. Indeed, neither was interactive, in contrast to telephone communications. With regard to the latter, the author clearly echoed a series of arguments by Licklider, writing:

> Considering people somewhat mechanistically, we might view their use of the telephone as inter-human resource sharing. To solve a problem, a man will call those people who have bits of data which he needs and will call on specialists for opinions, thus making use of other human resources. This is achieved because the media is appropriately responsive for human requirements and permits interactive conversation, thus eliminating the need for transmitting excessive detail, much of which may be unnecessary. Also, with an interactive dialogue, information does not need to be formatted in a standard way since details can always be clarified if misunderstood.

Predicting "teleconferencing, publishing, library services, and office paperwork filing and distribution," Roberts added:

> Communication between computers would most likely be effected in an analogous manner if a data communication system were made available which matched the needs of computers as well as the phone matches the needs of humans [...]. If it permitted truly interactive conversations between a large ensemble of computers the effect should be much the same in permitting remote access to specialized hardware and software resources, joint problem solving and the dynamic retrieval of data from remote files.[109]

---

107. In October 1971, for example, Licklider was chairman of a Network Working Group seminar intended "to formulate the problem of holding person-to-person conversations ('dialogues') over the network and engaging in various kinds of interactive cooperation" and subsequently he coordinated a committee, consisting of Robert Balzer, Robert Bressler, William Duvall and Warren Teitelman, to develop the issue. See Licklider Papers, Box 10, Folder "ARPA 1971."

108. See Lawrence G. Roberts, "Pattern Recognition With An Adaptative Network," paper presented in 1960 at the international convention of the Institute of Radio Engineers, later published in Uhr, *Pattern recognition*, p. 295; Lawrence G. Roberts, "Recent Development in Optical Character Recognition at M.I.T.," in *Optical Character Recognition*, ed. by George L. Fisher, Jr., Donald K. Pollock, Bernard Radack and Mary E. Stevens, Washington, DC, Spartan Books, 1962, p. 209; Roberts, "Machine Perception Of Three-Dimensional Solids." All three of these essays can be accessed at http://www.packet.cc/.

109. Lawrence G. Roberts, "ARPA Network Implications," *Educom*, 6, no. 3 (1971): pp. 5, 8, in http://www.packet.cc. See also Lawrence G. Roberts, "A Forward Look," *Signal*, 25, no. 12 (1971): pp. 77-81, in http://www.packet.cc.

5. Epilogue

From Arpanet to Internet

Arpanet's nodes rose from 29 in August 1972 to 58 in July 1977, and during this period traffic on the network increased tenfold, from 970,000 to 9.7 million packets.[1] Five years later, in March 1982, a report by the Network Information Centre listed 235 host computers.[2] Not long after in 1983, Roberts cited 400 hosts "in all the interconnected networks",[3] and in the same year the Internet Systems Consortium counted 562 of them. Subsequently, this number continued to rise exponentially – particularly in the second half of the 1980s – and in 1987 it saw a record 453.6% increase. In October 1989, on the eve of Arpanet's closure, the 1,961 hosts present in 1985 had become 159,000. Over the next decade, during the Internet boom years, the increase in the number of hosts continued uninterrupted, and by the year 2000 they had surpassed 93 million in number (Figure 24).

From the outset the growth in the number of hosts was, among other things, due to the birth of new networks, the first of which were the French Cyclades and Réseau à Commutation par Paquets (RCP) in 1973-1974. Others followed, including the American Telenet in 1975, the European Informatic Network (EIN) in 1976, the British Experimental Packet Switching System (EPSS) and the Canadian Datapac in 1977, the French Transpac and the Japanese DX-2 in 1978, and so on. The exact number of networks in existence at the various dates is more difficult to say with any accuracy, in part because some of them shut down after just a few years of existence, while others merged with different networks, but also and above all because of the various meanings associated each time with the terms net and network.

As these structures grew and came to include a growing number of nodes, they were also differentiated and organized into a sort of hierarchy. Beginning with Arpanet, which from early on extended beyond American borders by experimenting, as we will see, with new radio and satellite connections, supranational networks

1. DARPA, "A History of the Arpanet: The First Decade," p. III-89.
2. "Arpanet Directory," NIC 4900, March 1982, prepared for Defense Communications Agency, produced and published at the Network Information Centre, SRI, in Licklider Papers, Box 3, Folder "Arpanet Directory, NIC 4900, March 1982."
3. Lawrence G. Roberts, "The ARPANET and Computer Networks," p. 152.

Figure 24 – Internet hosts, 1981-2000

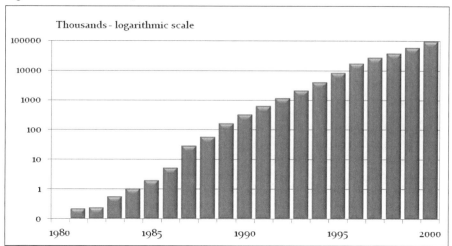

Source: Internet Systems Consortium, "Internet Host Count History," http://ftp.isc.org/www/survey/reports/2012/07/.

joined national ones. Furthermore, additional networks in each country became more common. These included regional and interregional networks (Wide Area Networks (WAN)), and more circumscribed metropolitan networks, the density of which was proportionate to the population. Finally, Local Area Networks (LAN) formed at the lowest level – at times in a single location and at times in multiple buildings in close proximity, such as on a university campus – and these replaced the systems formed by terminals connected to a single host.[4]

However, and in contrast with what is commonly believed, given that the networks' growth took place from the largest to the smallest and not vice versa, this multi-level framework was actually anything by rigid. Indeed, in order to connect with each other, many networks skipped a number of steps, thus provoking irregular and rather complex ramifications. Of the 42 networks connected to Arpanet in September 1981, for example, some were local to the BBN, SRI and Stanford University.[5] As for those outside of the United States, this was also the case for the network created by Davies at the National Physical Laboratory.[6]

---

4. The advantages of a structure like this were illustrated from 1973 onwards by Howard Frank, "The Practical Impact of the Recent Computer Advances on the Analysis and Design of Large Scale Networks," May 1973, http://www.dtic.mil/cgi-bin/Get TRDoc?AD=AD0767403 &Location=U2&doc=GetTRDoc.pdf.

5. Jon Postel, "Assigned Numbers," RFC 790, September 1981.

6. See R. A. Scantlebury and P. T. Wilkinson, "The National Physical Laboratory Data Communication Network," in *The Second International Conference on Computer Communications, Stockholm 1974, 12-14 August: Computer Communication Today and up to 1985*, Stockholm, The Conference, 1974, pp. 223-228, also in http://www.rogerdmoore.ca/PS/NPLPh/NPL1974A.html.

The situation was further complicated by the fact that various communication technologies were being used at this time, including various protocols, and thus not all of the networks had yet been interconnected.

Connections between the various networks developed less according to their geographical proximity and more on the basis of their affinities, which therefore need to be considered here. In 1986, John S. Quarterman and Josiah C. Hoskins analyzed networks with at least mail or news services that were connected to others with the same services and divided them into five categories: 1) research; 2) company-owned (such as the DEC and IBM); 3) cooperative, in other words developed by communities of users with similar interests; 4) commercial; and 5) meta networks "directed at extending network user communities by connecting existing and as yet unconstructed networks." However, as the authors pointed out, this only amounted to a theoretical classification because some networks fitted more than one category: for example, many cooperative networks were also research networks.[7]

In sum, it is difficult to establish the precise number of networks that existed at various dates. This also holds true for what had come to be called ARPA Internet,[8] around which the network of networks, in the strict sense of the term, was emerging. Two RFCs from 1986 and 1990, however, provide the order of magnitude and allow us to better understand the criteria used to count the networks at the time. The first counted 665 "networks" connected with Arpanet's protocols: 514 of these belonged to ARPA Internet and other US Department of Defence networks, while 151 of them were independent and mostly commercial.[9] The second RFC listed 4,226 networks connected to what was now commonly referred to as Internet. Of these networks, 2,203 or 51.2% were research networks, 1,108 (26.2%) were commercial and 916 (21.7%) were governmental, of which 567 (13.4%) military.[10] Compared to the early phase, the most relevant development was the birth and growth of commercial networks, but otherwise these figures suggest significantly that the scientific vocation that had characterized the first network was no less prominent.

What the authors meant by network remains to be seen. Another RFC, in which Mark K. Lottor of the Network Information Systems Centre retraced Internet's development from 1981 to 1991, provides clarification to this end.[11] In his assessment, he avoided using the term network and referred, on the one

7. John S. Quarterman and Josiah C. Hoskins, "Notable Computer Networks," *Communications of the ACM*, 29, no. 10 (1986): pp. 932-971. Another slightly earlier analysis of research networks is Lawrence H. Landweber, Dennis M. Jennings and Ira Fuchs, "Research Computer Networks and their Interconnection," *IEEE Communications Magazine*, 24, no. 6 (1986): pp. 5-17.

8. The expression appears for the first time in an RFC from 1980: Jon Postel, "Internet Message Protocol," RFC 759, August 1980.

9. Joyce Reynolds and Jon Postel, "Assigned Numbers," RFC 990, November 1986.

10. Sue Kirkpatrick, Mary Stahl and Mimi Recker, "Internet Numbers," RFC 1166, July 1990. Slightly different percentages can be found in Laura E. De Nardis, *Protocol Politics: The Globalization of Internet Governance*, Cambridge, MA – London, MIT Press, 2009, p. 153.

11. Mark Lottor, "Internet Growth (1981-1991)," RFC 1296, January 1992.

hand, to the number of hosts and, on the other, to the number of domains. At the time and as is the case today, a domain name was expressed in letters and it identified a registered user. It was assigned one or more IP (Internet Protocol) numerical addresses, and when there was more than one address, the numbers referred to existing subnets. Of the 727,000 hosts that Lottor counted in January 1992, for example, 715,143 had just one IP address, but 9,015 had two, 1,027 had three, 556 had four, and so on. From this it can be inferred that the above-cited RFCs were labeling IP addresses as networks, and that the domains provide an acceptable estimate of the number of interconnected networks in this period. The Domain Name System, which was proposed in 1983 by Paul V. Mockapetris[12] and introduced in 1984, was not actually completed until four years later and so no significant data exists on the system until July 1988. The 900 domains registered on this date rose over the next twelve months to 3,900, to 9,300 in October 1990, and finally to 17,000 in 1992.[13]

Such unbridled growth begs many questions, but a careful reconstruction of the development that lies behind these figures falls outside of the realm of this study and would require significant further research. Therefore, we will only focus on the most relevant aspects, which will also allow us to verify if the interpretive hypothesis presented in the introduction holds true. In order to do this, we will draw away from our meticulous analysis to make greater reference to existing literature on the subject than we have done until this point.

A good starting point would be a few works by Licklider, who returned as IPTO's director in January 1974 and remained in post until August 1975, after which he moved permanently back to MIT. Roberts had left ARPA in September 1973 to form a company affiliated with BBN, which not long after led to the birth of a private network, Telenet. Neither he nor Lukasik were able to find a person who could take over the management of the office and thus they turned to its founder. Aware of the importance of the undertaking, Licklider accepted the proposal, and he explained his motivation to the Director of MIT's Department of Electrical Engineering in the following manner: "Although my concurrence was somewhat reluctant, there was actually no question in my mind that, in terms of importance to the world, the arpa job was dominant."[14]

Licklider also wrote in 1974 that he believed that the 1970s would see a "socio-technological revolution." This revolution would continue for a further ten to fifteen years "before we can figure out the general outline of the ensuing regime," and would change "the basic paradigm of human communication" on both the technological (and here the author cited packet-switching) and social fronts. Licklider emphasized person-to-person communication, which would have greatly benefited from the mediation and support of a network, and he estimated

---

12. See Paul Mockapetris, "Domain Names: Concepts and Facilities," RFC 882, November 1983; Paul Mockapetris, "Domain Names: Implementation and Specification," RFC 883, November 1983.

13. Lottor, "Internet Growth (1981-1991)."

14. Joseph C.R. Licklider to Louis D. Smullin, November 5, 1973, in Licklider Papers, Box 1, Folder "JCRL, MIT, 'Leave of absence,' 1973-1974."

that over the next fifteen years between 10 and 25% of Americans would interact with a computer. Obviously these would not be programmers or people whose jobs were directly linked to such devices. Instead, he predicted that "many people will work directly with computers in the office, and many will use computers, probably mainly through telecommunication channels, in the home." Connections would take place through a "network of networks" that would include "a kind of computer supported telephone service and a mail service."[15] Continuing, Licklider envisioned that

> In the latter part of this decade and in the next, network-accessible databases will arise in many areas of government, business, and private life. Reservation services will include most hotels, motels, restaurants, theatres, and sports events, and advisory services will be available on-line along with reservations and ticketing. On-line shopping, linked to cable television and to all manner of consulting services and discount clubs, will create something of an upheaval in retailing. Urban and regional planners will have access to data on the number of vehicles of various types on various highways as a function of time of day and time of year – and so on.[16]

It would be superfluous to highlight once again the author's capacity for predicting the future, a talent that he shared with other protagonists of this story. For example, as early as 1967, Baran had predicted both the computer's entrance in the home and the sending and reception of messages, among many other things:

> We will speak to the computers of the future in a language simple to learn and easy to use. Our home computer console will be used to send and receive messages – like telegrams. We could check to see whether the local department store has the advertised sports shirt in stock in the desired colour and size. We could ask when delivery would be guaranteed, if we ordered. The information would be up-to-the-minute and accurate. We could pay our bills and compute our taxes via the console. We would ask questions and receive answers from "information banks" – automated versions of today's libraries. We would obtain up-to-the-minute listing of all television and radio programmes. We could use the computer to preserve and modify our Christmas lists. It could type out the names and addresses for our envelopes. We could store in birthdays. The computer could, itself, send a message to remind us of an impending anniversary and save us from the disastrous consequences of forgetfulness.[17]

If anything, Licklider's words allow us to better understand not just the multidisciplinary dimension that we have insisted upon, but also what allowed him, Baran and others to have such foresight. Licklider in fact spoke of the scenarios he foresaw as "projections,"[18] and we believe this is an illuminating term. Among the various entries for the word in the *Oxford Dictionary* (the projection of fixed or moving images, the representation of a three-dimensional body on a flat surface, etc.), the first definition given is "an estimate or forecast of a future situation or trend based on a study of present ones."[19] In contrast to the common but misguided

---

15. Licklider, "Potential of Networking for Research and Education," pp. 1-3.
16. *Ibid.*, p. 7.
17. Paul Baran, "The Future Computer Utility," *The Public Interest*, no. 8 (1967): pp. 77-78.
18. Licklider, "Potential of Networking for Research and Education," p. 10.
19. http://oxforddictionaries.com/definition/american_english/projection.

tendency of considering these people to be visionaries, their projections were founded on a deep understanding of the "state of the art"; on the potential and limits of the innovations occurring at the time they were writing.

Licklider had already highlighted some of these limits the year before during a presentation at a NATO convention in Great Britain on information science. One limit was that "if storage and processing belong to the computer field, transmission belongs to the communication field, and the two fields have been interacting as though they were superpower antagonists in a cold war." The author had therefore advocated for a "use- and user-oriented information science," which was necessary because "so much of the forward thrust of computers and networks has come from inside, that so many great potentials have been built up by technologists for users instead of by users or by technologists and users working together." Furthermore, he added, "great advances in human-factors aspects of information-systems design will have to be made before the potential users become actual users."[20]

Licklider had thus affirmed that "the present capability of the ARPANET is very great, and I believe that history will judge it to be as significant as the first automobile or the first airplane." But, he added, echoing Shakespeare, "'all that's past is prologue'" to two unresolved problems: the problem with the functionality of the system and the inconsistency of the network, and the problem with the creation "of the many additional resources that potential users will require." He believed that to solve these problems, it was necessary, among other things: 1) to define "an 'interaction language' or 'interaction protocol'" that could be implemented in every system; and 2) to develop "an effective way of determining 'user needs' and relating them to technical and economic feasibility." The latter suggestion was the most difficult of the two challenges, because "much of what has been said and written about user needs in related fields is pap; when asked what he needed most, the old farmer replied, 'A stronger mule.'"[21]

The following year, since "most of the services and systems that will make networks vital are in their infancy or have not yet been conceived," he confirmed that it would not be immediately useful to connect "real people who want to see a real network being used for real purposes" to a terminal. He believed that "the best strategy for any movement to attract users to networks seems to be to select users who will be creative and productive and will bring into being the services and systems that later users will require." What was now necessary to focus on, he concluded, "is the role of the user in the realization of potential."[22]

More than ten years later, in 1986, Roberts took up some of the points raised by Licklider in a presentation at a convention on the history of personal workstations. Speaking on Arpanet and other networks that had emerged by that

20. Joseph C.R. Licklider, "Psychological and Technological Dynamics of Information Science," in *Perspectives in Information Science: Proceedings of the NATO Advanced Study Institute on Perspectives in Information Science, Held in Aberystwyth, Wales, UK, August 13-24, 1973*, ed. by Anthony Debons and William J. Cameron, Leyden, Noordhoff, 1975, pp. 168-170.

21. *Ibid.*, pp. 171-173. The Shakespeare reference is to the first scene of the second act of *The Tempest*.

22. Licklider, "Potential of Networking for Research and Education," pp. 9-11.

point, he began with a comparison between the current situation and the state of things in 1964. He believed that the developments during the period were "in part a massive and evolutionary change in computer technology, and in part a modest and revolutionary change in telecommunication technology." The former consisted in the development and diffusion of microcomputers, whereas in the 1960s only large mainframes existed and just a few of these were time-shared. The latter began with Arpanet and "grew into a communications revolution called packet switching."[23]

Even if ARPA's network had grown independently of the telephone network,[24] according to Roberts, in the next twenty years "the basic fabric supporting all switched services (data, telephone and video) appear likely to become converted to packet switching, completing the revolution." In any case, while waiting for this to happen, already at the time "your terminal could well be a microcomputer networked with a very large, worldwide collection of other computers" and "virtually all the world is linked by packet switched communications service so that any terminal can access almost any computer in the world."[25]

PC, Networks and Protocols

For some time computers had been shrinking in size and cost while increasing in power, and in the 1970s the first PCs made their appearance. The inaugural event of this well-known story is usually pinpointed to the year 1975, when a small company in Albuquerque, New Mexico put Altair 8800 on the market. The machine was sold in its assembly box for less than 400 dollars (the equivalent of 1,700 dollars today), and was very successful in the California anti-conformist youth communities to which the computer's creators – H. Edward Roberts and his collaborators – belonged. Altair had little memory and was not very user-friendly, but was successful because it stood up to IBM and other large companies in the name of the freedom of circulation and use of new technologies. Two years later, Steve Wozniak and Steve Jobs presented Apple II, an innovative and easy to use PC with advanced graphics that cost about 500 dollars and was widely used. Others followed, beginning with IBM's personal computers in 1981.[26]

23. Roberts, "The ARPANET and Computer Networks," p. 143. Both Kleinrock and Roberts made similar observations to those made by Licklider. See Leonard Kleinrock, "On Communications and Networks," *IEEE Transactions on Computers*, C-25, no. 12 (1976): pp. 1326-1335 and Roberts, "The Evolution of Packet Switching."

24. Farber and Baran had already drawn attention to the problem in David Farber and Paul Baran, "The Convergence of Computing and Telecommunications Systems," *Science*, 195, no. 4283 (1977): pp. 1166-1170.

25. Roberts, "The ARPANET and Computer Networks," p. 143.

26. See Paul Freiberger and Michael Swaine, *Fire in the Valley: the Making of the Personal Computer*, New York, McGraw-Hill, 2000 [1984]; Roy A. Allan, *A History of the Personal Computer: The People and the Technology*, London, Ont., Allan Pub., 2001; Martin Campbell-Kelly and William Aspray, *Computer: A History of the Information Machine*, New York, Basic Books, 1996; Ceruzzi, *A History of Modern Computing*.

What Roberts did not say in 1986, which is no reason to overlook it, is that ARPA had also made a significant contribution to that "massive and evolutionary change in computer technology."[27] We have already discussed Wesley A. Clark's first machines and the DEC's PDPs that were also used on Arpanet, as well as Engelbart and his team's work. Regarding this point, however, we must mention at least one other innovation from 1973. That year a staff team at the Xerox Corporation that included various members of the IPTO community, including Butler W. Lampson, Chuck P. Thacker and Robert L. Sproull, created Alto. Alto was a personal workstation equipped with a microprocessor that Intel created in 1972 (which led to a significant reduction in costs), with a 128 KB RAM expandable to 512, a 2.5 MB hard disk, a graphic monitor and a mouse.[28] This is often considered the first PC, and it marked an important step forward with respect to existing minicomputers, but it was never marketed[29] and thus was used only at universities. Since these were the most active and advanced centres in the sector, however, the workstation nonetheless played an important role in dissemination. It was also connected to another significant development, the LAN, which was destined to become the standard in the field of local networks, and as we will see, made an important contribution to the development of networking.

That the advent of these machines and those that followed them was a wide-reaching phenomenon is demonstrated by the speed of their success alone, which was facilitated by the significant decrease in prices due to the entrance on the market of the first "clones" of IBM's PCs.[30] In the US, the cost of a desktop computer decreased by 23% per year in the period from 1976 to 1983, and 25% between 1983 and 1989.[31] According to the US Census Bureau, in 1984 there were 87,073 homes with personal computers, and this number rose to 94,061 in 1989 and 98,736 in 1993: from 8 to 15 to 23%;[32] these were essentially the percentages that Licklider had spoken of in 1974. In 1990 there were 21 PCs for every 100

27. Numerous authors emphasized this point both at the time and later, including, for example, Larry Press, "Before the Altair: The History of Personal Computing," *Communications of the ACM*, 36, no. 9 (1993): pp. 27-33.

28. Chuck P. Thacker, "Personal Distributed Computing: The Alto and Ethernet Hardware," in *Proceedings of the ACM Conference on The History of Personal Workstations*, ed. by White and Anderson, pp. 87-100; Butler W. Lampson, "Personal Distributed Computing: The Alto and Ethernet Software," in *Proceedings of the ACM Conference on The History of Personal Workstations*, ed. by White and Anderson, pp. 101-131.

29. See Douglas K. Smith and Robert C. Alexander, *Fumbling the Future: How Xerox Invented, then Ignored, the First Personal Computer*, New York, Morrow, 1988.

30. See Ryan, *A History of the Internet and the Digital Future*, p. 59. Between 1981 and 1985 5.7 million IBM or compatible PCs were sold, of which 3.8 million were sold in the US: Computer Industry Almanac Inc., "25-Year PC Anniversary Statistics," 2006, http://www.c-i-a.com/pr0806.htm.

31. Ernst R. Berndt and Neal J. Rappaport, "Price and Quality of Desktop and Mobile Personal Computers: A Quarter-Century Historical Overview," *The American Economic Review*, 91, no. 2 (2001): p. 271. Additional and more significant decreases took place between 1989 and 1994 (-35% per year) and between 1994 and 1999 (-40%).

32. US Census Bureau, "Computer and Internet Use, Appendix Table A, Households With a Computer and Internet Use: 1984 to 2009," http://www.census.gov/hhes/computer/.

Figure 25 – Xerox Alto

Source: http://archive.computerhistory.org/resources/still-image/Xerox/102710353.03.01.lg.jpg?rand=739988351.

people in the US, and more than 10 in Australia, Canada, Denmark, Finland, Great Britain and Sweden.[33] It is no less significant that already in January 1983, "Time" Magazine – a source both authoritative and sensitive to change – for the first time chose not a "person of the year" but a "machine of the year": the personal computer.[34]

With the development and distribution first of minicomputers and then of PCs, time-sharing entered a period of decline. When computers were less numerous and consisted in the more expensive mainframes that were used only by computer scientists and experts, time-sharing had been economically advantageous and had brought with it very significant innovations. In contrast, from the 1970s onwards, large systems became increasingly inconvenient, with the exception of those based on powerful machines used to process enormous quantities of data. These changes altered the direction of the computer industry, and in the early 1980s time-sharing "was killed by the rise of the PC."[35] They also took their toll on Arpanet, which was employed less and less for the use of remote hardware

33. UN Statistics Division, "Millennium Development Goals Indicators, Personal Computers per 100 Population," http://mdgs.un.org/unsd/mdg/SeriesDetail.aspx?srid=607.

34. See http://www.time.com/time/covers/0,16641,19830103,00.html. The 1981 cover had been dedicated to the US President Ronald Reagan, and the 1982 cover to the Solidarność leader Lech Walesa.

35. Campbell-Kelly and Garcia-Swartz, "Economic Perspectives on the History of the Computer Time-Sharing Industry," p. 31.

and software, and increasingly "for bringing people together."[36] However, the mere creation of minicomputers and PCs was not enough for this to occur: they also had to be interconnected, which depended on the developments of the first network and other kinds of networks in this period. We have therefore to explain these developments without minimizing the institutional and managerial changes involving Arpanet in the 1970s.

The first of various issues to be resolved in this period was that once Arpanet was up and running, it went from being an experimental research project to a structure that needed to be managed, which was not one of ARPA's tasks. The hypothesis of ceding control to AT&T ultimately came to nothing as the telephone company rejected the offer;[37] as Licklider put it, acting as a rival superpower in a cold war. A study conducted in 1973 by Cabledata Associates, a company founded by Baran, suggested forming "an industry group or consortium" to develop common standards and to keep it under "closer governmental supervision or regulation" to avoid the formation of an oligopoly.[38] However, this solution was also abandoned because various public structures, many of which were military, were using Arpanet. In July 1975 its management was assigned "until equivalent service could be provided on a military network"[39] to the Defence Communications Agency (DCA), the very same agency of the Department of Defence, that ten years earlier Baran had avoided entrusting his project.

In contrast to IPTO, DCA's staff did not include civilians, and from then on Arpanet's administration endured a major increase in bureaucratic and regulatory procedures. Furthermore, between January 1975 and December 1977, while under George H. Heilmeier's directorship, ARPA also became somewhat more militarized. Indeed, he "pressed IPTO to be more mindful of the military applicability of research and exploratory development projects," in an environment within which "the entire DOD had changed, and computer science had matured, so it was more difficult to sustain the IPTO philosophy."[40] These changes raised strong concerns in the Arpanet community, which Licklider expressed without mincing his words in an email from April 1975,[41] however these changes were not enough to halt the network's development. Indeed, on the one hand, the network was still unclassified, and on the other, the innovations that supported it were still being created by the research teams under IPTO's management – i.e. the users (as always) who among other things in 1973 had formed a Users Interest Working Group and in 1975 opened the first mailing list, Msggroup.[42] All this

36. Abbate, *Inventing the Internet*, p. 111.
37. See Roberts, "The Evolution of Packet Switching," p. 1310.
38. Paul Baran et al., "Arpanet Management Study," Cabledata Associates, Inc., 20 January 1974, p. IV, http://www.dtic.mil/cgi-bin/GetTRDoc?AD=AD0777747.
39. DARPA, "A History of the Arpanet: The First Decade," p. III-106.
40. Norberg and O'Neill, *Transforming Computer Technology*, pp. 19, 35-37.
41. Licklider wrote about Heilmeier: "The problem is that the frame of reference with which he enters the discussions is basically quite different from the frames of reference that are natural and comfortable, and familiar to most of us in IPTO – and, I think, to most of you." *Ibid.*, p. 48.
42. See David Crocker, Neigus, Feinler and Jean Iseli, "Arpanet Users Interest Working Group Meeting," RFC 585, 6 November 1973. Msggroup's archive can be found at http://

was exacerbated by the fact that in his second tenure Licklider persuaded BBN to publish the origin code for the software used to manage the IMP and the TIP[43] so that it could be completely overhauled with the usual collaborative procedures.

It is significant, on the other hand, that David C. Russell, who had a PhD in physics but was also an army colonel, succeeded Licklider as the office's director. In sum, the growing importance that the Department of Defence attributed to Arpanet had the dual effect of steering the network toward routine applications of a military nature[44] and weighing down its management with numerous rules,[45] while also promoting its growth, even when its strategic importance was reshaped by the creation of another network specifically designed for military installations. This network, which was promoted by DCA in 1976, was called Autodin II, and three years later it connected 160 hosts and 1,300 terminals.[46] The fact remains, however, that by the mid 1980s, ARPA was the largest single source of funding for computer science in the United States.[47]

In any case, certain projects with potential military applications, which were started, among other reasons, to obtain increased financing, had already seen significant development in IPTO's programmes. These projects were promoted by Robert E. Kahn, who in November 1972 had moved from the BBN to ARPA as programme manager and in 1979 took over management of the office. In addition to a few projects that aimed for voice transmission, particular attention was given to creating and promoting new ways to send digital messages, which also contributed to making 1972 and 1973 a turning point in Arpanet's history.

Among the various innovations that followed, one was the construction of a radio network,[48] and here as well it is important to note that the programme was the result of a spontaneous initiative. Indeed, the programme was the development of a project launched in 1968 by a team led by Norman M. Abramson at the University of Hawaii, Honolulu, which aimed to interconnect the university's various branches. The campuses were located on several different islands, and Abramson had the idea of using radio transmissions to overcome the difficulties created by malfunctions in local telephone lines. This small radio network was

---

web.archive.org/web/20011102110954/http:/www.tcm.org/msggroup/. The net's applications included a few computer games: see Keith Uncapher and Vinton G. Cerf, "The Arpanet: A User Perspective," 1974, http://archive.org/details/The ArpanetAUserPerspective.

43. See Hafner and Lyon, *Where Wizards Stay Up Late*, p. 235.

44. See Norberg and O'Neill, *Transforming Computer Technology*, p. 56; Abbate, *Inventing the Internet*, p. 136.

45. See for example Defense Communications Agency, "Arpanet Information Brochure," 13 March 1978, http://www.dtic.mil/dtic/tr/fulltext/u2/a482154.pdf.

46. Abbate, *Inventing the Internet*, p. 138.

47. Mark Stefik, "Strategic Computing at DARPA: Overview and Assessment," *Communications of the ACM*, 28, no. 7 (1985): p. 690. See also Ronald G. Havelock and David S. Bushnell, "Technology Transfer at DARPA: The Defense Advanced Research Agency: A Diagnostic Analysis," December 1985, http://www.dtic.mil/dtic/tr/fulltext/u2/a164457.pdf.

48. See Robert E. Kahn, "The Organization of Computer Resources into a Packet Radio Network," in AFIPS, *Proceedings of the May 19-22, 1975, National Computer Conference and Exposition*, New York, ACM, 1975, pp. 177-186.

called Alohanet and became operational in 1971. In December 1972, NASA's Ames Research Centre connected the network to Arpanet via satellite.[49]

A similar satellite connection was created in 1973 with the Norwegian Seismic Array (NORSAR),[50] a geological and seismic research centre created in 1968 as part of an agreement with Norway for the survey of underground nuclear explosions, which was also of military and strategic interest. Immediately afterwards, University College London was also connected.[51] From 1975 onward, connections with Norway and London merged in the Satnet project (Atlantic Packet Satellite Network),[52] and subsequently similar means were used to link other sites throughout the world. By experimenting with these networks overseas, the Arpanet community intensified its collaboration and sharing of resources with numerous groups of researchers active in Norway, Great Britain, France and later in other countries. As a result, a transnational community was formed that from 1977 to 1982 used a particular series of RFCs, the Internet Experiment Notes (IEN), which were also managed by Postel.[53] As such, they made the shaping of Internet a process that was no longer limited solely to the United States.[54]

As a result of these initiatives two new types of digital network were added to the original type that was connected through telephone lines: the first by satellite and the second by radio, PRNET,[55] whose significance for military aims Lukasik

49. See Norman Abramson, "The Aloha System: Another Alternative for Computer Communications," in *Proceedings of the November 17-19, 1970, Fall Joint Computer Conference*, New York, ACM, 1970, pp. 281-285; Norman Abramson, "Packet Switching with Satellites," in *Proceedings of the June 4-8, 1973, National Computer Conference and Exposition*, New York, ACM, 1973, pp. 695-702; Richard Binder, Norman Abramson, Franklin Kuo, Alan Okinaka and David Wax, "ALOHA Packet Broadcasting: A Retrospect," in *Proceedings of the May 19-22, 1975, National Computer Conference and Exposition*, New York, ACM, 1975, pp. 203-215.

50. See William C. Dean, "Seismic Array Analysis Center Quarterly Technical Summary, January-March 1973," 18 April 1973, http://www.dtic.mil/dtic/tr/fulltext/u2/760745.pdf; Yngvar Lundh, "Development of Internet Technology and Norwegian Partecipation," in *History of Nordic Computing 3, Third IFIP WG Conference, HINC 3, Stockholm, Sweden, October 18-20, 2010*, ed. by John Impagliazzo, Per Lundin and Benkt Wandler, New York, Springer, 2011, pp. 287-296; Pål Spilling, "The Internet Development Process: Observations and Reflections," in *History of Nordic Computing 3*, ed. by Impagliazzo, Lundin and Wandler, pp. 297-304.

51. See Peter T. Kirstein, "Early Experiences With the Arpanet and Internet in the United Kingdom," *IEEE Annals of the History of Computing*, 21, no. 1(1999): pp. 38-44.

52. See Robert E. Kahn, "The Introduction of Packet Satellite Communications," in *National Telecommunications Conference, Washington, D.C., November 27-29, 1979*, part 3, New York, IEEE, 1979, pp. 45.1.1-45.1.8, also at http://archive.org/details/TheIntroductionOfPacketSatelliteCommunication.

53. The IENs can be consulted at http://www.rfc-editor.org/ien/ien-index.html.

54. See Ronda Hauben, "The Internet: On its International Origins and Collaborative Vision. A Work In-Progress," (2004), www.columbia.edu/~rh120/other/misc/haubenpap.rtf; Sandra Braman, "Internationalization of the Internet by Design: The First Decade," *Global Media and Communication*, 8, no. 1 (2012): pp. 27-45.

55. See Robert E. Kahn, Steven A. Gronemeyer, Jerry Burchfiel and Ronald C. Kunzelman, "Advances in Packet Radio Technology," *Proceedings of the IEEE*, 66, no. 11 (1978): pp. 1468-1496.

had already emphasized before US Congress in 1973.[56] Since each of these networks functioned differently and they all needed to be rendered compatible with telephone networks, specific instruments had to first be created in order to interconnect them. Essentially, a new and more complex communications protocol had to be developed to satisfy these requirements. A group formed by Kahn, Cerf, Robert M. Metcalfe and the French computer engineer Gérard Le Lann created the protocol between 1973 and 1974. Le Lann was a member of the staff of Louis Pouzin, who had already been in contact with the Arpanet group and who created Cyclades, the first network outside of the US that became operational in 1973.[57]

The new protocol was called the Transmission Control Protocol (TCP), which, like others before it, evolved over time. This, however, did not prevent it from spreading quite quickly on Arpanet, where it started to replace previous protocols. As a result, a growing number of the network's nodes began to speak the same language, which was an essential condition for its growth. Subsequently in 1977 Cerf, Postel and Daniel Cohen further perfected the protocol, dividing it into two distinct but connected parts. The TCP continued to manage the sending and receipt of messages within Arpanet. Internet Protocol (IP), on the other hand, was responsible for transmitting data between different networks (telephone networks, whether via radio or satellite), routing them through specifically designed nodes called gateways.

In 1978 TCP/IP was finalized and with it the tool that allowed for effective interconnection among various networks. The protocol was officially adopted as the standard in 1983 and was used by many of the networks that had since been created in America. In reality, as we will see, TCP/IP's success in the US and in other countries was by no means automatic, and it occurred to the detriment of alternative solutions. For this reason, too, it is significant that the technology that led to Internet's creation was developed by users based on their interests, thanks in part to the relative freedom they were given by the American government, as well as to its promotion by the Department of Defence.[58]

Additional important consequences of the radio and satellite projects arose from their applications, which were usually unplanned. Metcalfe drew particularly on the work conducted for the Hawaiian radio network and the TCP, in order to design and create the structure of a local network. This was not an entirely new development; indeed, there were similar networks in Great Britain, where, since the network created by Davies at the NPL, they had spread in part to compensate for the delay with which geographically extensive networks connecting multiple

56. DoD Appropriations for 1974, *Hearings Before a Subcommittee of the Committee of Appropriations House of Representatives, Ninety-Third Congress, First Session, Subcommittee on Department of Defense,* Part 9. *Defense Agencies*, Washington, DC, US Government Printing Office, 1973, p. 1043.

57. See Louis Pouzin, "Presentation and Major Design Aspects of the CYCLADES Computer Network," in *Proceedings of the Third ACM Symposium on Data Communications and Data Networks: Analysis and Design*, New York, ACM, 1973, pp. 80-87; Louis Pouzin, "Le Project Cyclades (1972-1977)," *Entreprises et histoire*, no. 29 (2002): pp. 33-40.

58. See Miles Townes, "The Spread of TCP/IP: How the Internet Became the Internet," *Millennium – Journal of International Studies*, 41, no. 1 (2012): pp. 44-46.

centres were developed in surrounding areas. However, the LAN destined to become the most successful belonged to Metcalfe. This was called Ethernet and was launched in the late 1970s, but its creator had already begun work on the LAN in 1973 with the help of David R. Boggs, Lampson and Thacker. Originally, it had been planned to connect the Alto workstations of the Xerox Corporation.[59]

Ethernet's effects on the net's development were significant because it was administered Alohanet's procedure. Here, the packets, which on Arpanet were routed one by one, were not launched sequentially but simultaneously, for reasons dependent on radio technologies. Along with other technical innovations obtained from this type of network, this greatly increased the transmission speed first of Ethernet and subsequently of the entire networking. The role of the LANs proved to be essential also because of their limited extension, which also contributed to the high speed of communications. Ethernet was especially successful also because, in respect of the set-up that was popularized by various exponents of the IPTO community outside of universities, it was sold to agencies in the sector for a symbolic price. Thanks to this liberalization approach, Metcalfe's network became the standard in the field of LANs and brought significant economic savings.[60] Designed to connect mini and personal computers, to this day it is the most widely used technology for local networks.

Meanwhile, the TCP protocol, even before it became TCP/IP, had been developed and articulated in many different versions, some of which were specifically designed for personal computers. It was promoted by ARPA, but another important factor that contributed to its success was the spread of the Unix operating system. Unix's vocation was expressed in its name, inspired as it was by MIT's Multics system. While the latter had been designed for mainframes that were supposed to serve many users, Unix was imagined for personal workstations. Developed in AT&T's Bell laboratories in the late 1960s, it was a very flexible operating system that worked on many different computers and thus was well received by the academic communities. In the late 1970s Berkeley developed an advanced version of the system, which it shared with other schools. In a short space of time, the majority of universities adopted it, which was a decisive factor for TCP/IP's success, because this had been included in the system and distributed at no extra cost.

It is clear that the logic underlying these developments remained collaborative and non-profit, as it had been at the origins of the network.[61] It is no accident, moreover, that in 1982 William N. Joy, a computer scientist from Berkeley who had worked on Unix, joined SUN Microsystems, a company founded by two Stanford graduates to produce and market particularly powerful workstations, which were equipped with the version of Unix developed at Berkeley.

---

59. See Robert M. Metcalfe and David R. Boggs, "Ethernet: Distributed Packet Switching for Local Computer Networks," *Communications of the ACM*, 19, no. 7 (1976): pp. 395-404.

60. See Urs von Burg, *The Triumph of Ethernet, Technological Communities and the Battle for the LAN Standard*, Stanford, Stanford University Press, 2001.

61. See Peter H. Salus, *A Quarter Century of Unix*, Reading, MA, Addison-Wesley, 1994; Steven Weber, *The Success of Open Source*, Cambridge, MA, Harvard University Press, 2004, pp. 20-43.

Uniforms and Sneakers

According to Hans Dieter Hellige, it was ultimately the strange alliance "between uniforms and sneakers" created by Licklider and developed by Taylor in July 1968 with the 'graduate student's conference,' that gave Internet its superior historical importance.[62] Two of the most brilliant graduate students from each of the universities financed by IPTO had been invited to the conference. These were probably the individuals wearing the sneakers indicated in the above quote, but more generally Hellige's metaphor refers to the relationship that had taken shape between ARPA, the centres of excellence under ARPA's management and the other user communities that formed in the 1980s. Hellige further noted:

> If the network of networks acquired such wide reaching value, it was not only on account of the Pentagon and Arpanet/Internet's pioneers. This is proven by the post-1975 period, in which due to the military freeze, the continued expansion of the user population and the development of new applications were no longer pursued. The military could have closed the *organizational space* of the network's standardization, but not the *area of applications*, which slowed its growth. Here, the DARPA's alliance that had begun with Licklider and Taylor between uniforms and sneakers came to the rescue. The network cultures excluded from Arpanet developed in Bitnet, Fidonet and primarily Usenet, which was based on UNIX.[63]

Created in 1981 by Ira H. Fuchs of the City University of New York and Greydon Freeman of Yale University, Bitnet (Because It's Time Network) was an academic network financed by IBM, which by the end of the decade connected 3,000 computers at 450 research institutions, primarily in the US and Europe.[64] Fidonet, developed in 1983 by Thomas D. Jennings, was a network of "computer hobbyists ('hackers', in the older, original meaning)"[65] aimed at PC users and also "in the spirit of Bitnet utility to academic community." In 1986 it connected approximately 500 hosts, most of which had only one user each.[66] Finally, Usenet was a network created in 1979 by three Duke University and University of North Carolina graduate students, James T. Ellis, Tom Truscott and Steven M. Bellovin, to connect Unix machines via modem. It was called "a poor man's Arpanet," and thanks in part to DEC's support, in 1988 Usenet had 11,000 sites, some of which were in Canada, Australia and Europe, with traffic of 1,800 messages a day.[67]

The initial growth of these networks was slow, and they saw a true explosion only when they could connect among each other and above all to Arpanet. In 1980

62. Hellige, "Die Geschichte des Internet als Lernprozess."

63. *Ibid.*, p. 157.

64. See Vijay Gurbaxani, "Diffusion in Computing Networks: The Case of BITNET," *Communications of the ACM*, 33, no. 12 (1990): pp. 65-75; David A. Grier and Mary Campbell, "A Social History of Bitnet and Listserv, 1985-1991," *IEEE Annals of the History of Computing*, 22, no. 2 (2000): pp. 32-41; Gong, Qi and Li, "Lifelike Evolution of CSnet and Bitnet."

65. Thomas Jennings, "FidoNet History and Operation," 1985, http://www.wps.com/FidoNet/fidohist1.txt.

66. Quarterman and Hoskins, "Notable Computer Networks," pp. 942, 953.

67. *Ibid.*, especially pp. 958-959; Michael and Ronda Hauben, *Netizens*, especially chapters 2 and 3.

at the University of California at Berkeley, the first link was created that allowed Usenet users to access mailing lists and the RFCs of the first network. In the mid-1980s, Bitnet interfaced with Arpanet and with Usenet, whose newsgroups could be connected through Fidonet. These networks did not always use the same protocols, but specific software allowed them to interconnect and thus little by little a large community was formed that shared certain essential services.

Moreover, Bitnet, Fidonet and Usenet do not fully represent all that existed in this period. Among research networks, Computer Science Network (Csnet) had a particularly important role. The universities connected to Arpanet were points of excellence, but they made up only a small portion of the American academic system. Many electronic engineering departments had been excluded from the first network. Connecting other schools that were not involved with programmes financed by ARPA was not permitted and in any case would have been prohibitively expensive.[68] One must also consider that the DCA was primarily interested in developing military connections.

In 1979, on the initiative of Lawrence H. Landweber from the University of Wisconsin, eleven computer science departments commenced their work on a new network. Kahn and Cerf, who had been working at IPTO since 1976, offered to contribute to these efforts since the network was connected to Arpanet. Csnet was funded in 1981 by the National Science Foundation and administered by an organization with a branch at the BBN. Five years later, it had nearly 170 members from universities, government entities and industries, with connections in various parts of the world. Many of its nodes were also Arpanet hosts, and all of the sites of the so-called ARPA Internet could be reached from every part of Csnet.[69] In 1987, Bitnet and Csnet merged to form the non-profit Corporation for Research and Educational Networking.[70]

Meanwhile, in 1982 a Defence Data Network had been formed as the head of all the Defence Department's networks. On this basis between 1983 and 1984, the military installations covering 70% of Arpanet's nodes were moved to a separate network, Milnet.[71] For strategic reasons, Milnet branched out to Europe and in particular to the German Federal Republic, where the US had a number

---

68. In 1984, for example, an IMP cost 130,000 dollars: Peter J. Denning, "The Science of Computing: Computer Networks," *American Scientist*, 73, no. 2 (1985): p. 127.

69. See Douglas Comer, "The Computer Science Research Network Csnet: A History and Status Report," *Communications of the ACM*, 26, no. 10 (1983): pp. 747-753; Peter J. Denning, Anthony Hearn and C. William Kern, "History and Overview of CSNET," *Computer Communication Review*, 13, no. 2 (1983): pp. 138-145; Lawrence H. Landweber, "CSNET: A Brief History," 1991, http://diswww.mit.edu/menelaus.mit.edu/com-priv/1395; Quarterman and Hoskins, "Notable Computer Networks," 945; Dennis M. Jennings, Lawrence H. Landweber, Fuchs, Farber and W. Richard Adrion, "Computer Networking for Scientists," *Science*, 231, no. 4741 (1986): 943-950.

70. See Paul A. David, "The Evolving Accidental Information Super-Highway," *Oxford Review of Economic Policy*, 17, no. 2 (2001): 167.

71. Defense Communications Agency, "Arpanet Information Brochure," December 1985, http://www.dtic.mil/dtic/tr/fulltext/u2/a164353.pdf. The authors were Stephen Dennett, Elizabeth J. Feinler and Francine Perillo.

of military bases. In this way, the first network ceased to be Janus-faced (one military, one civilian) and the ground was laid for its management to be entrusted to a civilian structure.

This structure was the National Science Foundation, which in 1984 launched the Nsfnet project, a "network of networks," created to connect six university super-computers coordinated from its Office of Advanced Scientific Computation. With an operation that was considered to be a kind of "new Sputnik,"[72] the US Congress funded the initiative to address Japanese competition in the sectors, and it was immediately extended to Csnet. Then, based on an agreement with ARPA and with the support of the Department of Defence, little by little Arpanet's nodes were connected to Nsfnet,[73] until the former became a subnet of the latter. In 1989, Arpanet's structures – at this point obsolete – were phased out, its nodes became Nsfnet hosts and the first network was formally closed on 28 February 1990.

Not without reason, certain authors recognized many developments, if not outright spin-offs,[74] of Arpanet's technologies in Nsfnet; something that had previously been noted with regards to Csnet and the various commercial networks set up during the period. As for the size of the NSF's meta-network, David L. Mills and Hans-Werner Braun cited 63 networks connected to its backbone in 1987, which did not account for the underlying regional and consortium networks financed by the NSF. These networks were numerous, but nonetheless greatly inferior in number to the more than 250 networks that made up the "Internet system as a whole."[75] The fact remains that from the time that Arpanet and Nsfnet were interconnected, Internet's development was so rapid as to merit the use of adjectives like "phenomenal," "tremendous" and "exponential."[76] Without considering the various meanings attributed to the term "network" by a range of authors, it is obvious that the interconnection of various networks in a single system would have been greatly facilitated by a reduction in the number of

72. Eiichiro Kazumori, "Coordination and Decommissioning: NSFNET and the Evolution of the Internet in the United States, 1985-1995," Stanford Institute for Economic Policy Research, Discussion Paper n. 02-07, February 2003, 19, http://www.stanford.edu/group/siepr/cgi-bin/siepr/?q=system/files/shared/pubs/papers/pdf/02-07.pdf.

73. Jennings, Landweber, Fuchs, Farber and Adrion, "Computer Networking for Scientists." In table 2 the authors counted 43 out of 65 that were expected to be connected in September 1986.

74. For example, the expression was used in Denning, "The Science of Computing," p. 127, which in addition to Csnet mentions commercial networks such as the previously cited Telenet, Unidata and CompuServe.

75. David L. Mills and Hans-Werner Braun, "The NSFNET Backbone Network," *Computer Communication Review*, 17, no. 5 (1987): p. 191.

76. Karen D. Frazer, "NSFNET: A Partnership for High-Speed Networking. Final Report, 1987-1995," 1996, p. 35, http://www.merit.edu/about/history/pdf/NSFNET_final.pdf; Ivo Maathuis and Wim A. Smit, "The Battle Between Standards: TCP/IP vs OSI. Victory Through Path Dependency or by Quality?," in *Proceedings of the 3rd Conference on Standardization and Innovation in Information Technology*, ed. by Tineke M. Egyedi, Ken Krechmer and Kai Jakobs, Piscataway, NJ, IEEE, 2003, p. 169; Andrew S. Tanenbaum, *Computer Networks*, 4th ed., Upper Saddle River, NJ, Pearson Prentice Hall, 2003, p. 50.

protocols, and even more so by the adoption of a single standard. It is to this issue that we must therefore now turn our attention.

The "Protocols War"

Of the many protocols in use in the 1970s and 1980s, Arpanet's protocol eventually took prevalence over all the others. The beginning of its success can be pinpointed to 1983. It was in fact in this year that, following a difficult transition phase[77] and immediately prior to Milnet's separation, TCP/IP became the only protocol used on the Department of Defence networks. All other protocols were eliminated, with the exception, naturally, of those with separate functions, such as FTP. In addition, in the early 1980s the Department attempted to distribute TCP/IP in the private sector, and on the initiative of Colonel Heidi Heiden ARPA earmarked 20 million dollars for its development in the systems of computer producers. As a result, at the end of the decade the protocol was available to almost everybody on the American market.[78] However, as previously mentioned, the rise of TCP/IP was rather contested. Indeed, its success was hardly a given and was the final result of a protocol competition that was so heated that many commentators and scholars described it as a battle, a war and even a religious conflict.[79]

In the mid-1970s, networking was in full swing thanks in part to the arrival of proprietary and commercial networks, some of which were already operative, while others were still being developed. The first group included those announced in 1974 by large companies such as IBM and the DEC (respectively System Network Architecture, SNA, and Decnet), which used reserved protocols. The second group included Telenet, the BBN network managed by Roberts, which became operative in 1975, followed by Tymnet set up by Tymshare Inc. in 1976. Such networks were not limited to the US: in addition to Cyclades and RCP that were already active in France, various other networks were under construction in Europe, Canada, Japan and Australia. Many of these were promoted by the postal and telephone services of the various countries.

With the growth in the number and nature of stakeholders, various alternative strategies were outlined. Strengthened by their positions on the market, the largest companies aimed to develop proprietary technologies. In contrast, it was in the interest of small producers to develop standards that made various products

77. See Jon Postel, "NCP/TCP Transition Plan," RFC 801, November 1981; Network Information Center, SRI International, "Internet Protocol Transition Workbook," March 1982, http://www.dtic.mil/dtic/tr/fulltext/u2/a153607.pdf.

78. Janet Abbate, "Government, Business, and the Making of Internet," *The Business History Review*, 75, no. 1 (2001): p. 171

79. See William J. Drake, "The Internet Religious War," *Telecommunications Policy*, 17, no. 9 (1993): pp. 643-649; Peter H. Salus, "Protocol Wars: Is OSI Finally Dead?," *ConneXions*, 9, no. 8 (1995): 16-19; Abbate, *Inventing the Internet*, p. 179, which alludes to von Clausewitz's aphorism "politics with other means;" Maathuis and Smit, "The Battle Between Standards."

compatible. The telecommunications systems of various countries also had the same objective, and since many of these were state systems that intended to develop public networks, governments and international entities in the sector were directly involved in the question.

In particular, the International Telecommunication Union (ITU) played an important role. A structure under the ITU's direction, the Comité Consultatif International Télégraphique et Téléphonique (CCITT), developed a set of protocols in 1975 that, among other objectives, aimed to limit IBM's and other American producers' domination of the sector. This set was called X.25, was approved in 1976 and established itself as an international standard, after being adopted by the public systems of various countries as well as numerous small (especially European) producers, in addition to the American Telenet, which had contributed to its creation.[80] Although presented as alternative solutions, X.25 and TCP/IP were interfaceable. However, this implied a significant additional commitment to developing specific instruments. Over the following years an intense debate ensued about the merits and defects of one or the other, without ever arriving at a solution. Arpanet was favoured for the fact that its setup safeguarded the specificities of the various networks,[81] while CCITT's network aimed to render the defining characteristics homogenous and to control them. In addition, the first network had an end-to-end architecture that was not optimized for certain applications but provided a relatively neutral platform that allowed users to develop various services. This setup, which was inherited by Internet, promoted innovation, network growth and competition.[82] In addition, the various national authorities of the post offices, telegraphs and telecommunications did not predict that LANs could be connected to their networks. As a result, the majority of public operators and some commercial networks adopted X.25, while ARPA Internet and many private networks continued to use TCP/IP or other protocols.

Finally, the International Standard Organization (ISO) joined the mix, and in 1978 published another reference model, Open Systems Interconnection (OSI). It was a complex project articulated in seven protocol layers, the first version of which – developed in collaboration with the CCITT – was ready in 1984. Together with the consent of small producers and users who were interested in an open system,

80. In addition to Abbate, *Inventing the Internet*, in particular chapter 5, see Stuart L. Mathison, Lawrence G. Roberts and Philip M. Walker, "The History of Telenet and the Commercialization of Packet Switching in the U.S.," *IEEE Communications Magazine*, 50, no. 5 (2012): pp. 28-45.

81. Despite recognizing that a unified system would have allowed for greater integration and better performances, David Clark later argued that "it was necessary to incorporate the then existing network architectures if Internet was to be useful in a practical sense. Further, networks represent administrative boundaries of control, and it was an ambition of this project to come to grips with the problem of integrating a number of separately administrated entities into a common utility," David D. Clark, "The Design Philosophy of the DARPA Internet Protocols," *Computer Commununication Review*, 18, no. 4 (1988): p. 107.

82. See Milton Mueller, John Mathiason and Hans Klein, "The Internet and Global Governance: Principles and Norms for a New Regime," *Global Governance*, 8, no. 2 (2007): p. 247.

the recognized authority of the ISO allowed OSI to be formally adopted more or less everywhere.[83] Arpanet created a connection protocol also in the US and from 1983 onward the National Bureau of Standards launched a programme for the development of OSI. Four years later, the Department of Defence announced that those protocols would be adopted as military standards.[84] The Americans' cooperative attitude – which boiled down to the need to maintain good relations with allied countries, in this sector as in others[85] – did not change even in the face of the failed attempt by one of their representatives to get TCP/IP included in the suite of OSI protocols. Instead, X.25 was included, thus guaranteeing support for the system from postal and telecommunications entities in many countries. At the end of the 1980s, nothing suggested that all the existing networks would not come together on OSI standards. And yet, things did not go as planned, and it was TCP/IP that "ran away with the prize."[86]

Scholars largely agree on the reasons for this outcome, which many had not anticipated. First of all, the time factor was decisive. In 1980 Hubert Zimmermann, chair of the work group on OSI architecture wrote, "if standards come too late or are inadequate, interconnection of heterogeneous systems will not be possible or will be very costly."[87] In actual fact, while ISO was still busy deliberating on just one part of its protocols, and CCITT was issuing updated versions of its systems once every four years,[88] the producers and research communities needed fast solutions for the problems that arose as a result of networks' tumultuous development, and thus they used what was already available. In this way, anyone with their own protocols kept them, while Internet grew by drawing on the more simple, usable and more extensively tested TCP/IP, which not only allowed problems to be resolved step by step, but was also supported by LANs and desktop workstations.[89] In short, as has been written, "the TCP/IP architecture

83. In Europe the computer market, governments and the European Economic Community "saw the OSI program as an instrument of industrial policy to protect European manufacturers – which already were major vendors of proprietary network solutions – from the predominance of IBM and other U.S. firms," Committee to Study Global Networks and Local Values, Computer Science and Telecommunications Board, Division on Engineering and Physical Sciences, National Research Council, *Global Networks and Local Values: A Comparative Look at Germany and the United States*, Washington, DC, National Academy Press, 2001, p. 30.

84. See James Baldo and David O. Levan, "The Effects of the Transition from DoD to ISO OSI Communication Protocols," IDA Paper P-2041, November 1987, http://www.dtic.mil/cgi-bin/GetTRDoc?AD=ADA199005. Appendix C includes the memorandum of the Assistant Secretary of Defence Donald C. Latham, who released a directive on the matter on 2 July.

85. Miles Townes goes even further, writing that in this context "the important institutions are not ISO and CCITT," but NATO and OECD, Townes, "The Spread of TCP/IP," p. 46.

86. Campbell-Kelly and Garcia-Swartz, "The History of the Internet," p. 25.

87. Hubert Zimmermann, "OSI Reference Model – The ISO Model of Architecture Open Systems Interconnection," *IEEE Transactions on Communications*, COM-28, no. 4 (1980): p. 431.

88. See Ole J. Jacobsen, "The Trouble with OSI," *ConneXions*, 6, no. 5 (1992): p. 63.

89. See Tineke M. Egyedi, "'Tension Between Standardization and Flexibility' Revisited: A Critique," in "Proceedings of the 1st IEEE Conference On Standardisation and Innovation in Information Technology (SIIT), 15-17 September 1999, Aachen, Germany," http://www.tbm.

was a derivative of a working solution, while the OSI architecture was an (ex-ante) standardization solution."[90]

The Arpanet community's "organization design, knowledge management and adaptive governance" were also decisive.[91] As William J. Drake confirmed in 1993, "The debate is not merely about the comparative efficacy of two sets of standards, but it is rather between two competing visions of how international standardization processes and network development should be organized and controlled."[92] When compared, the two approaches were diametrically opposite: the first prevalent in Europe was top-down, while the second was bottom-up, as had long been practice in the United States.[93] The first was formal and the second was informal, as exemplified by the Network Working Group and the RFC.

In 1979, alongside these instruments, Cerf added an Internet Configuration Control Board that was coordinated by David D. Clark. In 1984, this was replaced by an Internet Activities Board that was divided into nine task forces. Of these, the Internet Engineering Task Force (IETF) in particular played a key role in the network's development. Created in 1986, this was a voluntary and informal entity whose ethos was summed in 1992 by Clark as follows, "we reject: kings, presidents and voting. We believe in: rough consensus and running code."[94] It is significant that these procedures had been considered an exemplary case "of a rule making process that meets Habermas's notoriously demanding procedural conditions for a discourse capable of legitimating its outcomes."[95]

The reasons for TCP/IP's success are clearly highlighted by a comparison between the IETF and the Joint Technical Committee created in 1987 by ISO and the International Electrotechnical Commission. The former was open to everybody, it distributed standards free of charge, and discussions took place primarily through email. The second was comprised of "the national standards

tudelft.nl/fileadmin/Faculteit/TBM/Over_de_Faculteit/Afdelingen/Afdeling_Infrastructure_Systems_and_Services/Sectie_Infomatie_en_Communicatie_Technologie/medewerkers/tineke_egeydi/publications/doc/SIITEgyedi.pdf; Salus, *Protocol Wars,* p. 17.

90. Tineke M. Egyedi, "Shaping Standardization: A Study of Standards Processes and Standards Policies in the Field of Telematic Services," Technische Universiteit Delft, Dissertation, 1996, pp. 231-233, http://www.tbm.tudelft.nl/fileadmin/Faculteit/TBM/Over_de_Faculteit/Afdelingen/Afdeling_Infrastructure_Systems_and_Services/Sectie_Informatie_en_Communicatie_Technologie/medewerkers/tineke_egeydi/publications/doc/tpm_egyedi_19960212.PDF.

91. Pierre Barbaroux, "Identifying Collaborative Innovation Capabilities within Knowledge-Intensive Environments: Insights from the ARPANET Project," *European Journal of Innovation Management,* 15, no. 2 (2012): pp. 232-258.

92. Drake, "The Internet Religious War," p. 643.

93. Egyedi, "Shaping Standardization," p. 13.

94. David D. Clark, "A Cloudy Crystal Ball: Visions of the Future," in "Proceedings of the Twenty-Fourth Internet Engineering Task Force," ed. by Megan Davies, Cynthia Clark and Debra Legare, Cambridge, MA, MIT, NEARnet, 13-17 July 1992), p. 543, http://www.ietf.org/old/2009/proceedings/prior29/IETF24.pdf. On this matter, see Andrew L. Russell, "'Rough Consensus and Running Code' and the Internet-OSI Standards War," *IEEE Annals of the History of Computing,* 28, no. 3 (2006): pp. 48-61; De Nardis, *Protocol Politics,* pp. 27, 47.

95. Froomkin, "Habermas@Discourse.Net," p. 752.

bodies, which represent the national interest," it functioned mostly "in face-to-face sessions" and its documents were sold in hard copies.[96] As David M. Piscitello and A. Lyman Chapin wrote, ISO and CCITT's standards were "difficult to identify, hard to acquire, challenging to read, and hideously expensive [...]. This simply doesn't make sense: makers want open systems, then they should be doing everything possible to make standards freely available and easy to access."[97]

In short, open source and user driven,[98] TCP/IP filled a gap and established itself as a de facto standard not just in the US – where the Clinton-Gore administration promoted the development of the Net[99] – but also elsewhere. As predicted by the staff of Internet,[100] the TCP/IP and OSI suites continued to coexist, but the number of countries that adopted the latter ceased to grow in 1993.[101] The former spread rapidly despite the opposition of many traditional operators, for which Internet represented a cultural, technological and organizational challenge. Finally, in 1994 "the sting was removed from the OSI-TCP/IP debate. Governments relinquished their 'OSI only' stance."[102]

The war, if this is what it had been, was over. The resort to bellicose metaphors to depict the competition between protocols is warranted, although only in a general sense. In 1993, David M. Piscitello and A. Lyman Chapin were clearer in their assessment, comparing OSI's defeat with that suffered by the Spanish Armada in 1588: "Sir Francis Drake demonstrated that small and manoeuvrable corsairs could defeat significantly larger warships. The TCP/IP community has a similar advantage over the OSI standards community."[103] The reference is undoubtedly more to the point, but an episode from the First World War may capture the situation even better. In the Battle of Caporetto, October 1917, the Austro-Hungarian and Germans defeated the Italian troops. Much blood had already been shed over the possession of the mountains in what today is Slovenian territory, which military strategy considered important for a decisive attack. At the time, the Austro-German divisions (one of which was under the command of the young Erwin Rommel) applied a new tactic: they advanced with little opposition through the valley, surprising and circumventing the Italians who were barricaded on the mountain peaks.[104]

96. Egyedi, "'Tension Between Standardization and Flexibility' Revisited."
97. David M. Piscitello and A. Lyman Chapin, *Open Systems Networking: TCP/IP and OSI*, Reading, MA, Addison-Wesley, 1993, p. 29. For their part, Campbell-Kelly and Garcia-Swartz speak of "ponderous and labyrinthine operating procedures" and "mountains of documentation" that rendered those standards "a risible target for the slightly anarchic ARPANET community," Campbell-Kelly and Garcia-Swartz, "The History of the Internet," p. 22.
98. Townes, "The Spread of TCP/IP," p. 46.
99. Campbell-Kelly and Garcia-Swartz, "The History of the Internet," p. 39.
100. David Clark, A Lyman Chapin, Vinton G. Cerf, Robert Braden and Russell Hobby, "Towards the Future Internet Architecture," RFC 1287, December 1991.
101. Maathuis and Smit, "The Battle Between Standards," p. 170.
102. Egyedi, "'Tension Between Standardization and Flexibility' Revisited."
103. Piscitello and Chapin, *Open Systems Networking*, p. 27.
104. See Nicola Labanca, *Caporetto. Storia di una disfatta*, Firenze, Giunti, 1997; Mark Thompson, *The White War: Life and Death on the Italian Front, 1915-1919*, New York, Basic Books, 2009.

If other sorts of images are preferred, Tineke M. Egyedi provided one that is no less fitting. She pointed out that she wrote her PhD dissertation on standardization in English, rather than Esperanto, and as an explanation she referred readers to the chapter comparing OSI and TCP/IP.[105] However, it goes without saying that the evolutionist metaphor that we have chosen as the basis of our study applies perfectly to the competition between protocols from the 1970s to the 1990s.[106] Indeed, during this period, fortune smiled on the solutions that best guaranteed the survival and development of the network because they answered the needs of developers and users. Having been created by a global and open community, such as that found in universities and research institutes, in an environment made favourable by the US government, the Internet faithfully reflected – if it can be said so – its "DNA."

As if to seal the entire deal, between 1993 and 1994 an innovation caused Internet to literally explode and become more user-friendly than even before: the World Wide Web. The web was invented by Tim Berners-Lee in 1990, and as is well known, it arose from a research community, on this occasion not in the US: the European Council for Nuclear Research (CERN) of Geneva. TCP/IP was introduced in 1985 and four years later was officially adopted. It is significant that the web's software was "designed to take advantage of the Internet's end-to-end architecture,"[107] and that it was put on the network in 1993 on the public domain of CERN.[108] In Geneva, a number of physicists used the Digital Equipment Corporation's operating system and Decnet, while others used Unix. Berners-Lee opted for TCP/IP because it could connect all of the systems.[109] As he himself noted, if one of the web's requirements was the hypertext that stemmed from the elaborations of Bush, Nelson and Engelbart, the other was Internet; "the task left to me," he noted, "was to marry them together."[110]

Governance of the Network

Licklider was not able to witness these developments because he died in 1990. However, in an important article on "Computers and Government" in 1979, he had predicted two different scenarios. In the first, more pessimistic scenario, progress

105. Egyedi, "Shaping Standardization," p. VIII.
106. On this point, Piscitello and Chapin argue, "just as the evolution of a species is influenced by external conditions – climate, in particular – network evolution toward a single open systems networking technology has been affected by the climate of the information-processing marketplace, which has too many networking choices," Piscitello and Chapin, *Open Systems Networking*, p. 506. Meanwhile, Gillies and Cailliau have similarly noted "the Internet grew in a way that would not have been unfamiliar to Charles Darwin or Alfred Wallace," Gillies and Cailliau, *How the Web Was Born*, p. 64.
107. Russell, "'Rough Consensus and Running Code' and the Internet-OSI Standards War," p. 56.
108. See Gillies and Cailliau, *How the Web Was Born*, p. 262.
109. Tim Berners-Lee, with Mark Fischetti, *Weaving the Web: The Original Design and Ultimate Destiny of the World Wide Web by its Inventor*, New York, Harper Collins, 2000, p. 19.
110. *Ibid.*, p. 6.

would not have been exceptional. The year 2000 would have seen "new sheet metal on a souped-up 1970s chassis," the federal government would not have pressed for the development of computers as it once did, and the research community would have "only minor effects outside the laboratory." Governments would use computers more than ever, but would continue to prioritize security, intelligence and command and control, with the result that the "controlled sharing of information in computer systems and networks" would be neglected. Without mincing words, Licklider deemed the national authorities of European telecommunications as reactionary. He had also been critical of the American government ("the technology of interconnection is years ahead of policy pertinent to the topic") and had expressed his concerns about the use that a repressive government could make of the network.

> From the point of view of mankind – if only mankind had a point of view – the important thing would seem to be a wise rather than a rapid or intensive development of computer technology. Such crucial issues as security, privacy, preparedness, participation, and brittleness must be properly resolved before one can conclude that computerization and programmation are good for the individual and for society.[111]

In the second scenario, on the other hand, "an international network of digital computer communication networks serves as the main and essential medium of informational interaction for governments, institutions, corporations, and individuals." In this vision, his projections had exceeded those of five years earlier. On the topic e-commerce, Licklider has in actual fact gone a bit too far, claiming that some could "receive delivery of small items through adjunct pneumatic tube networks," but otherwise he had only confirmed his capacity for accurate predictions.

In addition to increasing the development of knowledge and learning, better guaranteeing the safety of States and their citizens, and becoming the seat of stock markets, Multinet (as Licklider called it) would have made politics itself interactive, turning it into a "giant teleconference," in which millions of citizens would have actively participated. The network would have also allowed for forms of tele-medicine, increasing patient monitoring and support for the elderly and disabled, while also limiting their isolation. In addition, it would have made food quality control more efficient, helped with the rehabilitation of inmates and so on. The list of areas in which Licklider believed the network could have significant effects was long, "ranging from electronic games to virtual painting and sculpture."[112] His conclusions had been prudent, as trends in those years appeared to favour fragmentation, minimal reliability and the interests of various agencies and corporations, but this had not dampened his optimism.

> There is a feeling of renewed hope in the air that the public interest will find a way of dominating the decision processes that shape the future. That does not mean simply that everyone must vote on every question, for voting in the absence of understanding defines only the public attitude, not the public interest. It means that many public-spirited

---

111. Licklider, "Computers and Government," in *The Computer Age: A Twenty-Year View*, 4th ed., ed. by Michael L. Dertouzos and Joel Moses, Cambridge, MA – London, MIT Press, 1983 [1979], p. 105. The previous references in the text are on pp. 90, 103, 117, 118.
    112. *Ibid.*, pp. 91, 92, 114, 122.

individuals must study, model, discuss, analyze, argue, write, criticize, and work out each issue and each problem until they reach consensus or determine that none can be reached – at which point there may be occasion for voting. It means that many public-spirited individuals must serve government – indeed, must be the government. And it means that decisions about the development and exploitation of computer technology must be made not only "in the public interest" but in the interest of giving the public itself the means to enter into the decision-making processes that will shape their future.[113]

In the early 1990s the outcomes of the "protocols war" seemed to justify the "renewed hope" held by Licklider in 1979. The management functions performed by the Internet Activities Board and its task forces, including the IETF, were transferred in 1992 to a new non-profit organization promoted by a number of Arpanet veterans and led by Cerf, the Internet Society, which also guaranteed the continuation of RFCs. In this area some study and work groups oversaw the development of standards, dealt with the network's architecture and handled the various problems that had arisen from the nature and the growth of Internet, from spam to copyright issues. As for the web, in 1994 Berners-Lee set up a consortium at MIT to guarantee its optimal development based on its openness and its universal nature.[114]

With the support of the American government,[115] these entities were the expression of the user-designer community, but Internet's development introduced new figures onto the scene, especially private businesses. This was because during the same period the Internet's supporting structure in the US, already open to commercial uses, was privatized by the government and by the National Science Foundation.[116] In 1994 the NSF assigned the management of the Domain Name System to a private company, provoking a controversy that dragged on for several years. Finally, responsibility for questions relating to Internet was moved to the US Department of Commerce, which in 1998 placed domain management into the hands of a private non-profit company with headquarters in California, the Internet Corporation for Assigned Names and Numbers (ICANN). Under ICANN's management was the Internet Assigned Numbers Authority (IANA), which handled IP addresses and was administered by Jon Postel at the University of Southern California, until his death in 1998.[117]

---

113. *Ibid.*, p. 126.

114. For a detailed analysis of the structures in this period see Lee A. Bygrave and Terje Michaelsen, "Governors of Internet," in *Internet Governance: Infrastructure and Institutions*, ed. by Lee A. Bygrave and Jon Bing, Oxford – New York, Oxford University Press, 2009, p. 95. On the World Wide Web Consortium see Andrew L. Russell, "Constructing Legitimacy: The W3C's Patent Policy," in *Opening Standards: The Global Politics of Interoperability*, ed. by Laura De Nardis, Cambridge, MA – London, MIT Press, 2011, p. 159.

115. See Shirley M. Radack, "The Federal Government and Information Technology Standards: Building the National Information Infrastructure," *Government Information Quarterly*, 11, no. 4 (1994): pp. 373-385.

116. See Kazumori, "Coordination and Decommissioning;" Massimiliano Neri, "Historical Analysis of the Microeconomic Processes Associated with the Development of the Internet," Ludwig von Mises Institute, Working Paper, 2007, http://mises.org/journals/scholar/neri.pdf.

117. See Nicolas Adam, "L'ICANN et la gouvernance d'Internet: une histoire organisationnelle," Centre Études Internationales et Mondialisation, Cahier de recherche 07-01, November 2007, http://www.ieim.uqam.ca/IMG/pdf/AdamN_ICANN-FINAL-2007.pdf;

Selected by the American government and placed under its supervision, this model of governance was founded on voluntary contractual relations that were arranged from the bottom-up between various private subjects, including researchers, planners, businesses and users. Although the majority of Internet's hosts and 45.2% of its users were concentrated in the United States, during the boom of the 1990s other countries acquired an increasingly large piece of the pie: in 1998, 22.1% of users were based in the European Union and another 16% were located in Asia.[118] These developments translated to the creation within ICANN of a Governmental Advisory Committee, but that did not lessen the pressure from international entities and many governments, who aimed to end the US's unilateral control and supported a different governance model based on the stipulation of formal treaties.[119] Under the aegis of the United Nations, a World Summit on the Information Society was formed by the International Telecommunication Union between 2003 and 2005, at the end of a long preparatory phase that began in 1998. The makeup of participants during preliminary meetings is significant, as it demonstrates the clear prevalence of governments, but also the strong growth of non-governmental entities that feared losing their spaces for self-management.[120]

At the 2005 World Summit, a definition of network governance emerged as "the development and application by Governments, the private sector and civil society, in their respective roles, of shared principles, norms, rules, decision-making procedures, and programmes that shape the evolution and use of the Internet."[121] Sometimes deemed a "non definition," it actually acknowledged the role of the various subjects involved and reflected the authors' desire to create an essentially multi-stakeholder governance model, which had been tested since 2006 by a new organism: the Internet Governance Forum.[122] The construction site was however so complex that some compared it to that of the Tower of Babel.[123]

Rebecca E. Casey, "ICANN or ICANN't Represent Internet Users," Virginia Polytechnic Institute and State University, Master of Arts in Political Science, 2008, http://scholar.lib.vt.edu/ theses/available/etd-08272008-093846/unrestricted/CaseyRThesis.pdf. The official documents can be consulted at the National Telecommunications & Information Administration, US Department of Commerce, http://www.ntia.doc.gov/page/docicann-agreements.

118. The World Bank, "World Development Indicators," April 2012, http://databank. worldbank.org/databank/download/archive/WDIandGDF_excel_2012_04.zip.

119. On these two models see Lee Bygrave, "Contract vs. Statute in Internet Governance," in *Research Handbook on Governance of the Internet*, ed. by Ian Brown, Cheltenham, Edward Elgar, 2013, pp. 168-197.

120. See John Mathiason, *Internet Governance: The New Frontier of Global Institutions*, London – New York, Routledge, 2009, pp. 105, 110, 122-123; Amanda Hubbard and Lee Bygrave, "Internet Governance Goes Global," in Bygrave and Bing, eds., *Internet Governance*, pp. 217-218.

121. World Summit on the Information Society, "Report from the Working Group on Internet Governance," 3 August 2005, http://www.itu.int/wsis/docs2/pc3/off5.pdf.

122. See Elena Pavan, *Frames and Connections in the Governance of Global Communications: A Network study of the Internet Governance Forum*, Lanham, MD, Lexington Books, 2012.

123. Jovan Kurbalija, *An Introduction to Internet Governance*, 4th ed., Msida – Genève, Diplo Foundation, 2010, p. 29, http://archive1.diplomacy.edu/poolbin.asp? IDPool=1060.

Simply listing the dozens of structures involved in Internet governance would mean to essentially lose oneself in a thick jungle of acronyms, and much time would be needed to illustrate their areas of expertise and mutual relationships. Suffice to say that this construction site is still ongoing.

This is in part due to the fact that the legal, political and institutional problems posed by Internet and complicated by its most recent developments are innumerable and have no easy solution, starting with the relationship between concepts of governance and government. Governance, wrote for example Milton J. Mueller,

> is often (mis)interpreted as implying a kind of top-down regulation or control of the Internet. The term governance, however, gained currency in international relations precisely because it was weaker than government; it denotes the coordination and regulation of interdependent actors in the absence of an overarching political authority. In international relations the term global governance suggests that some steering and shaping function exists, but is less hierarchical and authoritative. Thus, Internet governance is the simplest, most direct, and inclusive label for the ongoing set of disputes and deliberations over how the Internet is coordinated, managed, and shaped to reflect policies.[124]

In part, a definitive solution has naturally not been found, as still to this day there exist many contrasting perspectives, opinions and interests.[125] Without going into the merits of the most recent debates, for our purposes it is sufficient to note that the High Level Ministerial Meeting held on 5 November 2012 in Baku under the aegis of the UN, ITU, UNESCO, ICANN and the Internet society also reiterated that "the Internet Governance Forum and the multi-stakeholder model are essential to ensure a sustainable, robust and open global Internet for all."[126] In spite of everything, the network of networks still maintains the user-oriented set-up that characterized its origins all those many years ago.

124. Milton L. Mueller, *Networks and States: The Global Politics of Internet Governance*, Cambridge, MA, MIT Press, 2010, pp. 8-9.

125. There is also an extensive literature on the topic. Without claiming to provide an exhaustive list, among more recent studies, besides those already, see Davide De Grazia, *Il governo di Internet*, Milano, Franco Angeli, 2010; Rolf H. Weber, in collaboration with Mirina Grosz and Romana Weber, *Shaping Internet Governance: Regulatory Challenges*, Berlin, Springer, 2010; Mikkel Flyverbom, *The Power of Networks: Organizing the Global Politics of the Internet*, Cheltenham – Northampton, MA, Edward Elgar, 2011; Eric Brousseau, Meryem Marzouki and Cécile Méadel, eds., *Governance, Regulations and Powers on the Internet*, Cambridge, Cambridge University Press, 2012; Robin Mansell, *Imagining the Internet: Communication, Innovation, and Governance*, Oxford, Oxford University Press, 2012; Rebecca McKinnon, *Consent of the Networked: The Worldwide Struggle for Internet Freedom*, New York, Basic Books, 2012.

126. "Baku Declaration of the High Level Ministerial Meeting on 'Addressing the Challenges of a Hyperconnected World,'" Baku, Azerbaijan, 5 November 2012, http://www.intgovforum.org/cms/2012/Book/Baku%20Declaration%20Final%20version.pdf. The guidelines adopted by the meeting, which took place one day before the VII Convention of the Internet Governance Forum, were essentially confirmed by the ITU conference held in Dubai on 13 and 14 December 2012. See International Telecommunication Union, "Final Acts World Conference on International Telecommunications (Dubai, 2012)," p. 20, http://www.itu.int/en/wcit-12/Documents/final-acts-wcit-12.pdf.

Acknowledgments

Our deepest gratitude goes first of all to the staff of the following archives and libraries where most of our research was carried out: the National Archives, College Park, MD; the MIT Institute Archives and Special Collections, Cambridge MA; the Library of Congress, Washington D.C.; the Columbia University Libraries, New York, NY; the Libraries of the Department of Information Engineering and Mathematics and the Department of History and Cultural Heritage at the University of Siena. In particular, we would like to thank Kenneth Schlessinger and Robin E. Cookson at the National Archives, Nora Murphy at the Massachusetts Institute of Technology and Ilaria Betocchi at the University of Siena.

We received useful feedback from participants at three seminars held between 2009 and 2010 where we presented summaries of our study: the first at the "Scuola Galileiana" at the University of Padova; the second held at the Department of Historical Sciences at the University of Bologna; the third promoted by the Departments of Politics, Institutions and History and Communication Studies at the University of Bologna. In addition, during the 2011-2012 Academic Year, the students of the Advanced Degree in Modern History at the University of Siena did much to put our work to the test.

The friends and colleagues who have provided us with assistance are too numerous to count. Some gave us information and material; others served as readers of chapters, providing us with suggestions and criticism that were always constructive. We are very much indebted to these individuals, although – as is always the case – we bear full responsibility for the final product. In particular, we would like to thank Sebastiano Bagnara, Mariarosa Bricchi, Mario Del Pero, Nando Fasce, Marcello Flores, Giovanni Gozzini, Gianni Guastella, Nicola Labanca, Roberta Mazzanti, Ilaria Porciani, Federico Romero, Fabrizio Tonello and Elisabetta Vezzosi.

Abbreviations

ACE	Automatic Computing Engine
ACM	Association for Computer Machinery
AFIPS	American Federation of Information Processing Societies
AIEE	American Institute of Electrical Engineers
ARDC	Air Research & Development Command
ARPA	Advanced Research Projects Agency
AT&T	American Telephone and Telegraph Company
B2B	Business-to-business
B2C	Business-to-consumer
BBN	Bolt, Beranek and Newman
CBI	Charles Babbage Institute
CCITT	Comité Consultatif International Télégraphique et Télephonique
CERN	Organisation Européenne pour la Recherche Nucléaire
CPU	Central Processing Unit
CTSS	Compatible Time Sharing System
DARPA	Defense Advanced Research Project Agency
DCA	Defense Communications Agency
DEC	Digital Equipment Corporation
DIS	Distributed Information Systems
DNA	Deoxyribonucleic Acid
DoD	Department of Defense
DTIC	Defense Technical Information Center
EDVAC	Electronic Discrete Variable Calculator
EIN	European Informatic Network
ENIAC	Electronic Numerical Integrator and Calculator
EPSS	Experimental Packet Switching Network
EU	European Union
FTP	File Transfer Protocol
GPD	Gross Domestic Product
GPO	General Post Office
IANA	Internet Assigned Numbers Authority
IAS	Institute for Advanced Study
IBM	International Business Machines Corporation
ICANN	Internet Corporation for Assigned Names and Numbers

ICT	Information and Communications Technology
IDA	Institute for Defense Analyses
IEEE	Institute of Electrical and Electronic Engineers
IEN	Internet Experiment Note
IETF	Internet Engineering Task Force
IFIP	International Federation of Information Processing
IMP	Interface Message Processor
IP	Internet Procotol
IPTO	Information Processing Techniques Office
IRE	Institute of Radio Engineers
ISO	International Standard Organization
ITU	International Telecommunication Union
JOSS	Johnniac Open Shop System
LAN	Local Area Network
LINC	Laboratory Instrument Computer
MAC	Multiple Access Computer, Machine-Aided Cognition
MIT	Massachusetts Institute of Technology
NARA	National Archives and Records Administration
NAS	National Academy of Sciences
NASA	National Aeronautics and Space Administration
NATO	*North Atlantic Treaty Organization*
NIC	Network Information Center
NLS	oN Line System
NOAA	National Oceanic and Atmospheric Administration
NORSAR	Norwegian Seismic Array
NPL	National Physical Laboratory
NSF	National Science Foundation
NWG	Network Working Group
OECD	Organisation for Economic Co-operation and Development
OLIVER	On-Line Interactive Vicarious Expediter and Responder
OSI	Open Systems Interconnection
PAL	Psycho-Acoustic Laboratory
PC	Personal Computer
R&D	Research and Development
RAM	Random Access Memory
RAND	Research and Development
READMSG	Read Message
RCP	Réseau à Commutation par Paquests
RFC	Request for Comment
RG	Record Group
SAGE	Semi Automatic Ground Environment
Satnet	Atlantic Packet Satellite Network
SDC	Systems Development Corporation
SDS	Scientific Data Systems
SIGCOMM	Special Interest Group on Data Communications

SNA	System Network Architecture
SNDMSG	Send Message
SRI	Stanford Research Institute
SUN	Stanford University Network
TCP	Transmission Control Protocol
TCP/IP	Transmission Control Protocol/Internet Protocol
TIP	Terminal Interface Processor
UCLA	University of California at Los Angeles
UCSB	University of California at Santa Barbara
UN	United Nations
UNESCO	United Nations Educational, Scientific and Cultural Organization
UNIVAC	Universal Automatic Computer
US, USA	United States of America
USAF	United States Air Force
USSR	Union of Soviet Socialist Republics
W3C	Word Wide Web Consortium
WAN	Wide Area Network
WWW	World Wide Web
XDS	Xerox Data Systems

Index

Printed in Szczecin, Poland
by Booksfactory
July 2017